Zimbabwe
An Introduction to
the Economics of Transformation

Zimbabwe
An Introduction to
the Economics of Transformation

by

Peter Roussos

Baobab Books
Harare

BAOBAB BOOKS

About the author

Peter Roussos has been teaching economics in Zimbabwe for the past seven years. At present he is head of Economics at the Harare Polytechnic and principal lecturer in Development Studies in the Bachelor of Technology programme. He has taught economics at O Level, A Level, Diploma level (to CIS and NID students) and at degree level.

Other works by the same author include *Introduction to Commerce,* (Book 1) published by the Curriculum Development Unit of the Ministry of Education, Zimbabwe; and *Multiple Choice Questions in Economics,* which is a revision text for students of economics. Peter Roussos has also written numerous articles on the Zimbabwe economy that have been published in local journals and newspapers.

Published by Baobab Books, Harare, Zimbabwe, 1988
© **Pete Roussos**
Artist: Donatus Bonde
Typeset by Thompson Publications (Pvt) Ltd.
Design and Lay-out by Maviyane Project
Printed by National Printing and Packaging
ISBN 0-7974-0793-6

DEDICATION

This book is dedicated to all those who helped play a part in its creation; to my family, without whose support I could not have even begun the work, and whose support means that I have to continue working; to my students, who helped with a lot of the spadework and who provided enough criticism of early drafts to have buried me; to my employer; to my editor, who provided me with the determination to finish the book, if only to get her off my back; to my parents, who convinced me from an early age that I had something to say and whose love and hard work ensured that I had the means to say it; and finally to all the people of this country, without whom I would have had nothing to write about.

Contents

List of Tables

Chapter One

Chapter Two

List of Graphs

List of Boxes

Main Acronyms used in the Text

ACP	—	African, Caribbean and Pacific group of countries (signatories to the Lomé Convention).
ADA	—	Agricultural Development Authority
ADB	—	African Development Bank
AECI	—	African Explosives and Chemical Industries
AFC	—	Agricultural Finance Corporation
AGRITEX	—	Department of Agricultural Extension (Ministry of Lands, Agriculture and Rural Settlement)
AMA	—	Agricultural Marketing Authority
ARDA	—	Agricultural and Rural Development Authority
BCCZ	—	Bank of Credit and Commerce, Zimbabwe Ltd.
BIAO	—	Banque Internationale pour l'Afrique Occidentale
BSAC	—	British South African Company
CONEX	—	Conservation and Extension Department (part of Ministry of Agriculture until 1981)
CMB	—	Cotton Marketing Board
CPI	—	Consumer Price Index
CSC	—	Cold Storage Commission
CSO	—	Central Statistical Office
CZI	—	Confederation of Zimbabwe Industries
DEVAG	—	Department of Agricultural Development (part of Ministry of Agriculture until 1981)
DCZ	—	Discount Company of Zimbabwe
DMB	—	Dairy Marketing Board
EEC	—	European Economic Commission
EPO	—	Exclusive Prospecting Order
ESC	—	Electricity Supply Commission
FFYNDP	—	First Five Year National Development Plan
FNB	—	First National Bank of Boston
GDE	—	Gross Domestic Expenditure
GDI	—	Gross Domestic Income
GDO	—	Gross Domestic Output
GDP	—	Gross Domestic Product
GMB	—	Grain Marketing Board
GNI	—	Gross National Income
GNP	—	Gross National Product
GOP	—	Gross Operating Profit
GOS	—	Gross Operating Surplus
IDAC	—	Industrial Development Advisory Committee
IDC	—	Industrial Development Corporation
IMF	—	International Monetary Fund
IPCORN	—	Industrial Promotion Council for Rhodesia and Nyasaland — re-named in 1964 Industrial Promotion Corporation of Central Africa
LME	—	London Metal Exchange
LMS	—	Lomagundi Mining and Smelting
MBCA	—	Merchant Bank of Central Africa
MFEPD	—	Ministry of Finance, Economic Planning and Development
MLARR	—	Ministry of Lands, Agriculture and Rural Resettlement
MMCZ	—	Minerals Marketing Corporation of Zimbabwe
MPC	—	Mining Promotion Council

NCI	—	No Currency Involved
NCD	—	Negotiable Certificate of Deposit
NDP	—	National Development Plan
NI	—	National Income
NRZ	—	National Railways of Zimbabwe
OECD	—	Organization of Economic Co-operation and Development
POSB	—	Post Office Savings Bank
PSIP	—	Public Sector Investment Programme
PTA	—	Preferential Trade Area
PUPS	—	Paid-Up Permanent Shares
R&SS	—	Department of Research and Specialist Services (Ministry of Lands, Agriculture and Rural Resettlement)
RBZ	—	Reserve Bank of Zimbabwe
SADCC	—	Southern African Development Co-ordinating Conference
SDR	—	Special Drawing Right
SEDCO	—	Small Enterprises Development Corporation
SLA	—	Sabi-Limpopo Authority
SMW	—	Statutory Minimum Wage
TILCOR	—	Tribal Trust Lands Development Corporation
TMB	—	Tobacco Marketing Board
TNDP	—	Transitional National Development Plan
TTL	—	Tribal Trust Lands.
UNIDO	—	United Nations Industrial Development Organisation
UNIVEX	—	Universal Exports
ZDB	—	Zimbabwe Development Bank
ZFC	—	Zimbabwe Fertilizer Corporation
Zimphos	—	Zimbabwe Phosphates
ZISCO	—	Zimbabwe Iron and Steel Corporation
ZMDC	—	Zimbabwe Mining Development Corporation
ZSE	—	Zimbabwe Stock Exchange
ZIMCORD	—	Zimbabwe Conference on Reconstruction and Development

INTRODUCTION

One of the primary reasons for writing this book was the difficulty that I, as a teacher, experienced in locating relevant materials for current and topical economics courses. It was reasonable to assume that other teachers in the field would also have had such difficulties; and so I decided to collate all the information that I had assembled while teaching.

In an effort to make the information immediately available to a wide range of teachers, students and practitioners of economics the original material was published as weekly articles in a local financial newspaper. The series ran from May to November, 1986. This book is an expanded and updated version of those articles.

The book is an attempt on my part to chart and comment on the transitional path of the Zimbabwean economy. Having said that, the question arises, 'transformation or transition to what?' The stated aim of government is to build 'a socialist and egalitarian society' in Zimbabwe. Government has furthermore said that such a transition would be effected through raising the living standards of the poor rather than dropping those of the rich. Growth would therefore be necessary before equity would be possible, and such growth would be achieved through the maintenance and, in many cases, strengthening of the capitalist economic base while slowly expanding government participation and ownership of the economic assets.

The expansion of government ownership does not necessarily transfer wealth or economic control to the mass of the people. The danger of simply replacing one elite with another is very real and would have the effect of limiting the benefits of the transition to a small group of people. Although this is a fundamentally important issue, I believe that it must remain secondary to breaking the hold of international capital on the local economy and establishing local control, be it government or private; to gearing the development of Zimbabwe to the needs of the Zimbabwean people rather than those of the international economy; and to consolidating the Zimbabwean nation. Once this has been achieved then the nation would be in a position to chart its own path of development.

This book is therefore an attempt to introduce the Zimbabwean economy; to explain how the wealth is generated and distributed; to explore patterns of ownership in the economy; to highlight dependencies and weaknesses; to introduce possible growth strategies; all with the objective of exploring the potential for development within the government's framework of 'growth with equity'. I write this book in the firm belief that without a thorough understanding of the workings of the economy the question of transition remains purely academic. An introduction to the economics of transformation must therefore involve an understanding of the nuts and bolts of the economy — which I have attempted to provide.

The first chapter deals with the historical development of the economy from the pre-capitalist Shona and Ndebele economies to the post-1980 reconstruction. Chapter Two deals with National Income accounting and draws some tentative conclusions based on the empirical data presented. The subsequent chapters deal with the five major sectors of the economy: agriculture; manufacturing; mining; money and banking; and the foreign sector. The historical development of each of these sectors, their characteristics, problem areas, relations with government, and future prospects are dealt with.

Many different people read the initial drafts and made valuable comments which played a part in the final version. Special thanks must go to the representatives of the Chamber of Mines; the Confederation of Zimbabwe Industries; the Commercial Farmers Union; the RAL Merchant Bank; and the Central Statistical Office for the comments made on the initial drafts of Chapters Three to Seven. The advice provided by both Andre Proctor and Rob Davies on Chapters One and Two respectively was very useful and led to substantial revisions.

The final text of the book remains, however, my responsibility.

Chapter 1

THE BACKGROUND TO THE PRESENT

The Present — the Birth of a new Nation

On the 18th April, 1980, ninety years after the arrival of the colonialists and fifteen years after the unilateral declaration of independence by the Smith government (UDI), the new Zimbabwean nation was born.

At the time of Independence the new government inherited an economy of great contrasts. On the one hand there was a sophisticated infrastructure capable of producing a wide range of agricultural, mining and manufactured products, both for the domestic and the export market but, on the other hand, there were also severe inequalities in income, capital and land holdings and access to basic services such as education and health which the new government had promised to redress.

The years of UDI had necessitated a large degree of self-sufficiency, but had also left a legacy of outdated capital stock and a war-damaged infrastructure.

Growth with Equity

On coming to power the new government espoused the policy of 'Growth with Equity' in an effort to overcome the legacy of imbalance. This policy statement outlined the Government's development objectives. The policy instruments with which government was to implement and achieve these objectives were as follows:

- a) the establishment of a socialist society;
- b) rapid economic growth;
- c) balanced development and equitable distribution of income and productive resources;
- d) economic reconstruction;
- e) the development of human resources;
- f) rural development;
- g) worker participation;
- h) the development of an economic infrastructure and social services;
- i) fiscal and monetary reform.

Expansionary Policy

The additional growth which was to finance the equity (as the government did not envisage reducing standards of living, but rather raising those of the 'have-nots') was to be attained by building on to the existing infrastructure. Together with favourable external conditions — a high gold price, improving terms of trade (the terms of trade are the relationship between import and export prices: if the terms of trade are improving it means that export prices are rising faster than import prices) and the lifting of sanctions — the government introduced a number of measures designed to stimulate the local economy. These included increased foreign exchange allocations which were introduced in the expectation of a rapid growth of exports and large inflows of foreign capital, increased agricultural producer prices to stimulate output, and expansion in the road and rail systems to pave the way for new investment (i.e. growth). On the equity side the government increased minimum wages, rapidly expanded the health and education services and launched an agricultural resettlement scheme.

These domestic expansionary policies, together with large amounts of foreign borrowing (and favourable weather conditions) resulted in bumper crops and a real growth rate of 13% in the 1980-81 period. (See Table 1).

TABLE 1: Real Growth in the Zimbabwe Economy: 1980-86

Year	1980	1981	1982	1983	1984	1985	1986
Nominal GDP	3 226	4 049	4 609	5 081	5 700	6 700	7 770
Growth rate (%)	27	22,5	13,8	10,2	12	17,5	16
Real GDP (%) (1980 Z$m)	11	13	Nil	- 3,5	1	6	3

Export Performance

The rise in minimum wages increased domestic demand, which together with the increased foreign exchange allocations, led to a rapid rise in imports. In order to maintain a balance of payments equilibrium (exports = imports) the increased level of imports had to be met by an expansion of exports.

Exports earnings have to pay, not only for the importation of merchandise, but also for the net importation of capital (i.e. capital flowing in *less* capital flowing out) and the net importation of services (i.e. service and income receipts *less* service and income payments). Although Zimbabwe's capital account almost always reflects a net inflow of capital, the services account always reflects a net outflow. The net outflow (deficit) on the services account increased from $213m in 1979 to $542m in 1983.

(See Table 9, Chapter 7).

In the event, export earnings were far below what was needed in order to maintain equilibrium. The reasons for the rather poor export performance were as follows:

The consequence of the drought: the three years after the 1980-81 agricultural season were drought years which not only reduced Zimbabwe's capacity to export agricultural products, but also necessitated spending valuable foreign exchange on food imports.

Decreased demand for exports: the world recession led to reduced output levels in the First World and, as a consequence, less demand for our exports in both the mining and manufacturing spheres.

Increased domestic demand: this was partly due to the increased minimum wage which meant that some goods which would have been exported were diverted to the domestic market.

Domestic inflation: this was due to the expansion of government spending which resulted from the effort to increase social services and develop the infrastructure, the rise in minimum wages (not linked to increasing productivity levels), and the expansion of domestic credit.

The rising prices at home reduced the competitiveness of our exports abroad, thereby further reducing export earnings.

TABLE 2: Levels of Inflation : 1979-86

Year	CPI HIG*	CPI LIG*	Average CPI	Rate of Inflation
1975	67	63,4	65,2	
1976	71,8	69,5	70,7	8,4%
1977	76,7	74,8	75,8	7,8%
1978	81,6	82,2	81,9	8,0%
1979	90,7	93,5	92,1	12,5%
1980	100	100	100	8,6%
1981	113,6	111,5	112,6	12,6%
1982	133,4	122,7	128,0	13,7%
1983	152,6	149,4	151	17,9%
1984	171,5	180	175,8	16,4%
1985	198,2	196,2	197,2	12,1%
1986	215,1	220,9	218	10,5%
1987*				13,0%

2

Note: HIG = High Income Group
LIG = Low Income Group
The average CPI Consumer Price Index is the mid-point between the HIG and LIG CPI's.
The rate of inflation is the percentage increase in CPI from year to year.
The figure for 1987 is for January only.

Exchange rate movements: the 1980-81 period saw an appreciation of the Zimbabwe dollar which, in turn, made our exports more expensive. The subsequent depreciation of the dollar in the last quarter of 1982 brought the price of our exports down, but increased the price of our imports.

Contractionary Policy

The above factors led to the large current account deficits experienced during the 1980-81 periods (see Graph 1) and brought about a major reappraisal of government economic policy. The new policy measures were designed to cut back domestic demand, reduce inflation, reduce imports and expand exports.

The measures introduced by the government were:

The reduction of domestic demand: the bank rate was drastically increased from 4.5% in 1980 to 9.0% in 1981 as part of a tight monetary policy designed to control consumer spending (i.e. cut demand) and thereby reduce inflation. The freezing of wages between 1982 and mid-1985 caused a decline in real wages and, therefore, a further decline in domestic demand.

Export promotion: exporters were granted automatic foreign exchange allocations for required inputs as part of an incentive scheme to increase the volume of exports. The 25% depreciation of the Zimbabwe dollar and a shift to a more flexible system of exchange rate management were meant to make Zimbabwean exports more competitive. The wage freeze and the tight monetary policy helped to ease inflation which, in turn, made our exports more competitive.

GRAPH 1: Balance of Payments: 1978 - 85

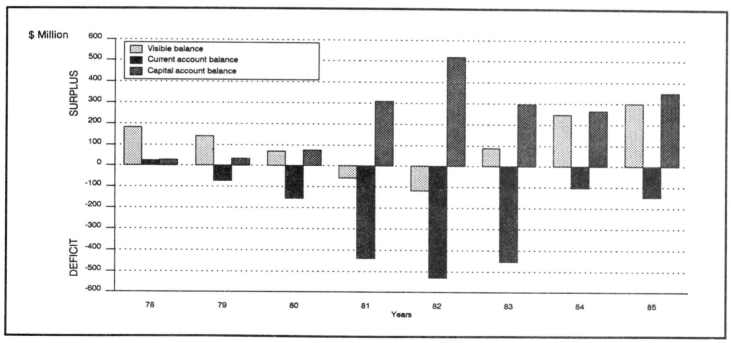

3

Controls on foreign exchange: foreign exchange allocations to importers were cut back and temporary restrictions were placed on the remittance of profits, dividends and capital, in an attempt to conserve scarce forex.

As a result of the introduction of these measures the current account deficit was significantly reduced (see Graph 1), inflation dropped from 23.7% in 1983 to 9,1% in 1984, and the dramatic rise in net service payments (contributed to by our rising external debt) was brought under control.

Deficit Financing

Social spending continued to increase both as a result of the government's commitment to income redistribution, and in an effort to mitigate against the effects of the drought and the recession. Despite the return to positive growth rates after 1983 the budget deficit has remained at about 10% of the Gross Domestic Product (GDP). Even the 6% real growth experienced in 1985 was not enough to pay for parastatal subsidies, expanding social services, and escalating defence requirements which arose as a result of increased instability in the region. A continuation of the budget deficit will erode all the benefits reaped from the tight monetary policy imposed in 1982, and will drive the economy back into a state of high inflation, increased levels of domestic demand and balance of payments deficits.

The years since Independence have seen dramatic changes in the Zimbabwean economy. The new government has had to cope with the rebuilding of a war-ravaged economy, with the costs of implementing its policies of 'Growth with Equity', and with the restraint imposed by the world recession and the three year drought. In the face of this, the government has managed to restore the damaged power and transport infrastructures, and significantly expand social services, as well as develop a viable peasant farming sector, while maintaining the commercial farming sector and begin the economic reintegration of Zimbabwe into the world economy. The long-term prospects for the Zimbabwean economy depend on its ability to pay for development programmes from its own resources, i.e. to finance the move towards greater equity from the expansion of the domestic economy.

Background to the Present

The previous section dealt with the developments in the economy since Independence. Although many of these developments represent a major break with previous economic policy, in order to fully understand the difficulties and successes of present economic policy one needs to have an understanding of the past.

The rest of this chapter will deal with the process of industrialization in Zimbabwe. The economic history of the country will be divided into three periods: pre-colonial, colonial and post-colonial.

The pre-Colonial Period (pre-1890)

The basic unit of production in the pre-colonial economy was the family unit known as the homestead. Production within the homestead was divided along sexual lines with the young men being responsible for herding the cattle and protecting the fields from wild animals, and the older men generally being responsible for the heavier work such as clearing the land, making the tools and weapons, and hunting. Women, on the other hand, did much of the essential work such as child care, planting, reaping, the making of meal, cooking, preparing beer, and making pottery.

Each homestead belonged to a lineage (all the people in a lineage shared the same ancestors) and each lineage was part of a community.

Wealth in the pre-colonial economy was held in the form of cattle. Although individual homesteads owned cattle, wealth was not really private property. Most cattle belonged to the lineage, so that if cattle were to be traded outside of the lineage, permission had to be sought from the elders of the lineage.

As some lineages grew in wealth and power (through the accumulation of cattle) a ruling class of chiefs and senior lineages began to emerge. They gained control of the bulk of each community's cattle, iron production, gold mining and trade. This ruling class began to extract tribute from the ordinary people in the society. Young men were taken from their own homesteads to herd and guard the rulers' herds or to help in the building of the rulers' houses; young women were required to dig and carry clay for the rulers' houses and to make and decorate the dagga work; hunters had to give one tusk from every elephant they killed to their ruler; miners had to give part of each day's extraction of gold to the ruler. [1] Thus emerged the tributary mode of production which was the dominant mode in the period prior to the penetration of capital.

The tribute that was appropriated by the ruling classes formed the surplus that was used in trade. The tributary system further enabled the early inhabitants of Zimbabwe to resist the first attempts at European penetration (the Rozvi armies defeated the Portuguese in 1693 and drove them from Zimbabwe). The tribute that was appropriated by the ruling classes formed the surplus that was used in trade between different groups of people in the region and with the forerunners of colonialism, merchant capital. Merchant capital was primarily interested in trade and, unlike mining or industrial capital (which came later), had no interest in settling permanently in the area.

1   Garlake, P. and Proctor, A., **People Making History,** Zimbabwe Publishing House, Harare, 1985.

4

The pre-Colonial Shona Economy

The traditional Shona economy was mainly geared towards subsistence (i.e. growing crops for their own consumption), together with the specialized production of crafts (iron smelting), the growing and curing of tobacco and gold mining. The peoples inhabiting the Zimbabwe plateau in the 19th century were known for their participation in local, regional and long-distance trade. Although crop cultivation was the major activity of this period — rapoko and mhunga being the major crops cultivated — cows, sheep, goats and fowls were also kept.

The Shona used a land rotation system which involved the clearing and planting of an additional acre of land each year. When land fertility declined on a piece of land, it would be allowed to lie fallow for 10-15 years. Given that there was a plentiful supply of land, this was an efficient agricultural system.

Trade in the pre-Colonial Shona Economy: the major products used for trading purposes in early Zimbabwe were iron products, salt and tobacco. The Njanja people of Wedza mountain were renowned for their iron work. Their hoes were reputed to last twice as long as any other hoes produced in Zimbabwe at that time.

The Shangwe people, living in what is now called Gokwe, specialized in the manufacture of a special type of tobacco which was sold by European traders far beyond the borders of Zimbabwe. The major products traded by the Shona outside Zimbabwe were gold, copper and ivory. The majority of trade taking place was in gold which was sold to Portuguese settlements in the Tete area. The Nguni invasions in the early nineteenth century and the passing of the Gold Trade Ordinance (in the Colonial period) which prohibited Africans from buying or selling gold, effectively put an end to the gold trade.

The pre-Colonial Ndebele Economy

Cattle played an important role in the Ndebele economy with the size of the Ndebele herd reaching about 250 000 by 1890. Ndebele settlements were also characterized by extensive fields of Indian corn, beans, melons, pumpkins, potatoes and peas. The missionary T.M. Thomas, who spent the years 1859-70 living with the Ndebele, noted that in some areas, cotton was grown, and that tobacco was grown in every village that he knew of.

Throughout the 19th century Ndebele trade was geared towards mitigating the effects of the frequent droughts in Matabeleland. Beads, cattle and goats were traded for corn, which was bought mainly from the Shona of eastern Matabeleland and western Mashonaland.

The Ndebele also obtained large quantities of iron products from their northern neighbours. The Ndebele state consumed vast quantities of iron which was used for making spears, hoes, knives and axes.

Much of the Ndebele external trade was governed by the political needs of the Ndebele state. During their stay in the Transvaal the Ndebele under Mzilikaze bought firearms from the Cape Colony. When the Boer-Ndebele conflict prohibited the further purchase of firearms from the Cape, Mzilikazi turned to the Portuguese for supplies of guns and ammunition.

Until the 1870s the sale of ivory was the most prominent and lucrative of the Ndebele kingdom's exports. In the 1880s and 90s the main Ndebele goods traded were cattle, sheep, goats, animal skins and elephant tusks. These goods were exchanged for European-style clothes, guns and ammunition, and tinder-boxes.

The Colonial Period

The colonial period began with the arrival of the settler invasion force in present-day Harare in September 1890 who followed the rumours of extensive gold deposits, north of the Limpopo. Mining capital in the form of Rhodes' British South Africa Company (BSAC) was the organizing body behind it. Rhodes claimed to have entered into a treaty with Lobengula — the Rudd Concession of 1888 — in which he was said to have given Rhodes' men 'all his land and all his cattle'. The 196 men of the invading column were each entitled to 3 000 acres of land and 15 gold claims, for the role they had played in the conquest of the Shona peoples. By February 1891 some 7 000 gold claims had already been marked off. Frustration soon followed when the expectation of a 'second Rand' proved futile. This prompted the settlers to attack the Ndebele in the hope of finding greater mineral resources in Matabeleland. By December 1893, the conquest of the Ndebele people completed, the settlers, once again, simply annexed vast areas of their land and cattle. In the process, missionaries also acquired approximately a quarter of a million acres of land by 1900.

Pioneer invasion force enter Zimbabwe.

On the land that was left, 'Native Reserves' were established. By 1896 all the Reserves in Matabeleland had been marked out, and by 1902 Reserve land throughout the country totalled 20 million acres. An acute shortage of labour for the newly established mines and the settler farmers led to the establishment of the Labour Board of Southern Rhodesia in 1899, and later the Rhodesian Native Labour Association which had the task of recruiting foreign labour (mostly from Northern Rhodesia and Nyasaland) to serve the local economy. That the Shona and the Ndebele peasants did not respond to the labour needs of the cash economy, was the result of their own self-sufficiency. They were able to expand their own production in accordance with the needs of the newly created markets. (It is interesting to note that it was only in 1912 that the food supplies of the commercial farmers to the mines exceeded that of the peasant farmers.)

By 1912 the myth of a 'second Rand' had been shattered and agriculture began to rival mining as the principal activity in the region. In line with this realization the Company (the BSAC still administered Southern Rhodesia at this stage) began to concentrate more of its resources on agriculture.

The Company followed the same strategy in agriculture as it did in mining. It encouraged the flotation of companies and the consequent introduction of large agricultural capital from Britain into Southern Rhodesia.

More European farmers were recruited and placed on land that had formerly been allocated to the Reserves; more research and extension services were provided, and in 1912 the Land Bank was set up with a share capital of $250 000.

The effect of these policies and subsequent measures adopted by the first colonial government served to boost European agriculture at the expense of the peasant economy. The viable economies which existed prior to the arrival of the Pioneer Column had been virtually destroyed by the 1930s.

The Struggle between Settler Capital and International Capital

The arrival of the BSAC in what became known as Southern Rhodesia represented the penetration of international capital into the region, and in order to establish itself, it entered into an alliance with settler capital. The Company had been granted a Royal Charter in 1899 by the British Government which authorized it to make treaties and promulgate laws as well as to maintain a police force and to undertake public works in the name of the British Empire. Effectively, this made the Company the government of the day in Southern Rhodesia.

By 1902 the alliance between the settlers and the company began to weaken. Tensions had arisen over the percentage of shares reserved in all companies for the BSAC, over the small number of elected legislative council members, and over the high cost of living. Although the Company managed to appease the settlers by granting concessions, the tensions between settler capital (the small mine owners and settler farmers) and the Company (the large mine owners) continued. In the 1920 elections the Responsible Government Association which represented a loose coalition of farmers, trade unionists and small traders swept to victory over the representatives of large capital who, with the Company, looked to union with South Africa to safeguard their interests. The settler state that emerged found itself powerless to act against the representatives of international capital which had Southern Rhodesia firmly in its grip. International capital, through the BSAC, had almost total control of base mineral mining; it owned the railway system; it controlled the only colliery in the country and it was entrenching its control over the gold-mining industry through a handful of large, company-owned mines. The contradictions between the different fractions of capital, (see Box 1) although important, remained secondary to their common interest in the exploitation of labour and the maintenance of the social and political conditions necessary for the continued extraction of surplus. The passing of the Land Apportionment Act in 1930 further undermined the position of the African peasantry in relation to the commercial farmer and ensured a continuous supply of migrant labour into the wage economy.

The Effects of the Depression 1930-33

The shrinking of international markets which came about as a result of the great depression and the consequent fall in commodity prices hit the Rhodesian economy very hard. The cut-backs in chrome and asbestos production meant the loss of thousands of jobs for black miners while white farmers were hard hit by the sharp reductions in the maize price and an outbreak of foot-and-mouth disease which brought all meat exports to a halt. The national income fell from £13,7m in 1929 to £8,7m in 1931 as the effects of depression spread to all sectors of the economy.

The Reform Party

In 1933 settler capital once again tried to oust international capital from the driving seat. The Reform Party and later the United Party under Godfrey Huggins, through a policy of control boards and subsidies, managed to stabilize settler agriculture and save it from certain ruin. By 1937 only poultry and pigs remained outside the state's ambit of control; all other products from European farms fell under the control boards. In 1938 the state moved into the meat industry through the establishment of the Cold Storage Commission (CSC).

The Reform Party's policies in the mining sector were aimed largely at the small worker and included the provision of cheap power through the Electricity Supply Commission (ESC), a government loan fund and tax exemptions for small miners. Despite Huggins' claims to represent the interests of the 'small people' against those of the big companies, after nearly two decades of self-government (since the granting of responsible government in 1923) the grip of the large companies remained as strong as ever. By the late 1930s the country still had a typical colonial economy based on the extraction and export of raw materials; industrialization had yet to take place.

The decline in the gold price in the early 1940s eliminated large numbers of small miners in the gold industry and led once more to the dominance of the large companies in gold mining. In 1945 large mines produced approximately 46% of the total gold output; ten years later this increased to 60%. The growing importance of the large miners led to closer working relations with the government to the detriment of the small miners.

The War Years (1939-45)

The advent of the Second World War meant that imports from the advanced capitalist countries were severely cut back, which

7

created the opportunity for the development of local industry. In 1940 the Industrial Development Advisory Committee (IDAC) was formed, and in 1942 Southern Rhodesia's iron and steel works were nationalized. The purchase of the railways by the state from the BSAC in 1947 was seen as part of an infrastructural policy to establish a base on which private capital could then build its own industry.

By the end of the Second World War there were 385 manufacturing establishments employing some 34 500 people, which represented a 100% increase in manufacturing employment since 1938. The government had laid the basis for the diversification of the economy beyond primary production, and had paved the way for a take-off into the sustained growth which was to occur after the war.

Settler capital was increasingly being confined to relatively small-scale operations in the agricultural and mining sectors and remained dependent on cheap migrant labour for its profitability. International capital, on the other hand, moved into the rapidly expanding secondary industry which demanded a more stable and educated labour force. A better paid work force meant an expanding domestic market for a developing industrial sector which had not yet been able to capture international markets. The agricultural and mining sectors, producing mainly for the export market, had nothing to gain from the increasing wage levels and in the case of the small-scale operators, were directly threatened. The process of industrialization therefore sharpened the

---

BOX 1: Stages in the Development of Capitalism

When capitalism first developed its dominant form was merchant capital, and the methods of production used remained those of pre-capitalist production. This period is known as 'the period of Merchant Capital', or the 'period of manufacture'. All that is necessary for the existence of merchant capital is that the production and exchange of commodities can take place on a sufficient scale, conditions which in themselves pre-date the rise of specifically capitalist production.

The surplus appropriated by the ruling class in pre-capitalist societies (see section ....) in the form of rent or forced labour formed the basis for trade with merchant capital. Because the 'costs of production' were not clearly defined in the pre-capitalist mode (since the ruling classes did not pay for labour or raw materials — they simply took what they wanted) there was scope for very large profits in trade which mainly accrued to merchant capital (i.e. to the traders). It was because of the magnitude of the profits and the possibilities for monopolizing trade that Marx stated: 'The independent development of merchant capital stands in inverse proportion to the general economic development of society'. *Capital* (Vol III).

The commercial empires that developed between the 16th and 18th centuries were driven mainly by attempts to monopolize trade. The methods of production used in many of the areas controlled by merchant capital were often pre-capitalist. Where the pre-conditions for capital production existed, merchant capital amassed large numbers of inividual producers in one place where they began to work jointly. This enabled the division of labour to take place and the costs of production to be reduced.

The next stage in the development of capital was brought on by the development of modern industry. Mechanization — or machinofacture — meant that the tools were taken out of the workers' hands and regulated directly by machines. Productivity increased dramatically as mass production had now become possible. The increased volume of production and the dramatic fall in prices which followed mechanization necessitated a greater volume of trade. The monopolistic restrictions on trade which were established in the period of merchant capital had to be swept aside as *industrial capital* rose to dominance.

Finance capital is capital which is controlled by banks and employed by industrialists. With the development of industry an increasing proportion of capital ceases to belong to the industrialists who employ it. The banks, who channel the money to industry, have increasingly been transformed into industrial capitalists. This bank capital, which is turned into industrial capital, is known as finance capital. The increasing concentration of this capital through the banks has led to the creation of huge financial monopolies at the centre of which is the ability to mobilize large amounts of capital.

Although in the period of competitive capitalism, it is possible to distinguish between financial and industrial capital, in the period of monopoly capitalism this distinction disappears. Finance capital, therefore, represents the fusion of industrial and bank capital.

Today it is the multinational corporations who represent finance capital. These companies are not controlled by the banks but their head offices perform many of the functions of bank capital in (a) raising money (often through the selling of shares) and (b) chanelling money from one subsidiary to another.

The development of modern capitalism is the story of the emergence and rise to dominance of these different 'fractions of capital'. The present-day hegemony of finance capital does not entail the eradiction of the other fractions of capital, but rather their subordination to its needs. Modern day capitalism, therefore, encompasses various fractions of capital (including mining capital, industrial capital, agricultural capital, etc...) which, although competing for the right to control the state, (and therefore for hegemony over the other fractions of capital) are united in their opposition to the working class.

contradictions between settler and international capital. The rapid industrialization of the 1940s had also strengthened the black working class which by 1948 (the year of the general strike) became a force to be reckoned with. Once again the primary contradiction — that between capital and labour — overshadowed the secondary contradictions between the fractions of capital (see Box I) and necessitated the partnership of a 'Federation' in order to deal with the increased level of working class militancy. The Second World War saw the reduction of foreign capital inflows and the technical and managerial skills on which the economy relied. This necessitated a greater drive towards self-sufficiency with local capital playing the major role. The services sector was expanded, the economic infrastructure was developed, and the state actively promoted import substitution. As a result of these measures a range of industries emerged which began to use local raw materials to produce manufactured goods: tanned leather, fencing materials, cables, plywood, cutlery, surgical instruments, furniture, chemicals and chemical products, metals and transport equipment are only a few of the examples of locally produced goods which emerged during this period. These new industries produced mainly for the domestic market.

Protective tariffs and subsidies for domestic manufacturing enterprises were introduced in an effort to further promote industrialization.

This early period was characterized by a strong reliance on foreign capital. By the end of the war total foreign investment was estimated at $120 million. (The total National Income (NI) during this period was in the region of only $200m). Foreign investment accounted for 45% of taxable corporate income and about half this capital was controlled by the British South Africa Company.

The post-War Years (1945-50)

The world-wide demand for strategic materials such as chrome, and the expanding market for Southern Rhodesian tobacco, led to a rapid growth in foreign trade. However, the major exports of the economy in this period continued to be agriculture and mining products, i.e. tobacco, maize, cattle, gold, chrome, asbestos, and coal.

The shortage of skilled workers and technical know-how was, to some extent, alleviated by the policy of attracting immigrants from Britain, Southern Europe and South Africa. The high standard of living offered to them contrasted starkly with the low wages paid to the largely migrant (local and foreign) work-force. This disparity and the profits that arose therefrom, was to play a crucial role in the economy over the next few decades.

Rural resources were increasingly inadequate and drove many of the young into wage employment. The poor and insufficient land, low rainfall and over-use of soil — due to over-population and over-stocking — intensified the problem. Productivity levels continued to drop and what little was produced was difficult to market due to the lack of roads, delivery vehicles or rail transportation. The net effect was one of rural poverty which drove the wage-earners into the urban areas for ever-increasing periods.

Formation of Rhodesia and Nyasaland heightened tension in the region as there was a prevailing fear in Nationalist circles this would simply entrench white majority rule.

The Federal Period (1953-63)

The Federation brought together Southern Rhodesia, Northern Rhodesia and Nyasaland and came into being in 1953. The attempt by the British Colonial Office to create a super-federation completely ignored the sentiments of nationalist elements in all three member states. Particularly in Nyasaland and Northern Rhodesia there was a prevailing fear in nationalist circles that the Federation would mean an entrenchment of white-majority rule. It was only in Southern Rhodesia that the idea of a Federation was greeted with enthusiasm by those entitled to vote.

Economically, Federation brought many advantages to the member states. It widened the resource base, expanded the market to allow for economies of scale (i.e. mass production), expanded resources and employment and led to higher standards of living. Nyasaland's major contribution was its agricultural products and its labour force; Southern Rhodesia contributed a manufacturing base, while Northern Rhodesia's copper brought in foreign exchange. In terms of National Income, the potential market increased from South Rhodesia's $340m; an increase of about 85%.

The Federation's budget was derived from income and indirect taxes. The key function of the Federal government was to finance infrastructural developments such as the Kariba Hydro-Electric Project, the jointly owned Rhodesia Railways, posts and telecommunications, roads, bridges, and housing.

Southern Rhodesia, being the most industrialized economy, also received the bulk of the Federal budget, with the Kariba Project being the most visible and the most expensive of the Federation's projects.

In the years 1953-64 the number of industrial units increased by only 7,5%; industrial employment decreased by 1% but industrial output increased by 173% (see Table 3 below). This increase was only bettered during the UDI period when the value of gross output increased by 239%.

The Federation also attracted increased capital inflows from abroad. The estimated net increase in foreign investment between 1953 and 1963 was $700m. This represented a 250% increase over the previous ten years. Of this total 65,7% came from outside the country, the balance representing reinvestment of profits from multinationals that were already operating in Southern Rhodesia.

The rise of black nationalism in both Nyasaland and Northern Rhodesia under Banda and Kaunda eventually led to the collapse of the Federation when the two northern territories withdrew.

TABLE 3: Industrial Units, Employment and Gross Output in selected Years: 1938-75

Year	Units	Employment	Gross Output ('000)
1938	381	42 100	16 272
1945	459	55 900	37 212
1952	1 172	126 000	176 176
1960	1 141	130 000	336 813
1964	1 260	125 000	480 200
1968	1 344	143 000	605 038
1971	1 570	184 000	935 931
1975	n.a.	215 000	1 624 802

4

With its collapse in 1963, Southern Rhodesia inherited all the assets within her borders. This included a highly sophisticated money market which was developed to service the entire Federation. Trade between Southern Rhodesia and her two northern neighbours had risen from 21% of total exports in 1953 to 30,5% in 1963. Despite the end of Federation, these trade links continued (at least until the war in Rhodesia led to the closure of the border with Zambia). The common currency, common customs duties and special protection tariffs were all lost, as were the advantages of Zambia's foreign currency earnings from copper sales.

There can be little doubt that the Federation greatly strengthened the economy of Southern Rhodesia, and that this was partly at the expense of the economies of the two Northern territories. The growth rate of the manufacturing industry in Southern Rhodesia was, for example, significantly above the Federal average, while that of the Northern territories was significantly below.

Nyasaland's supplies of cheap labour and Northern Rhodesia's copper played no small part in financing the increased volume of investment in the Federation, much of which was located in Southern Rhodesia. The benefit of the expanded market was also felt mostly by the latter which was in a position to exploit the large captive market; the more backward industries of the Northern territories did not, by comparison, receive any protection from their relatively more advanced southern neighbour. The infrastructural development that took place in the years of Federation laid the basis for the growth and diversification of industry that was to take place during the years of UDI.

The next 15 years were to be difficult years for the whole region as the war in Southern Rhodesia was to drag her neighbours into this internal conflict.

The rise of black nationalism in both Nyasaland and Northern Rhodesia under Banda and Kaunda eventually led to the collapse of the Federation.

The Early UDI Period (1965-74)

The rise to power of the Rhodesia Front represented the end of the partnership between settler and multinational capital which had been forged during the period of Federation. The winds of change that were sweeping through Africa forced changes at the level of colonial policy and in the methods of accumulation used by multinational capital in order to retain access to the wealth of the colonies. Political power was to be sacrificed in the interests of maintaining control of British investments and the right to repatriate profits. This realignment, which effectively meant the granting of independence to the colonies, while clearly in the interests of multi-national capital was not in the interests of settler capital which depended on its political power for its profitability. Majority rule would threaten the cheap labour policy and hence the surival of settler capital.

TABLE 4: Total GDP and Growth Rate: 1954-79

Year	Growth Rate
1954	
1955	8,9%
1956	13,9%
1957	10,7%
1958	3,4%
1959	6,7%
1960	6,0%
1961	6,6%
1962	1,9%
1963	2,3%
1964	3,5%
1965	7,1%
1966	- ,4%
1967	8,6%
1968	5,3%
1969	15,5%
1970	7,0%
1971	13,0%
1972	11,8%
1973	9,2%
1974	16,3%
1975	7,5%
1976	8,0%
1977	1,5%
1978	3,3%
1979	16,4%

5

The old contradictions between settler capital and international capital re-emerged and the coming to power of the Rhodesian Front and the unilateral declaration of independence represented a brief period of hegemony for settler capital. The sanctions that followed UDI meant, in economic terms, a shift from the external market-orientated policy (of export dependent growth) to one of internal self-augmentation (growth through import substitution).

Table 4 shows the annual growth from 1954 to 1979. This period can be divided into four distinct sub-periods: the Federal years (1954-64) which saw growth at a rate of 6,4% p.a.; the early part of UDI (1965-74) during which the economy grew at 9,3% p.a.; the latter UDI or war period (1975-78) in which growth slowed to 5,1% p.a.; and the year of the Internal Settlement in which growth rocketed to 16,4%. (Note that the following two years, 1980 and 1981, saw even higher growth rates of 20,6% and 21,8%).

TABLE 5: Selected Growth Rates in the UDI Period: 1964-74

Growth rate p.a.	9,34%
Real growth rate p.a.	7,4%
Per capita growth rate	3,8%
Growth in manufacturing sector p.a.	9,4%
Growth in government services p.a.	12,9%
Growth in agricultural sector p.a.a	7,4%

6

Table 5 gives a breakdown of the 9,3% growth achieved in the first ten years of UDI. The economic significance of this period is emphasized by the achievement of a higher growth rate than even the Federal period, when the market expanded greatly and external funds poured into the country. The comparatively slow rate of agricultural growth during the 1964-74 period was mainly due to the effect of sanctions on the marketing of Rhodesian tobacco.

Increasing State Participation

The state greatly increased its participation and control of the economy during this period. The Industrial Development Corporation (IDC) was established to assist new and selected existing enterprises with long-term (over five years) capital and managerial supervision. The Industrial Promotion Corporation of Central Africa Limited (IPCORN) provided medium-term capital and managerial advice. The Agricultural Finance Corporation (AFC) was created by merging the Agricultural Land Bank and the Agricultural Loan Fund. The Mining Council provided finance to new mining initiatives and the expansion of deserving old mines. Universal Exports (UNIVEX) found new markets for exports, expanded old markets and evaded sanctions. The Industrial Tariff Committee helped decide which old and new industries qualified for protection, to what extent, and for how long. The Industrial Projects Committee was established to determine what new industries needed priority consideration and which individual industrialists were to be accorded the sole franchise for producing the commodity/range in question.

The 1965 National Development Plan

The 1965 National Development Plan emphasized the increase in real per capita income. The long-term aim was to reduce dependence on external borrowing. Domestic savings were to be mobilized to finance growth without retarding private enterprise's capacity to expand. The plan encouraged and supported investments in foreign exchange earning production, and supported the inflow of capital and skilled manpower. A strong and stable currency was to be maintained and a sound balance of payments position was aimed for. The first condition of growth was stipulated to be the maintenance of capitalism.

Foreign Investment

Total foreign investment (excluding that from South Africa and Portugal) fell from about 33% prior to UDI to 20% six years later. This is especially significant in the light of the very high growth rates achieved during the early UDI period. British investment was 89,5% of the total; United States investment was 3,8%, followed by the Netherlands (3,4%) and Canada (less than 3%). Until 1977 there were at least 152 British, American and Canadian parent companies with investments in Rhodesia. Together they controlled 399 subsidiaries.

Rise in Production

Between 1964 and 1975 maize production increased by 95%; electricity consumption rose by 228%; commercial vehicles on the road increased by 180% while passenger vehicles increased by 87%; the national herd increased in size by 86%; iron production rose by 29% and steel production by over 84%. In 1963 manufacturing's contribution to GDP was 17,2%, compared to 20,1% in South Africa. In 1975 the local manufacturing sector's contribution to GDP was 24,8%, compared to 23,7% in South Africa. So successful was Rhodesian industrialization that some South African manufacturers of clothing, footwear and radios protested against the flood of Rhodesian exports.

The War Economy (1976-79)

The effects of the closure of schools, hospitals and clinics, the sabotage of road and railway routes and the policy of establishing protected villages forced many peasants to migrate to the urban areas in search of income.

The rural economy, both peasant and commercial, was affected by the war. The curfews, the reduced availability of draft animals, the spread of tsetse-fly as a result of the breakdown of veterinary services, all had their effect on rural production. In the commercial sector, many white farmers deserted their lands in the face of guerilla activity.

External trade also suffered as transport problems, bottlenecks and sanctions, white emigration and the world recession began to bite. In the seven years from 1974 to 1980 the balance of payments account only reflected a positive balance in 1976.

Despite the slow-down in the growth rate (see Table 4) in the last few years of UDI, the overall economic performance was excellent. The degree of success can be attributed to the continuity of sound economic policy and close collaboration between the UDI government and private enterprise. The economic base inherited from the Federal period was also an important factor, together with the ability to circumvent sanctions and shift resources from primary to secondary production.

References

1. Central Statistical Office (CSO) *Quarterly Digest of Statistics*, Harare, 1986.
2. *ibid.*
3. Ministry of Finance, Economic Planning and Development, *Socio-Economic Review 1980-1985*, Zimbabwe, Harare, 1986. Note that the 1985 figures are for the first three quarters only and are provisional.
4. Makoni, Tonderai, 'The Rhodesian Economy in a Historical Perspective, Part II', printed in *Zimbabwe Towards a New Order - an Economic and Social Survey*, working Papers, United Nations, 1980, p.48.
5. *ibid.*, Statistical tables, Annex 1, p.2.
6. *ibid.*, p.55

Chapter 2

ZIMBABWE'S NATIONAL INCOME

In this chapter we will examine the creation, production and distribution of Zimbabwe's wealth, i.e. we will look at who produces the wealth, how much is produced and how it is shared amongst the people of Zimbabwe.

Gross Domestic Product — a Measure of Wealth

The most common measure of wealth used is the Gross Domestic Product. This is a measure of all the goods and services produced within a given economy in one year. GDP can be calculated by:

— adding the total value at factor cost (i.e. market price *plus* subsidy *less* indirect tax) of the goods and services produced within each sector of the economy counted without duplication and before providing for depreciation. It is, therefore, essentially the sum of the 'value added' at each stage of production (see Box 1 on 'What is Value Added?'). Gross Domestic Output (GDO) is calculated by adding the value added of the agricultural sector to the value added of the manufacturing sector to the value added of the mining sector, etc. for all sectors of the economy.

— adding the incomes generated by the factors of production, land, labour, capital and entrepreneurship skill, i.e. rent, wages, interest and profit. This is then called Gross Domestic Income (GDI).

— adding the market expenditure by final consumer, the purchase of goods and services by government departments (government current expenditure), and the total investment expenditure by both government and the private sector. Goods produced within Zimbabwe but not sold within the country (exports) are then added in while goods sold, but not produced within Zimbabwe (imports) are subtracted. The total then gives us Gross Domestic Expenditure (GDE).

BOX 1: What is Value Added?

In order to illustrate the concept of 'value added' the production and sale of bread will be used as an example.

The production of bread goes through four distinct stages:

Stage 1	Let us assume that the farmer grows his own seed and produces his own manure for the growing of his wheat crop. The farmer, using labour, fertilizer and seed as the only inputs, then grows wheat to the value of $10 000. The $10 000 represents the return to the farmer (profit) and the wages earned by the workers. The total value of the wheat is added into the National Income calculation as it was all generated by the farmer. 'Value added' in this case is, therefore, equal to $10 000.
Stage 2	The farmer sells his wheat (for $10 000) to the miller, who then grinds it into flour. The miller has additional expenses over and above the cost of the wheat; he pays rent for the mill, transport and electricity costs, wages, and has to make a profit for himself. These additional expenses come to $5 000. The miller then sells his output (the flour) to a baker for $15 000. Note, however, that the miller only added $5 000 of value to the $10 000 worth of wheat which he purchased from the farmer. The miller's contribution to NI is, therefore, $5 000. This is the 'value added' of the miller. If we were to calculate the miller's contribution to NI being $15 000 the wheat produced by the farmer would have been added in twice, thereby overstating NI by the value of the wheat. This is known as 'double counting' which is an error.
Stage 3	The baker pays $15 000 for the flour from the miller and similarly adds 'value' to the flour by baking it into bread. If the additional expenses incurred by the baker amount to $5 000 (which would include additional inputs, wages, electricity, transport, profit for the baker, etc.) then the value of the baker's final product (i.e. the bread) would be $20 000. The baker's contribution to value added is, therefore, $5 000.
Stage 4	The retailer does not further process the bread, but incurs expenses in the distribution of the bread. The retailer's mark-up is the price the consumer pays for the convenience of the retailer's service. If the retailer adds 5% to the cost of the bread in order to determine his selling price (that 5% would cover all the retailer's expenses plus profit) then the final market value of the bread would be $21 000. The value added of the retailer (in respect of the sale of bread) would be $1 000.

Note that the sum of all the value added generated in the production and sale of bread is equal to the final market value of the bread (i.e. $21 000).

In any one year the total of value added must equal the total spending on consumer and investment goods and the incomes earned by those who produced these goods and services. We can therefore say that GDO = GDI = GDE (see Box 1).

The Equality of the Three Methods

Figure 1 indicates the equality of the three methods of calculating Zimbabwe's income. The first Pie Chart depicting National Income shows the contribution of the different factors of production. Chart B shows the contribution made by each sector of the economy to the national output; note that the total for National Output is equal to the total for National Income. Chart C deals with National Expenditure, showing the contribution of consumption expenditure; government expenditure and investment expenditure; note that in this case we deduct net exports and net indirect taxes in order to arrive at the common total of $5 081m. (1983 figures have been used throughout this chapter as this was the latest period for which final figures were available at the time of writing).

FIGURE 1: Zimbabwe's National Income: 1983

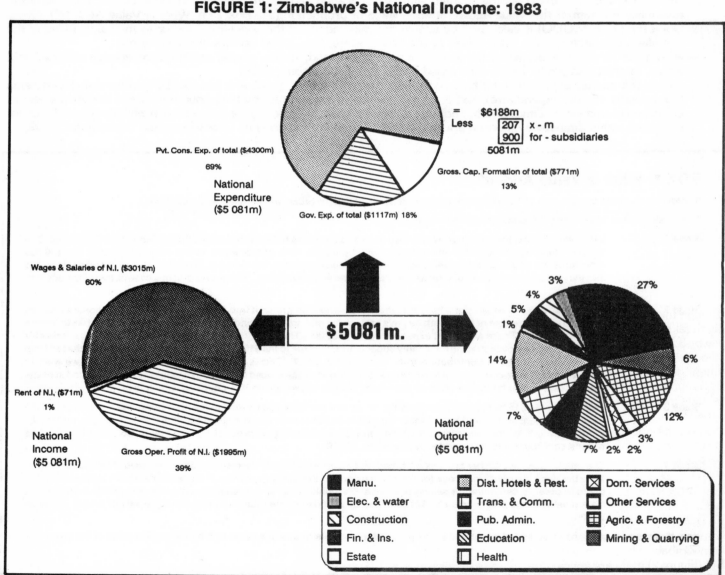

Calculating Zimbabwe's real Wealth

Table 1 shows the growth of Zimbabwe's wealth over the past six years. Note that the 1984 figures are provisional while the 1985 and 1986 figures are projected. Table 1 highlights the difference between nominal and real GDP.

Nominal GDP is calculated at current prices (and, therefore, includes inflation) while real GDP is calculated according to a base year (1980 in the case of the above table). Real GDP, therefore, has the effect of keeping prices constant throughout the period being examined (eliminating the effects of inflation) enabling one to calculate the real increase in output rather than the increase in prices.

TABLE 1: Real Growth in the Zimbabwean Economy

Year	1980	1981	1982	1983	1984	1985	1986
Nominal GDP	3 224	4 055	4 620	5 236	5 952	7 303	8 232
Growth Rate % (Z$m)	21,4	25,7	13,9	13,3	13,6	22,6	12,7
Inflation*	8,6	12,6	13,7	17,9	16,4	12,1	10,5
ReL GDP (1980 $m)	3 224	3 569	3 618	3 465	3 555	3 887	3 894
Real GDP Growth (%)	10,9	10,7	1,3	- 4,2	2,5	9,3	0
Real GDP per head (1980 $m)#	453	488	481	448	447	475	463
Real GDP per head growth (%)	8	8	- 1,4	- 7	0	6	- 2,6

Based on population figures shown in Table 3.

2

* For inflation figures see Table 2 - Chapter 1

Although the real GDP figures give a more accurate reflection of growth than nominal GDP, neither of the above measures of growth take population increases into account. Growth in 1982 was żero (see Table 1); yet Table 3 indicates that the population grew by 3.3% in 1982. This means that although the wealth in real terms remained constant, there were an extra 264 000 mouths to feed in 1982. Effectively, therefore, we grew 3.3% *poorer* in 1982. The 'real GDP per capita' figures in Table 1 incorporates this element of population growth into the measurement of wealth. On average, the people of Zimbabwe each earned $428 in 1986, which represented zero growth in relation to 1985. Moreover, although the 'real GDP. per head (%) growth' figure gives the most adequate measure of growth, it still masks the vast disparities in income which exist between the high and low income groups in Zimbabwe.

Based on the population figures for the past 11 years (1971-81) given by the Central Statistical Office (CSO) it is possible to project the population growth rate for the next few years. The rate of population growth in Zimbabwe over the 1971-81 period was 3.3% p.a. Based on a continuation of the same trend for the next nine years the projected population figures to 1990 are shown in Table 3.

From Table 3 we can see that the average rate of population growth in Zimbabwe is in the region of 2,8% p.a. Table 1 shows that real GDP per capita growth (%) has averaged 1,6% over the 1980-86 period. Since 1982, real growth per head has averaged —0,7% p.a. This means that on average Zimbabweans have been getting poorer by 0,7% per year since 1982.

Averages, however, have a way of obscuring reality. To suggest that Zimbabwe has been getting poorer implies that everyone within Zimbabwe has been affected in the same way by the decline in the real GDP growth rate. Based on figures provided by the CSO (Figure 2) there are approximately one million communal farmers in Zimbabwe earning in the region of $280 p.a. (i.e. $23,3

TABLE 2: Total Population and Population Growth Rates: 1971-81 (figures in thousands)

Year	Population	Net Growth	Growth Rate (%)
1971	5590	190	3,5
1972	5780	190	3,1
1973	5980	200	3,5
1974	6180	200	3,4
1975	6390	210	3,4
1976	6600	210	3,3
1977	6810	210	3,2
1978	7020	210	3,1
1979	7240	220	3,1
1980	7480	240	3,3
1981	7730	250	3,3

3

TABLE 3: Projected Population Growth Rate: 1982-2000

Year	Population (000's)	Growth Rate (% pa)
1982	7 517 165	
1983	7 730 726	2,80
1984	7 952 765	2,87
1985	8 182 477	2,88
1986	8 419 299	2,89
1987	8 662 506	2,88
1988	8 912 554	2,88
1989	9 169 900	2,88
1990	9 433 857	2,87
1995	10 838 057	2,97
2000	12 375 111	2,83

4

per month) and another 377 400 domestic and agricultural workers who earn less than $80 per month. Fifty per cent of our work-force, therefore, earn less than $50 per month and almost 70% earn less than $100 per month. A tiny proportion of the labour force (1,5%) earns over $700 per month. The distribution of income is a far more important indicator of the standard of living in Zimbabwe than the real GDP figures, especially when we consider that the poverty datum line for a family of four living in an urban area was estimated to be $277 per month in 1986.

Despite the inadequacies of GDP and GDP per capita figures as a standard of comparison between countries, or even as a measurement of standard of living within one country, they continue to be widely used for precisely this purpose. The remainder of this chapter will, therefore, continue to make use of this indicator, but will also draw on alternative indicators that have been developed (see page 48 on Quality of Life Index.)

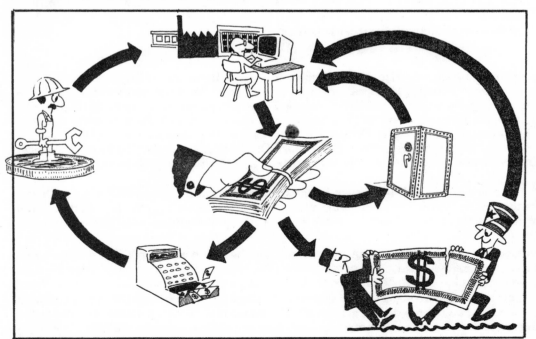

Diagram 1 illustrates the circular flow in income and expenditure throughout the economy. Pictures 1 and 2 represent the labour which is sold to commerce and industry. Picture 3 shows the money earned by the workers which is then spent in order to buy the goods and services produced by commerce and industry.

The worker cannot spend his/her entire salary on the purchase of goods and services; some of the worker's money is taken by the government in the form of taxes (picture 6) while some money is saved (5). These two leakages from our circular flow are re-injected in the form of government investment and investment by the private sector (note the arrows from 6 and 5 back into 2).

BOX 2: Working with Current and Constant Prices

The following example illustrates the uses of current and constant prices:

Table A: The Production of Maize by Country X: 1980-86

(1) Years	(2) Bags	(3) Price/bag	(4) Total Production (current prices)	(5) Total Production (constant prices)
1980	100	$25.00	$2 500.00	$2 500.00
1981	150	$30.00	$4 500.00	$3 750.00
1982	200	$35.00	$7 000.00	$5 000.00
1983	150	$50.00	$7 500.00	$3 750.00
1984	100	$75.00	$7 500.00	$2 500.00
1985	200	$35.00	$7 000.00	$5 000.00
1986	250	$30.00	$7 500.00	$6 250.00

Looking only at column 4 on the above table, i.e. total production at current prices, it would appear that the production of maize has increased steadily from 1980 to 1983, after which it slowed down and then decreased slightly in 1985 — only to regain its previous level in 1986.

The problem with these figures is that they reflect the current price of maize which includes the year on year inflation (in order to get one bag of maize in 1980 one had to pay $25; in 1983, by contrast, one had to pay $50 for the same bag of maize). Column 3 gives an indication of the fluctuating price of a bag of maize. From a price of $25 the price rises steadily to the 1984 level of $75. One reason for this could be a shortage of maize due to a drought. Because the price is rising faster than the drop in production we find that the total production of maize measured in monetary terms actually increases (column 4) despite the fact that less maize is now being produced.

If we are interested in the level of production rather than the current value of production then we can either ignore price and look only at the number of bags produced (i.e. column 2), or we can hold price constant and then see what happens to total product (see column 5).

Although the figures given in column 2 are a useful indicator of the level of production, this is not a very practical measure when working with many different commodities.

The use of constant prices is a more useful method of measuring changes in productivity. The figures in column 5 have been calculated by assuming that the price of a bag of maize remains constant over the 1980-86 period at $25 per bag. The increase in total production measured by column 5 is, therefore, the result of an increased production of maize, and not a result of price increases. Column 5 now shows a different picture to column 4; we now find that total product declines in 1983 and 1984. This is a decline in real terms, i.e. in the number of bags of maize produced. Similarly, the increase in total production from 1985 to 1986 came about as a result of an increase in the production of maize and is, therefore, a real increase.

Expressing total production at constant prices, therefore, eliminates the effects of inflation. The figures in column 5 can be referred to as 'deflated' or 'real' figures.

FIGURE 2: Structure of the Labour Force in Zimbabwe

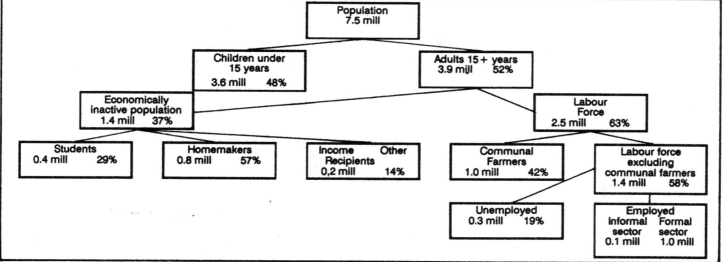

Graph 1 shows Zimbabwe's real and nominal GDP for the years 1980-86. The real figures (shaded bars) have been deflated using 1980 as the base year. In 1981, for example, nominal GDP was $4 049m (total bar); real GDP was $3 645m (shaded bar); while real GDP per capita was $472. (See Table 1 for figures). The size of the shaded bars on Graph 1 indicate that in 1980 terms we are only producing marginally more in 1986 than we were in 1981. The dramatic rise in GDP shown by the rise in nominal figures only reflects price rises (inflation). More important, however, is the falling trend shown by the 'real GDP per capita' line on the graph; this was calculated by dividing the 'real GDP (1980 Z$m)' figures given in Table 1 by the projected population figures given in Table 3. Since the rate of population growth has exceeded the rate of growth of the economy, per capita GDP has been falling.

GRAPH 1: Zimbabwe's Gross Domestic Product: 1980 - 86

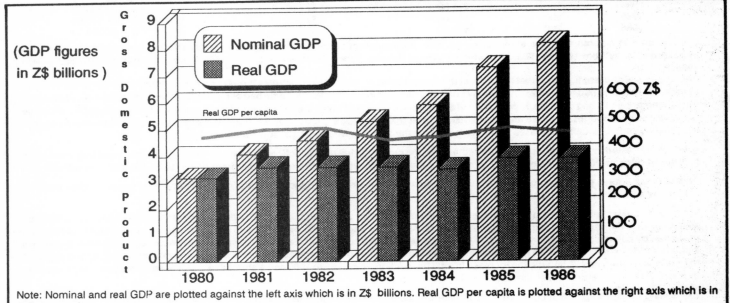

(GDP figures in Z$ billions)

Note: Nominal and real GDP are plotted against the left axis which is in Z$ billions. Real GDP per capita is plotted against the right axis which is in dollars.

The Calculation of Gross Domestic Product

As was noted earlier GDP can be calculated in three different ways: using the nation's *output;* adding up the rewards to the factors of production, i.e. the *incomes earned*; or calculating the total *expenditure* on both producer and consumer goods. Each of these methods will be examined in more detail using Zimbabwean National Income data.

Gross Domestic Output

The Pie Chart B in Figure 1 indicates what each sector of the economy contributes to the national income. At a glance we can see that the manufacturing sector is the single largest sector, followed by the distributive sector and then by agriculture. (Note that the distributive sector has moved into second place largely because of the effects of the drought on the agricultural sector. In the years preceding the drought, and in 1984 and 1985 the agricultural sector once again assumed its place as the second largest sector in the economy).

Table 4 provides the figures from which Pie Chart B was drawn. (The figures given in column 1 are the nominal figures (current prices); the figures given in column 3 are 1980 figures; while the figures in column 4 are 1983 figures which have been deflated and expressed in 1980 terms (i.e. at constant prices). Columns 3 and 4 are provided for the purpose of comparison.) By comparing columns 3 and 4 we can calculate the *real* rate of growth in each sector of the economy, as opposed to the *nominal* rate of growth which can be calculated by comparing columns 1 and 3. Column 2 gives the contribution of each sector to total output. Agriculture and forestry, therefore, generated 12% of the nation's total output in 1983.

Columns 5 and 6 give an indication of the difference between real and nominal rates of growth. Using only nominal (current) figures the fastest growing sector in the economy appears to be the construction sector, followed by education, electricity and

TABLE 4: Gross Domestic Output: 1980 + 1983

Economic Sector	1983 at current prices	% of total	1980 at current prices	1983 at constant (1980) prices	Nominal growth (%)	Real growth (%)
	(1)	(2)	(3)	(4)	(5)	(6)
1. Agriculture and forestry	592	12	458	469	+ 30	+ 2
2. Mining and quarrying	284	6	285	283	0	0
3. Manufacturing	1 385	27	802	852	+ 73	+ 6
4. Electricity and water	134	3	70	68	+ 91	- 3
5. Construction	194	4	87	89	+ 123	+ 2
6. Finance and insurance	274	5	159	211	+ 72	+ 33
7. Real estate	59	1	43	42	+ 27	- 2
8. Distribution, hotels and restaurants	737	14	451	392	+ 63	- 13
9. Transport and communications	364	7	211	223	+ 73	+ 6
10. Public administration	375	7	290	336	+ 29	+ 16
11. Education	343	7	169	310	+ 103	+ 83
12. Health	109	2	71	92	+ 54	+ 30
13. Domestic services	88	2	65	60	+ 35	- 7
14. Other services, n.e.s.	316	3	173	215	+ 87	+ 24
Less imputed banking service charges	- 173		- 108	- 120		
Gross Domestic product	5 081	100%	3 226	3 522		

7

water, and manufacturing. The real (constant) figures display a different reality: education, with a real growth rate of 83% is by far the fastest growing sector of the economy, followed by finance and insurance, health and public administration. The construction sector, with a nominal growth of 123%, has a real growth of only 2%, the rest of the nominal growth being inflation. Electricity and water, with a nominal growth of 91%, in fact declined by 3% in real terms (i.e. real growth was *minus* 3%). The major growth areas of the economy were, therefore, all in the service sector, with the social services being especially well represented.

Analysis of Output according to the Stage of Production

Table 4 can be further aggregated (or grouped) into the following sectors:
— the primary sector, or extractive industry;
— the secondary sector, or manufacturing industry;
— the tertiary sector, or services industry.

This enables us to assess the level of development of the economy. Development in this case being measured by the relative contribution of the different sectors to total output. The primary sector (agriculture, mining, fishing, etc.) usually dominates the economies of Third World underdeveloped countries, the secondary sector (manufacturing) that of Second World/developing countries, and the tertiary (service) sector, that of First World countries. (Note that it is the services provided by the private sector and not by the government that are relevant in this case).

From Table 4 we get the following:

TABLE 5: Output per Sector: 1983

Primary Sector		18%
Agriculture	12%	
Mining	6%	

Secondary Sector		31%
Manufacturing	27%	
Construction	4%	

Tertiary Sector		51%
Electricity and water	3%	
Finance and industry	5%	
Real estate	1%	
Distribution, hotels	14%	
Transport and communication	7%	
Public administration	7%	
Education	7%	
Health	2%	
Domestic services	2%	
Other services	3%	

Table 5 shows that it is the services sector which contributes the bulk of our total output. The 51% contribution of the services sector can be further sub-divided into services provided by the government, and services provided by the private sector, as is shown by Table 6:

TABLE 6: Sub-division of the Services Sector: 1983

Services provided by Government		Services provided by the Private Sector	
Electricity and water	3%	Finance and Insurance	5%
Public administration	7%	Real estate	1%
Education	7%	Distribution	14%
Health	2%	Domestic services	2%
* Transport and communication	7%	** Other	3%
Total	26%	Total	25%

9

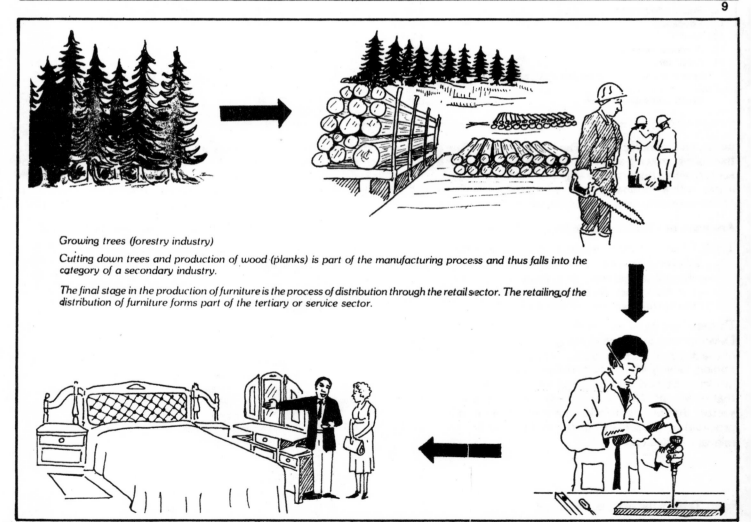

Growing trees (forestry industry)

Cutting down trees and production of wood (planks) is part of the manufacturing process and thus falls into the category of a secondary industry.

The final stage in the production of furniture is the process of distribution through the retail sector. The retailing of the distribution of furniture forms part of the tertiary or service sector.

The Stages in the Production of Furniture

Table 6 is significant, as some of the services provided by government might well be a drain on the economy. The expansion of the public service in order to absorb school-leavers would, for example, be reflected in a larger service sector. This, however, is not necessarily contributing to the growth of the economy. The provision of electricity and water and health and education are, however, vitally important economic services provided by government. Because these services are subsidized they are understated in our National Income data. The effect of the subsidized services on the standard of living in Zimbabwe is, therefore, greater than is reflected by the figures.

Note that the government's contribution to Gross Domestic Product is not limited to its 26% contribution to the services sector. The government is also involved in the primary and secondary sectors.

Material and non-Material Production

The Ministry of Finance, Economic Planning and Development (MFEP&D) categorizes the Gross Domestic Output/Product according to material and non-material production. Table 7 below shows the categorization and the contribution of each sector (and category) to national growth.

TABLE 7: GDP at Factor Cost by Industry of Origin: 1974-85

	1974	1975	1976	1977	1978	1979	1980	1981	1982	1983	1984	1985	Plan targets
Agriculture and forestry	15,6	14,7	16,5	14,0	15,5	15,3	14,2	13,6	13,7	13,3	13,6	16,1	16,2
Mining and quarrying	9,4	9,6	10,5	10,7	10,2	10,1	8,8	7,4	7,8	8,0	8,3	7,6	4,5
Manufacturing	23,5	23,3	22,1	22,7	22,0	24,1	24,9	24,2	24,1	24,2	23,0	23,4	28,5
Electricity and water	2,9	3,0	2,7	2,0	2,5	2,2	2,2	1,9	1,7	1,9	2,0	2,1	2,1
Construction	5,3	5,0	4,0	3,8	3,2	3,1	2,7	2,7	2,7	2,5	2,4	2,3	3,7
Distribution, hotels and restaurants	12,3	12,1	11,4	11,7	8,4	11,7	14,0	14,5	12,4	11,1	10,5	10,7	15,4
Transport and communication	6,7	6,3	6,1	5,7	5,8	6,0	6,5	6,6	6,5	6,3	6,5	6,3	6,5
TOTAL MATERIAL PRODUCTION	75,7	73,9	73,3	70,6	70,8	72,4	73,3	71,0	68,9	67,5	66,3	68,4	76,8
Finance and insurance	4,5	6,1	6,2	6,7	6,0	5,1	4,9	5,7	6,6	6,0	5,6	5,1	4,4
Real estate	3,0	2,6	2,3	2,3	1,9	1,7	1,3	1,4	1,2	1,2	1,2	1,1	*
Public administration	5,6	6,3	7,1	8,5	9,7	9,6	9,0	9,2	9,1	9,5	10,2	9,8	8,2
Education	4,1	4,3	4,3	4,8	4,4	4,4	5,2	6,5	6,5	7,8	8,8	9,4	9,16
Health	1,9	2,0	2,0	2,4	2,4	2,3	2,2	2,4	2,4	2,6	2,7	2,5	1,5
Domestic services	2,4	2,4	2,4	2,5	2,4	2,2	2,0	1,7	1,7	1,7	1,7	1,5	1,5
Other services	5,4	5,4	5,3	5,7	5,7	5,7	5,4	5,1	5,6	6,1	6,1	5,5	1,5
TOTAL NON-MATERIAL PRODUCTION	26,8	29,0	29,6	32,7	32,5	31,0	30,0	32,0	34,3	35,9	37,2	34,7	23,2
Less imputed banking charges	- 2,5	- 2,9	- 2,9	- 3,3	- 3,3	- 3,4	- 3,3	- 3,0	- 3,2	- 3,4	- 3,5	- 3,1	*
Total GDP	100	100	100	100	100	100	100	100	100	100	100	100	100

* Included in other services.

10

As is evident from Table 7, the trend has been for the non-material sectors to grow at the expense of the material sectors. Virtually all the material sectors show a decline over the 1974-85 period in contrast to the consistent growth experienced in the non-material sector over the same period. 1985 is a notable exception, as shown by Graph 3, which indicates the rate of growth year by year in the material and non-material sectors and in total GDP.

The expansion of the non-material sector at the expense of the material sector is not a post-Independence phenomenon. Graph 3 shows that the non-material sectors grew faster than the material sectors between 1974-78 as well as between 1980-84. The lack of investment by the private sector — which controls almost all of material production — is likely to be the culprit. Graph 2 shows the growth in the social services sector (i.e. education, health and public administration). Since 1974 this sector's contribution has doubled (increasing from 11,6% in 1974 to 21,4% in 1985).

GRAPH 2: % Contribution of the Pub. Admin. Education and Health Sectors to GDP: 1974-85

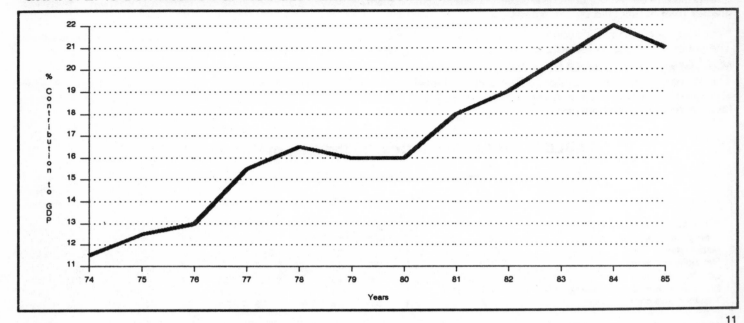

GRAPH 3: Real Growth in the Material and Non-material Sectors

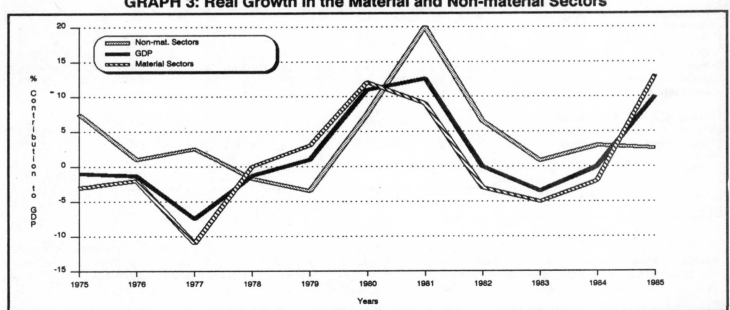

The imbalance between the material and non-material sectors, if continued, could have adverse effects on Zimbabwe's future development. Although the extension of social services to the mass of our people is long overdue, (and is of course central to the government's policy of growth with equity) the extension of such services is dependent on the ability of the material sector to continue to generate a surplus. If the material sector was expanding, then the increased tax revenues would be able to support a growing social services sector; if, on the other hand, the material sector is either remaining the same size or shrinking, then the only way to expand social services is either to increase the rate of taxation on the material sector, or for government to borrow money. The former option would threaten the viability of the material sector now, the latter would threaten its viability in the future (as the inflationary effects of deficit financing begin to be felt).

Employment and Output

TABLE 8: Employment Changes from 1980-84

Sector	1980	1984	% of total	Net change
1. Agriculture	327 000	265 500	26	- 61 500
2. Mining	66 000	55 000	5	- 11 000
3. Domestic service	108 000	98 000	9	- 10 000
4. Education	41 900	84 400	8	+ 42 500
5. Public administration	71 100	88 300	9	+ 17 200
6. Distribution	70 300	81 500	8	+ 11 200
7. Manufacturing	159 400	166 700	16	+ 7 200
8. Construction	42 200	46 900	4	+ 4 700
9. Transport and communication	45 00	49 900	5	+ 4 300
10. Other	77 200	96 600		+ 19 400
Totals	1 00 900	1 033 000	100,0%	+ 24 100

13

Table 8 shows the proportion of the labour force employed in each sector of the economy. The agricultural sector remains the largest employer, accounting for 26% of total employment (down from 32% in 1980). The second largest employer is manufacturing with 16% of the labour force. Breaking down the employment figures into people employed in the primary, secondary and tertiary sectors (as categorized in Table 5) we find that although the primary sector employs 34% of the labour force, it only generates 18% of the total output (which is consistent with the low productivity ratios of the primary sectors — see Table 9). The secondary sector employs 32% of the total labour force and generates 31% of the total output, while the tertiary sector employs 34% of the total labour force and generates 51% of the total output (see Table 9).

TABLE 9: Employment per sector*: 1984

Sector	No. employed	% employed
Primary sector	320 000	34%
Secondary sector	295 100	32%
Tertiary sector	320 200	34%
	936 000	100%

14

* Excluding "Other" (96 600).

The relationship between the number of people employed in each sector of the economy and the total output produced in that sector gives an indication of productivity in that particular sector. The figures alone do not, however, explain why one sector may be more productive than another and it would be dangerous to make simplistic assumptions. The much higher productivity in

25

manufacturing does not necessarily mean that workers in agriculture are less efficient or less educated. A more detailed examination of the two sectors might show that the difference in productivity was more related to the use of capital equipment and more scientific management structures than simply in the level of motivation or degree of education of the workforce.

TABLE 10: Relationship of Employment to Output: 1984

	(1)	(2)	(3)	(4)	(5)
Sector	(000's) Employees	% of Total	($m) Output	% of Total	Productivity Ratio
1. Agriculture	271,2	26	673	12	0,46
2. Mining	54,5	5	330	6	1,2
3. Manufacturing	166,3	16	1 565	28	1,75
4. Electricity and water	7,3	1	161	3	3,0
5. Construction	45,3	4	203	4	1,0
6. Finance and insurance	15,7	2	309	7	3,5
7. Distribution	80,2	8	791	13	1,6
8. Transport	50,1	5	403	7	1,4
9. Public administration	88,9	9	396	7	0,7
10. Education	83,8	8	423	7	0,87
11. Health	19,9	2	132	2	1,0
12. Domestic services	98,0	9	87	1	0,1
13. Other services	55,2	5	149	3	0,6
	1 036,4	100%	*5 686	100%	

15

* Imputed banking service charges ($199m) have been subtracted from 13 (Other services) in order to get the total output figure of $5 685m.

Table 10 enables us to compare the output and employment levels for all sectors of the economy, and by dividing the total output per sector (column 3) by the total employment in that particular sector (column 1) we get an average output per worker — the productivity ratio (column 5).

An examination of column 5 shows that the biggest employer in the country — the agricultural sector — has the second lowest productivity ratio. The two most productive sectors of the economy, finance and insurance and electricity and water, together only employ 3% of the total labour force. The electricity and water sub-sector, being a public sector monopoly, has an unfair advantage as it can increase its rates without fear of competition.

Setting aside the foreign exchange constraints, Table 10 indicates that for Zimbabwe to maximize its rate of economic growth, resources should be concentrated in those sectors which have the highest productivity ratios and employ the largest number, i.e. the manufacturing, distributive and transport sectors. As a whole the service·sectors (9 to 12) have a noticeably lower productivity ratio than the material sectors (1 to 8) with the exception of agriculture. Furthermore, the primary sectors (see Table 5) have, on average, a lower productivity than the secondary sectors, which in turn have a lower productivity than the tertiary sectors. The social services sectors (9 to 11) are also amongst the least productive sectors.

Population Growth and Employment

Graph 4 shows the relationship between population growth in Zimbabwe and the level of job creation (employment). Both sets of figures have been reduced to indices for ease of comparison. If all the people are to be employed, the two curves on the graph should have the same slope. Using 1964 as the base year, the graph shows that except for the years 1965 and 1966, the early UDI years saw employment generation grow at a faster rate than population growth. From 1975 the trend changed and population grew at a faster rate than employment; from 1981 the size of the work-force remained constant at 1 035m while the population continued to grow. The explanation of these trends lies in the performance of the economy in the above period. The import-substitution policies of UDI boosted local production and hence local employment. By 1975, however, the war began to take its toll and the economy entered a downturn. The 1984 level of employment (at 1 035m) was still below the 1974 level of 1 039m and the 1975 peak of 1,05m. Since 1975 the population of Zimbabwe has grown by 2,25m people (36%) while the size of the work-force has remained more or less constant.

GRAPH 4: Comparison of Population Growth Rate and Employment Creation: 1964-84

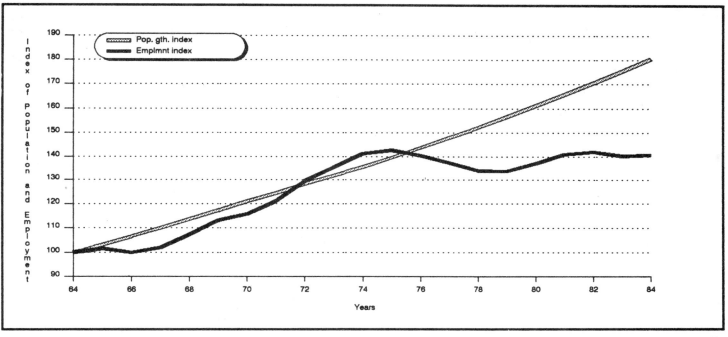

FIGURE 3: The Components of Gross Domestic Income

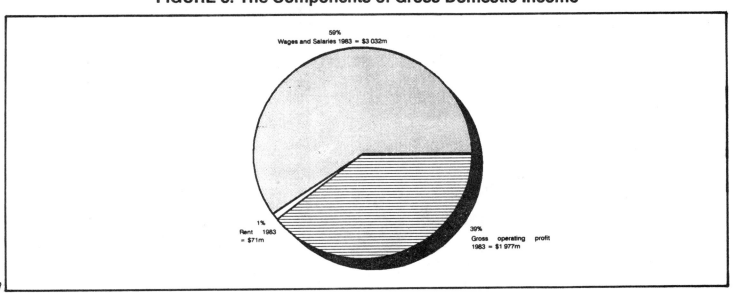

Gross Domestic Income

It has been previously shown (page 16) that the total of goods produced in an economy must equal the total of the wages, salaries, profits and rent earned in any one year and must also equal the total of consumption, investment and government expenditure. Simply stated this means that GNP = GNI = GNE. The previous section dealt with the Gross National Output, its constituents, and its relationship to employment, level of development, etc. This section will examine Gross National Income.

Figure 3 shows the relative contribution of labour and capital to the national economy. The total of $5 081m represents the Gross Domestic Income at Factor Cost. Indirect taxes and subsidies have not yet been taken into account and Net Investment Income paid abroad has not yet been subtracted. Table 11 shows the calculation of Zimbabwe's GDI for the past ten years, and the derivation of Gross National Income from Gross Domestic Income (at factor cost). By subtracting depreciation from Gross National Income it is possible to calculate Net National Income.

(The figure for depreciation of national assets is, however, not calculated in Zimbabwe — all the National Income tables give only gross values and not net values).

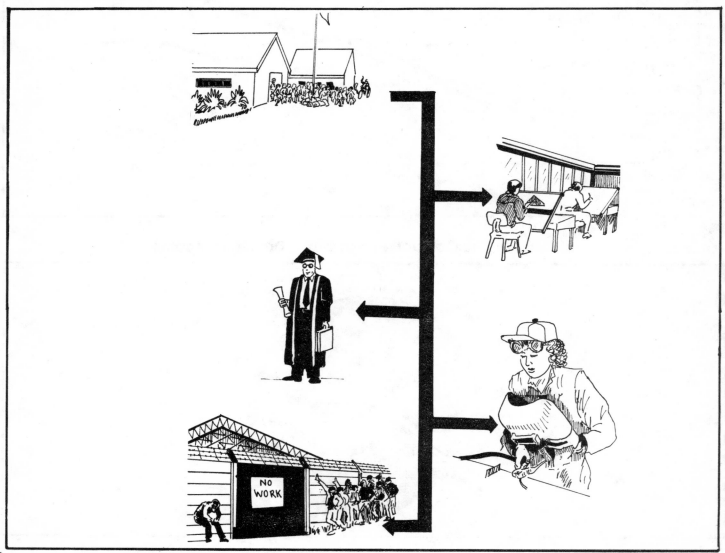

TABLE 11: National Income: 1974-83

$ million

Item	1974	1975	1976	1977	1978	1979	1980	1981	1982	1983
Wages and salaries	905	1 049	1 154	1 249	1 380	1 563	1 902	2 328	2 797	3 032
Rent	54	56	60	63	60	58	60	70	70	72
Rented dwellings (private)	17	17	18	18	16	16	15	20	18	19
Imputed for owner-occupied dwellings	22	21	23	24	22	20	18	24	25	26
Central and local government	15	18	19	21	22	22	27	26	27	27
Gross operating profit	832	799	849	759	817	1 033	1 264	1 651	1 741	1 977
Unincorporated enterprises	227	217	236	229	161	182	225	303	308	249
Companies (non-financial)	525	524	538	471	591	781	1 013	1 295	1 428	1 632
Financial institutions	34	42	43	49	54	57	85	90	111	136
Public Corporations (non-financial)	69	49	70	56	62	61	30	59	23	86
Central and local govt. enterprises (non-financial)	19	19	18	19	18	34	19	25	17	47
Less imputed banking service charges	- 42	- 52	- 56	- 65	- 69	- 82	- 108	- 121	- 146	- 173
Gross domestic income (factor cost)	1 791	1 902	2 064	2 069	2 257	2 651	3 226	4 049	4 609	5 081
Plus indirect taxes	129	137	170	223	238	262	317	504	709	960
Less subsidies	- 59	- 41	- 68	- 94	- 134	- 90	- 100	- 120	- 169	- 60
Gross domestic income (market prices)	1 861	1 998	2 166	2 198	2 361	2 823	3 443	4 433	5 149	5 981
Less net factor income paid abroad	- 40	- 46	- 59	- 48	- 41	- 54	- 47	- 115	- 194	- 250
Gross national income (market price)	1 821	1 952	2 107	2 150	2 320	2 769	3 396	4 318	4 955	5 731

18

TABLE 12: Composition of National Income: 1974-83

Item	1974	1975	1976	1977	1978	1979	1980	1981	1982	1983
Wage and salaries	50,0	55,2	55,9	60,3	61,5	58,8	59,0	57,3	60,2	59,3
Rent	3,4	3,2	3,1	3,3	2,9	2,4	1,9	1,7	1,5	1,4
Gross operating profit	46,2	41,6	40,9	36,4	35,6	38,7	39,2	41,0	38,3	39,3
Gross domestic income	100,0	100,0	100,0	100,0	100,0	100,0	100,0	100,0	100,0	100,0

19

The trends in Table 11 are easier to discern from Table 12 in which the three components of Gross Domestic Income are presented as percentages. The figures from Table 12 are represented graphically in Graph 5. Table 12 shows that labour has increased its contribution to National Income from 50% in 1974 to a peak of 61,5% in 1978 and back to its current level of 59,5% in 1983. As is to be expected, the years in which labour's contribution is at its peak (1977 and 1978) are also the years in which the contribution of capital is at its lowest. The years 1977 and 1978 represented the climax of the war and in such periods capital is usually on the retreat.

GRAPH 5: Proportionate Contributions to National Income: 1974-84

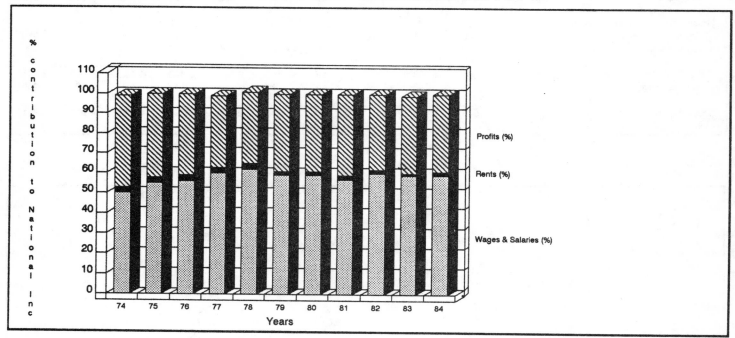

20

Wages

Table 13 gives an indication of the average standard of living in Zimbabwe. The figures in column 3 have been calculated by dividing the Gross National Income (column 1) by the total population. This gives us an average income *per person* for the whole of Zimbabwe.

Bearing in mind that 50% of the population is under the age of 15 and, therefore, not working, and that of the remaining 4,1 million people (1983 figures) only 1,03 million are employed in the formal sector, the wages earned by approximately one-eighth of the country support the entire population. The figures of $696 per capita (GNI in current prices) or $456 per capita (in constant prices) are not an accurate reflection of wages, but do reflect the standard of living of the population as a whole, wage-earners and dependants. (The reason the per capita GNI figures given in Table 13 are different from the per capita GDP figures given in Table

TABLE 13: Gross National Income: 1983

Year	Current (1983) Prices			Constant (1980) Prices	
	GNI at current prices ($m) (1)	Total Pop. (000's) (2)	Per capita GNI (3)	GNI at 1980 prices (4)	Per capita GNI (5)
1974	1 821	6 180	295	2 928	474
1975	1 953	6 390	306	2 915	456
1976	2 108	6 600	319	2 936	445
1977	2 151	6 810	316	2 804	412
1978	2 230	7 020	318	2 733	389
1979	2 658	7 240	367	2 931	405
1980	3 396	7 480	454	3 396	454
1981	4 318	7 730	559	3 801	492
1982	4 957	*7 985	621	3 716	465
1983	3 742	*8 249	696	3 763	456

* 1982 and 1983 population figures have been estimated based on a 3,3% pa growth rate on 1981 figures.

1 is that Table 1 deals with *Domestic* product whereas Table 13 deals with *National* income — see Table 11 for the difference between *domestic* income and *national* income).

Table 14 attempts to overcome the problem of dividing a wage earned by a small work-force by the entire population by calculating the average earning per worker rather than the average standard of living. The former is calculated by dividing the total wages earned in a particular year by the total workforce in that year i.e. dividing column 1 by column 2 to get column 3. Table 14 also compares average earnings at current prices (money values) with average earnings at real prices (constant/deflated figures). The latter calculated in column 5 is approximately four times the size of the average real earnings per person in Zimbabwe (Table 13, column 5).

Over the years 1974 to 1983 the trend in per capita Gross National Income can best be measured by looking at the real values — Table 13, column 5. This shows that standard of living (as measured by per capita real GNI) declined between 1974-78, rose sharply between 1979-81, and then dropped again in the 1982-83 period. The standard of living in 1983 was basically the same as that in 1975 despite fairly large rises in nominal Gross National Product (GNP). The major reason for the lack of improvement in

TABLE 14: Average Earnings per Worker: 1983

Year	Current (1980) Prices			Constant (1980) Prices	
	Total of wages wages & sal. ($m) (1)	Work Force (000's) (2)	Ave. earnings per worker pa (3)	Wages & sal. 1980 p's ($m) (4)	Per capital av. earnings (5)
1974	904	1 040	869	1 453	1 397
1975	1 050	1 050	1 000	1 567	1 493
1976	1 154	1 033	1 117	1 607	1 556
1977	1 248	1 012	1 233	1 627	1 608
1978	1 332	986	1 351	1 632	1 656
1979	1 494	984	1 518	1 647	1 674
1980	1 902	1 010	1 883	1 902	1 883
1981	2 319	1 038	2 234	2 041	1 967
1982	2 774	1 046	2 652	2 079	1 988
1983	3 105	1 033	2 919	1 976	1 913

the standard of living over this period is the rapid rise in population growth which was not matched by an equal rise in job opportunities (see Graph 4).

The rising trend in average earnings per worker in both money and real terms is largely a result of the static size of the work-force. As prices have risen, wages have risen but the size of the work-force has declined (see column 2, Table 14). Rising wages together with a shrinking work-force has meant higher wages for the lucky few who still have jobs. This does not mean that the standard of living — even of the salaried workers — is rising, as the fewer people in jobs have ever-growing numbers of unemployed relatives to support, thus effectively reducing their own standard of living.

Profits

Figure 4 indicates who earned the profits in 1983 the clear majority being earned by non-financial companies. The outer circle indicates which of the profits are earned by government (the public sector) and which are earned by the private sector (5% as against 94%). Government's contribution to gross operating profit has in the past ten years fluctuated between 10% in 1974 and 2% in 1982. Overall it can be said that the government contributes relatively little to the total profits earned.

FIGURE 4: The Composition of Gross Operating Profits

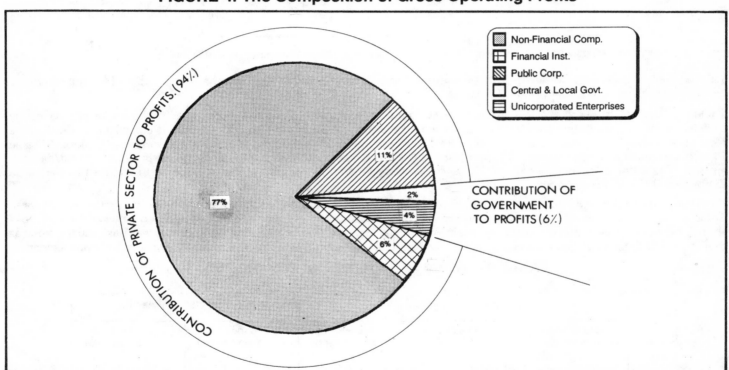

Table 15 below gives an indication of the contribution of government and the private sector to gross operating surplus (GOS) in each sector of the economy. Government's total contribution to GOS in 1983 ($175m) before the deduction of imputed banking service charges amounted to 8% of all profits earned in the economy. From Table 15 it is clear that 55% of this surplus came from the electricity and water sub-sector; another 38% from manufacturing; and 24% from finance and insurance. The losses made in the other sectors (primarily transport and communication) bring down the public sector's total contribution.

Three major sectors, manufacturing, agriculture and distribution contribute 30%, 16% and 28% respectively to the private sector Gross Operating Surplus. These three sectors, therefore, produce three-quarters of the surplus produced in the entire economy.

Contrasting government's contribution to value added (see Table 16) with its contribution to gross operating surplus, we find that in 1983 government produced 25.5% of the value added, yet generated only 8% of the GOS.

TABLE 15: Contribution of Government and Private Sector to Gross Operating Surplus

Sector	Government ($m)	Government (%)	Private Sector ($m)	Private Sector (%)	Total ($m)
Agriculture and forestry	1	0,3	312	99,7	313
Mining and quarrying	1	1	98	99	99
Manufacturing	66	10	609	90	675
Electricity and water	96	100	-	0	96
Construction	- 1	0	41	100	40
Finance and insurance	42	31	94	69	136
Distribution	- 4	0	557	100	553
Transport and communication	- 21	0	95	100	74
Education	-	0	- 1	100	- 1
Health	-	0	33	100	33
Other services	- 5	0	129	100	124

24

Profit as a reward to the enterpreneur for risk-bearing.

TABLE 16: Contribution of Government and Private Sector to Gross Domestic Product: 1983 figures

Sector	Government ($m)	Government (%)	Private Sector ($m)	Private Sector (%)	Total ($m)
Agriculture and forestry	24	4	568	96	592
Mining and quarrying	3	1	281	99	284
Manufacturing	109	8	1 275	92	1 384
Electricity and water	134	100	0	0	134
Construction	55	28	139	72	194
Finance and insurance	53	19	221	81	274
Real estate	-	0	59	100	59
Distribution	13	2	724	98	737
Transport and communication	192	53	172	47	364
Public administration	375	100	0	0	375
Education	275	80	68	20	343
Health	-	59	45	41	109
Domestic services	-	0	89	100	89
Other services	262	17	262	83	316
Less Imputed Banking Service Charges	- 53		- 120		- 173
TOTAL	**1 298**	**26**	**3 783**	**74**	**5 081**

25

Gross Domestic Expenditure

The previous two sections have dealt with the calculation of National Income using the Income and Output methods. This section will deal with the Gross National Expenditure. On page ... we said that GNO = GNI = GNE. This is based on the fact that every dollar earned is a dollar spent. Saving, too, represents an expenditure, as what is saved by the consumer is borrowed by business people and invested in productive activity. The goods that are not bought in the course of the year are added to stocks, which is a form of investment.

FIGURE 5: The Basic Components of Gross National Expenditure

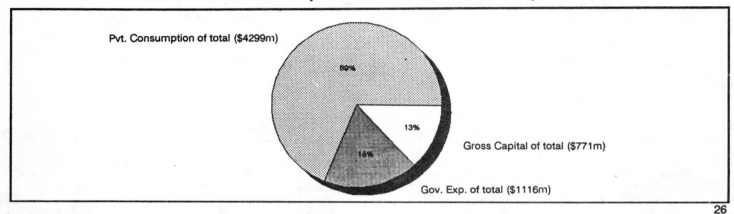

Pvt. Consumption of total ($4299m)

69%

13%

16%

Gross Capital of total ($771m)

Gov. Exp. of total ($1116m)

26

Figure 5 graphically shows that total consumer expenditure *plus* total government expenditure *plus* total investment (Gross Capital Formation) will give us the Gross National Expenditure.

In order to arrive at the figure of $5 080m for Gross National Expenditure at factor cost, we work with the 1983 figures from Table 17. The first step is to calculate Gross Domestic Expenditure by adding Private Consumption to Consumption of private non-profit bodies

1.	Private consumption	4 260	
	Consumption of private non-profit making bodies	39	
	Total Private Consumption		4 299
2.	Net Government Current Expenditure		1 116
3.	Gross Fixed Capital Formation	1 051	
	Less total increase in stocks	280	
	Net Capital Formation		771
	Gross Domestic Expenditure (at market prices)		6 186
4.	add Exports of Goods and Services		1 338
			7 524
5.	less Imports of Goods and Services		−1 544
	Gross Domestic Product (at market prices)		5 980
6.	less indirect taxes		960
	add subsidies		60
7.	Gross Domestic Product (at factor cost)		5 080
	less net investment income paid abroad		250
8.	Gross National product at factor prices		4 830

(The figure of $5 081 given in the Pie Chart is very close to the total GDP at factor cost worked out above; the difference is due to rounding off).

Consumption Expenditure

Comparing the current prices with the constant (1980) prices which are given at the bottom of Table 17 we see that much of the growth in the figures has been due to inflation. Private consumption expenditure shows a drop in the late seventies, returning to the 1974 level only in 1979.

The 1980-81 period saw private consumption expenditure grow by 14% p.a. This was largely due to the increase in minimum wages, the reduction in sales tax and the return to peace. Since 1982 the rate of growth in private consumption expenditure fell to 5% p.a. due to the demand restraint measures introduced by the monetary authorities, the wage freeze, the drought and the rising consumer prices.

The Components of Consumption Expenditure

Figure 5 is based on the total of Private Consumption Expenditure given in Table 17 (i.e. $4 260m in 1983 and $1 110 in 1974), and all prices are current prices. The diagram gives an indication of what Zimbabwean residents spent their money on in these years. Noticeable trends are the decline in expenditure on food (from 26% to 21%); the increased spending on luxuries like alcohol, tobacco and cigarettes; a rise in the spending on fuel, light and water; a doubling of the expenditure on health and education and a drop in the expenditure on housing. Without adequate data on the changing distribution of income in Zimbabwe it is difficult to determine the exact reasons for these changes. A decrease in the proportion of income spent on an essential item such as food and an increase in the spending on luxuries such as alcohol and cigarettes could on the one hand indicate an increase in the standard of living (as people would then spend more on luxuries and less on necessities); or it could indicate a rise in the incomes of the rich relative to the poor, i.e. an increasing maldistribution of income. The static size of the labour force in recent years (see Table 14, column 2) and the consequent increase in the rate of unemployment suggest that the latter may well be the case in Zimbabwe.

Private consumption expenditure increased by 43% in real terms over the 1980-83 period after remaining virtually constant in the 1974-79 period.

The 6% rise in spending on fuel, light and water mainly reflects the rise in fuel prices, and only partly, the increased availability of these services.

TABLE 17: Expenditure on the Gross National Product at Market Prices

$ million

Item	1974	1975	1976	1977	1978	1979	1980	1981	1982	1883
(at current prices)										
Private consumption	1 110	1 211	1 346	1 385	1 526	1 922	2 295	2 943	3 363	4 260
Consumption of private non-profit bodies	28	29	29	32	34	34	35	35	37	39
Net government current expenditure	221	256	319	382	451	537	677	763	973	1 116
Gross fixed capital formation	421	468	427	379	341	395	528	830	1 030	1 051
Increase in stocks										
Before revaluation adjustment	269	148	85	24	- 21	148	177	645	481	599
Revaluation adjustment	- 178	- 91	- 124	- 56	- 52	- 206	- 166	- 458	- 426	- 879
Total Increase in stocks	91	57	- 39	- 32	- 73	- 58	11	187	55	- 280
Domestic expenditure	1 871	2 021	2 082	2 146	2 279	2 830	3 546	4 758	5 458	6 186
Exports of goods and service	n/a	590	617	610	675	798	1 043	1 117.	1 141	1 338
Less Imports of goods and services	n/a	613	533	558	593	803	1 146	1 442	1 450	1 544
Net export of goods and services	- 10	- 23	84	52	82	- 5	- 103	- 325	- 309	- 206
Gross domestic product	1 861	1 998	2 166	2 198	2 361	2 825	3 443	4 433	5 149	5 980
Less net investment income paid abroad	- 40	- 46	- 59	- 48	- 41	- 54	- 47	- 115	- 194	- 250
Gross national product	1 821	1 952	2 107	2 150	2 320	2 771	3 396	4 318	4 955	5 730
(at constant (1980) prices)										
Private consumption	1 948	1 969	1 980	1 823	1 778	1 963	2 295	2 548	2 599	2 812
Consumption of private non-profit bodies	41	37	37	33	43	35	35	31	27	29
Net government current expenditure	326	348	393	425	599	615	677	791	845	907
Gross fixed capital formation	938	899	728	559	442	443	528	723	780	649
Increase in stocks	159	62	- 48	- 77	- 95	- 73	11	220	22	- 193
Domestic expenditure	3 412	3 315	3 090	2 763	2 767	2 983	3 546	4 313	4 273	4 204
Net export of goods and services	- 23	- 48	142	84	125	- 5	- 103	- 327	- 312	- 176
Gross domestic product	3 389	3 266	3 232	2 847	2 892	2 978	3 443	3 986	3 961	4 028
Less net investment income paid abroad	- 92	- 94	- 107	- 78	- 59	- 57	- 47	- 116	- 194	- 205
Gross national product	3 297	3 172	3 125	2 769	2 833	2 921	3 396	3 870	3 767	3 823

27

The consumption spending on both education and health has doubled while that on housing has dropped. The fixed prices on low-cost housing would probably be one of the major reasons for the drop in housing expenditure. Zimbabweans' consumption expenditure on durable goods (10%) is higher than that in the UK (9%); the major reason for this is more than likely the high prices of these durable goods due to their scarcity in Zimbabwe.

Government's Recurrent Expenditure

Government expenditure shows a continual rise from 1974 to 1983, despite the drop in real Gross National Product in this period. Spending on the war no doubt contributed to the rise in government current spending in the 1974-79 period, while increased expenditure on social services became the dominant element of government's recurrent expenditure in the post-Independence period. Despite efforts to cut back on its expenditure, the budget deficit has continued to rise.

FIGURE 6: Components of Consumers Expenditure in 1974 and 1983

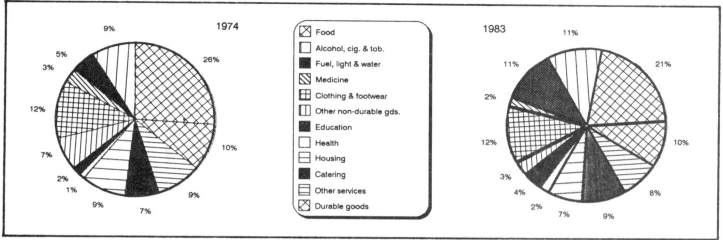

*Catering includes hotel accommodation and meals internal and abroad. Note: Non-residents expenditure not included.

Central government's current expenditure is made up of recurrent spending which is essentially spending on goods and services and transfers (see Table 18). Transfer payments are particularly important as they have formed the major component of current expenditure since 1983. The dramatic rise in interest costs reflects the rapid rise in public debt. The share of these payments in total current expenditure increased from 9% in 1980-81 to 16% in 1985-86. The proportion of government current expenditure on subsidies dropped sharply in 1979-80 but has steadily increased ever since (see Graph 6). The transfers listed under 'grants and transfers' are in the form of grants mostly for salaries, particularly in education and health. The constant proportion of salaries and allowances in current expenditure since 1980 is therefore somewhat misleading; if all salaries for education were included in this category it would be significantly higher.

One problem with an expanding civil service is efficiency.

TABLE 18: Central Government Budget Account: Expenditure, Z$ 000, 1977/78 - 86/87

	1977-78	1978-79	1979-80	1980-81	1981-82
Expenditure					
Recurrent Expenditure					
Goods and Services	410 953	481 833	613 587	605 151	769132
Salaries, wages and allowances	228 101	274 019	331 143	374 500	473 502
Subsistance and Transport	24 402	28 552	37 392	3 331	41 225
Incidental Expenses	22 803	18 504	19 975	21 354	26 268
Other recurrent expenditure	135 607	160 758	225 077	175 986	228 107
Transfers	334 826	323 675	357 862	531 290	689 049
Interest	42 489	53 754	70 431	99 815	139 327
Subsidies	119 351	122 799	91 376	106 418	138 152
Parastatal Bodies	3 601	2 201	4 097	13 498	15 169
Pensions	99 721	55 613	69 653	72 248	74 650
Grants and Transfers	69 664	89 308	122 305	239 311	321 751
Capital Expenditure	59 730	54 398	54 920	65 801	113 043
Land Purchase	311	307	2 601	3 844	21 597
Buildings	25 293	20 213	16 022	24 244	37 987
Land Development	2 643	1 205	1 388	1 864	2 163
Civil Engineering	22 554	21 760	20 746	27 923	39 950
Plant and Machinery	8 171	10 513	14 141	6 484	6 957
Office Equipment	734	358	514	1 414	4 358
Other Cap. expen.	24	42	48	28	31
Total Expenditure	744 569	859 906	1 026 369	1 202 242	1 571 224
Less Revenue	610 180	580 194	675 981	950 876	1 364 482
Budget Account Deficit/Surplus	- 134 789	279 712	350 388	251 366	20 674

	1982-83	1983-84	1984-85	1985-86	1986-87*
Expenditure Recurrent Expenditure					
Goods and Services	918 376	1 077 871	1 149 600	1 403 358	1 725 215
Salaries, wages and allowances	568 021	624 768	686 495	864 373	1 050 000
Subsistance and Transport	51 183	64 797	76 294	62 301	73 526
Incidental Expenses	30 346	36 649	48 695	71 545	60 377
Other recurrent expenditure	268 826	351 657	338 116	405 139	541 312
Transfers	906 055	1 156 011	1 292 036	1 533 366	1 760 345
Interest	197 853	251 852	320 450	393 241	538 600
Subsidies	156 110	184 539	311 837	312 688	389 802
Parastatal Bodies	28 484	56 002	69 841	115 888	46 809
Pensions	75 373	73 954	81 762	92 799	104 073
Grants and Transfers	448 235	589 664	508 146	618 750	681 061
Capital Expenditure	187 620	198 096	199 624	200 014	342 807
Land Purchase	28 251	6 548	7 082	5 688	6 520
Buildings	82 822	81 276	75 440	74 465	162 626
Land Development	2 639	7 096	5 319	3 704	37 775
Civil Engineering	58 774	88 109	76 629	98 572	113 964
Plant and Machinery	10 808	12 567	13 944	13 908	14 247
Office Equipment	3 312	2 165	18 169	3 630	3 900
Other Cap. expen.	14	335	41	47	3 775
Total Expenditure	2 012 051	2 431 978	2 641 260	3 136 738	3 828 528
Less Revenue	1 789 217	2 000 477	2 212 839	2 616 185	2 997 00
Budget Account Deficit/Surplus	222 834	431 501	428 421	520 553	831 528

* Estimates

It is government's policy to try and cover current expenditure from revenue receipts. Government borrowing would, therefore, only have to pay for capital expenditure. In the years prior to Independence spending on the war meant that revenue receipts (from direct and indirect taxes, etc.) only covered approximately 70% of current expenditure. In the years since Independence, government has managed to reduce the budget deficit to the position where revenue receipts cover approximately 90% of current expenditure; in the 1982-83 fiscal year the proportion was 98,1%, since then the rise in current expenditure has once again increased the deficit.

A more detailed breakdown of the sources of government revenue is given in Table 19. The size of the budget deficit can be calculated by subtracting the total expenditure figures from the total revenue figures (see the bottom line of Table 18).

GRAPH 6: Central Government Current Expenditure
(% Shares)

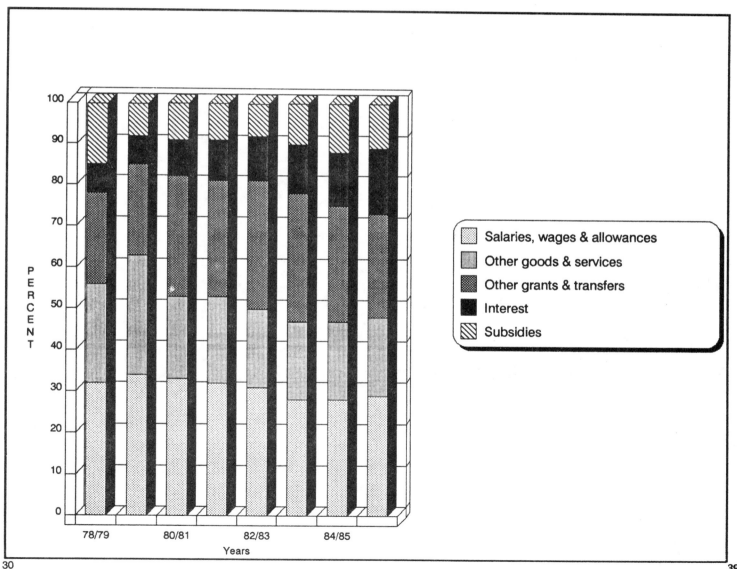

TABLE 19: Central Government Budget Account: 1983/84 - 86/87

	1983-84 Actual	1984-85 Actual	1985-86* Actual	1986-87 Estimates
REVENUE				
Taxes on Income and Profits				
Income Tax	775 937	867 841	1 030 682	1 220 000
Non-resident shareholders' tax	7 182	16 752	20 413	22 000
Non-resident's tax on interest	4 824	3 555	3 169	3 000
Resident shareholders' tax	5 428	5 852	7 416	10 000
Branch profits tax	1 336	1 483	1 000	2 000
Capital gains tax	6 861	6 418	3 905	8 000
Non-residents' tax on fees and royalties	1 179	2 390	3 190	3 500
Total	802 747	904 291	1 069 775	1 268 500
Taxes on goods and services:				
Sales tax	461 049	404 767	462 563	488 000
Customs duties	290 224	321 013	400 264	432 000
Excise duties	166 282	233 920	268 274	286 600
Betting tax	4 813	5 030	5 939	6 250
Other	813	957	768	950
Total	923 181	965 687	1 137 808	1 213 800
Miscellaneous Taxes:				
Stamp duties and fees	11 457	14 719	20 308	22 000
Estate duty	6 145	7 818	8 058	8 000
Holiday currency tax	-	9 557	10 008	13 500
Other	2	-	-	-
Total	17 604	32 094	38 374	43 500
Revenue from Investment and Property:				
Interest, dividends and profits	76 377	93 333	111 204	143 000
Rents	17 703	5 874	4 892	6 000
Royalties	-	-	-	-
Water supplies	452	-	-	-
Total	94 532	99 207	116 096	149 000
Fees: Deparmental facilities and Services:				
Agriculture	724	722	658	700
Civil Aviation	1 607	2 110	2 666	2 800
Companies, trade marks and patents	1 165	1 419	1 389	1 400
Education	14 450	19 385	23 330	27 400
Health	1 506	2 165	2 760	2 700
National Parks	1 454	2 270	3 072	3 000
Roads and Road Traffic	1 702	1 687	1 440	1 500
Water development	336	1	30	-
Other	2 842	4 397	3 936	4 500
Total	25 876	34 156	39 281	44 000
Recoveries of Development Expenditure	261	359	68	200
International Aid Grants	56 851	81 084	100 035	162 000
Other				
Pension contributions	48 514	53 512	69 352	74 000
Judicial fines	5 021	6 033	6 716	7 000
Sales of State property	16 540	17 040	16 883	18 000
Refunds of miscellaneous payments from Votes	3 531	5 804	9 876	7 000
Miscellaneous	5 818	13 572	11 921	10 000
Total	79 425	95 961	114 748	116 000
TOTAL REVENUE	2 000 477	2 212 839	2 616 185	2 997 000

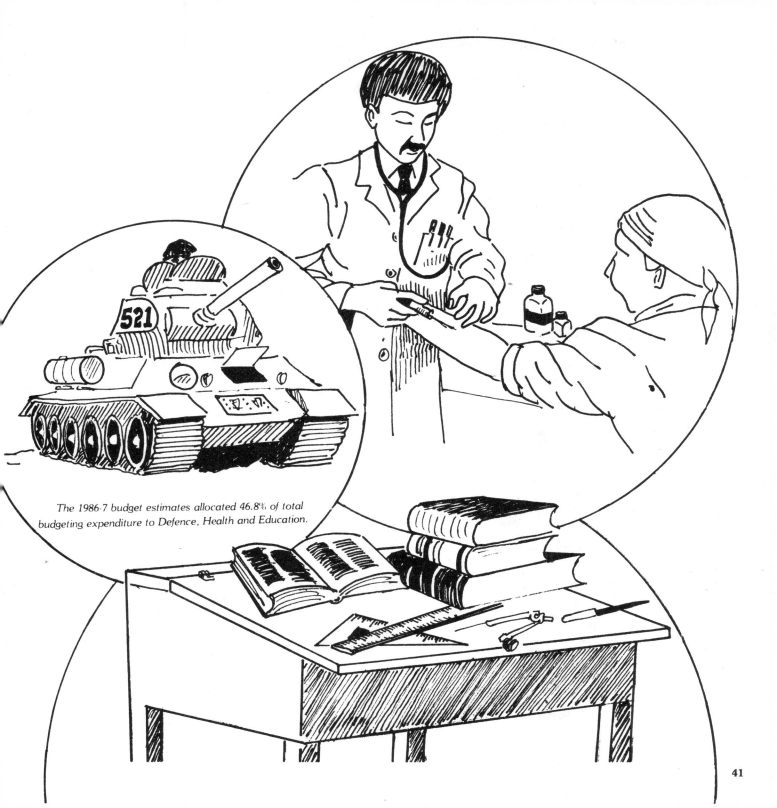

The 1986-7 budget estimates allocated 46.8% of total budgeting expenditure to Defence, Health and Education.

41

TABLE 20: Central Government Budget Account Expenditure by Vote*: 1983/84 —— 85 /86

	1983-84 Actual	1984-85 Actual	1985-86# Actual	Estimates
Constitutional and Statutory Appropriations:				
President	52	52	77	77
Parliament of Zimbabwe	78	97	108	129
Public Service	57 174	63 032	69 422	75 574
Finance, Economic Planning and Development	286 108	375 521	470 639	574 500
Audit	29	30	36	36
Local Government, Rural and Urban Development	396	429	430	450
Labour, Manpower Planning and Social Welfare	16 780	18 729	23 377	28 500
Justice, Legal and Parliamentary Affairs	716	605	814	905
Transport	396	429	427	450
Total	361 729	458 924	565 330	680 621
Vote appropriations:				
President	472	549	663	846
Parliament of Zimbabwe	3 464	4 270	6 105	9 263
Office of the Prime Minister and Cabinet	17 768	20 298	34 378	42 597
Public Services	10 102	11 442	13 013	17 513
Defence	414 726	393 235	504 644	639 521
Finance Economic Planning and Development	70 421	123 961	24 170	32 812
Central Statistical Office	1 949	2 009	2 332	2 861
Central Computer Services	3 806	4 623	3 933	9 722
Customs and Excise	4 583	5 423	6 370	8 027
Taxes	5 306	6 008	7 730	10 232
Vote of Credit	-	-	-	167 731
Audit	1 185	1 449	1 985	3 040
Industry and Technology	1 886	1 370	61 706	63 534
Trade and Commerce	34 153	23 688	20 367	11 731
Lands, Agriculture and Rural Resettlement	170 515	190 972	206 015	216 829
Research and Specialist Services	9 165	10 734	13 862	15 040
Agricultural, Technical and Extension Services	16 912	20 612	26 019	30 345
Veterinary Services	21 261	24 490	27 708	34 854
Surveyor-General	2 003	1 902	2 101	2 576
Mines	3 886	5 853	8 886	11 185
Transport	120 427	134 200	209 562	239 208
Foreign Affairs	17 306	23 361	28 805	33 264
Local Government, Rural and Urban Development	57 621	67 603	84 462	88 580
Labour, Manpower Planning and Social Welfare	121 172	50 760	28 555	23 548
Vocational Education	12 425	13 203	16 786	23 093
Health	136 645	155 497	191 038	227 398
Education	429 010	474 269	589 424	663 421
University	34 156	30 587	46 568	35 189

Cont.

Youth, Sport and Culture	7 535	10 759	10 904	14 072
Community Development and Women's Affairs	4 128	5 451	7 016	7 678
Home Affairs	10 170	13 127	13 921	11 851
Zimbabwe Republic Police	106 839	128 367	127 461	158 328
Justice, Legal and Parliamentary Affairs	10 204	11 300	13 587	16 151
Zimbabwe Prison Services	17 264	18 282	21 140	24 151
Information, Posts and Telecommunications	11 676	12 149	12 446	14 803
Natural Resources and Tourism	9 192	10 924	22 091	14 844
National Parks and Wild Life Management	9 945	10 655	14 444	16 237
Energy and Water Resources and Development	39 520	42 899	46 765	38 694
National Supplies	3 134	2 722	4 109	9 391
Cooperative Development	4 600	2 941	2 732	3 336
Public Construction and National Housing	113 717	110 392	107 605	154 411
Total	2 070 249	2 182 336	2 571 408	3 147 907
Total Expenditure	2 431 978	2 641 260	3 136 738	3 828 528
Less Revenue	2 000 477	2 212 839	2 616 185	2 997 000
Budget Account Deficit(-)/Surplus	- 431 501	- 428 421	- 520 553	- 831 528

32

* Budget Account Expenditure excludes Loan and Debt Appropriations which are reflected in the Financing Account (Table 18.5). # Provisional

Table 20 classifies the expenditure according to the votes given to the different ministries. The amount given to each ministry includes both capital and current expenditure.

Gross Fixed Capital Formation

Gross Fixed Capital Formation (in real terms) at $938m was substantially higher than the 1983 figure of $649m. The real figures indicate a dramatic decline between 1974 and 1978 (the war years), which is reversed between 1979 and 1982 when the figures once again begin to climb. The annual rate of growth in investment averaged 28% for 1980 and 1981, and then slowed down to about 8% in 1982 and fell in real terms by 17% in 1983 (see Table 17). Investment growth in the 1980-83 period averaged 9% which was significantly lower than the Transitional National Development Plan (TNDP) target of 23%.

Table 21 gives figures for Gross Fixed Capital Formation in the public and private sectors. Although investment from the public sector was noticeably lower than projected targets, what is important is that government's share of total investment has been increasing steadily (from 42% in 1978 to 54% in 1983) while private sector investment has been on the decline (see Table 21).

The reasons for the low levels of private sector investment include the recent recession which reduced available surpluses; poor performance of the export sector which in turn means that there is less foreign exchange available for the importation of capital goods or of raw materials which would activate further investment; and continued anxiety about Zimbabwe's socialist future. Government's investment levels have also been lower than expected. The reasons for low public sector investment include lower tax revenues accruing to government due to the economic recession; rapidly increasing recurrent expenditure which crowds out government investment expenditure; delays in utilizing the funds pledged in March, 1981 through the Zimbabwe Conference on Reconstruction and Development (Zimcord), which were expected to contribute almost 40% to the public sector investment programme; and inadequate identification of growth-generating investment areas.

External financing was expected to play a much greater role than it has in financing investment. In 1980, $157m entered Zimbabwe in the form of external financing; in 1982 the figure was $533m; in 1983 it was $457m. All these figures were below the

TABLE 21: Gross Fixed Capital Formation in the Public and Private Sectors: 1978-83
($ million)

	Public Sector						Private Sector					
	1978	1979	1980	1981	1982	1983	1978	1979	1980	1981	1982	1983
Agriculture and forestry	8	8	6	17	35	52	35	37	48	84	88	83
Mining and quarrying	-	-	-	-	-	-	59	83	83	133	94	89
Manufacturing	2	3	2	2	6	5	42	47	121	199	162	158
Electricity and water	18	14	26	47	133	156	-	-	-	-	-	-
Construction	-	1	1	4	8	8	3	5	12	13	19	20
Distribution, hotels and restaurants	1	-	1	3	4	7	18	24	43	47	43	20
Transport and communication	23	21	23	38	129	115	9	17	24	22	31	21
Total material production	52	47	59	111	315	343	166	213	331	498	437	391
Per cent. of total	36,4	34,6	36,4	46,8	61,5	59,4	83,8	81,6	90,4	84,0	84,4	82,7
Finance and insurance	-	-	-	-	1	1	9	32	14	34	37	40
Real estate	26	25	27	36	46	46	9	5	6	16	11	9
Public administration	21	18	21	26	33	52	-	-	-	-	-	-
Education	5	5	5	9	20	22	7	4	2	9	4	4
Health	6	7	7	6	5	7	2	1	1	1	4	4
Other services	2	2	2	2	14	11	5	6	12	35	25	25
General purpose investment by government	31	32	41	47	76	95	-	-	-	-	-	-
Total non-material production	91	89	103	126	197	234	32	48	35	95	81	82
Per cent. of total	63,6	65,4	63,6	53,2	38,5	40,6	16,2	18,4	9,6	16,0	15,6	17,3
TOTAL	143	146	162	237	512	577	198	261	366	593	518	473
Per cent. share in total GFCF	41,9	34,3	30,7	28,6	49,7	54,9	58,1	65,7	69,3	71,4	50,3	45,1

33

planned levels. The reasons for the lack of external financing include the rapid rise in the foreign debt immediately after Independence which intensified the debt service burden; the low utilization of external funds; the appreciating international exchange rates; rising rates of interest and poor export performance, which, together, would have made it very difficult to pay back money borrowed internationally for development purposes.

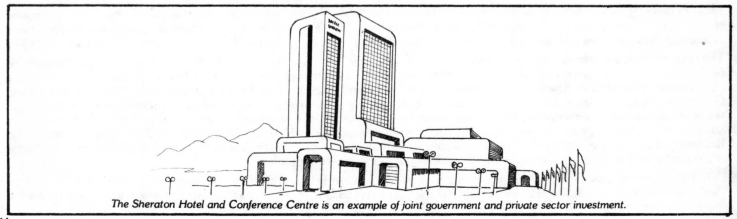

The Sheraton Hotel and Conference Centre is an example of joint government and private sector investment.

The Components of Investment Expenditure

Table 22 indicates the allocation of investment funds in the 1974-83 period.

TABLE 22: Gross Fixed Capital Formation 1974-83 (at current prices)

Item	1975	1975	1976	1977	1978	1979	1980	1981	1982	1983	%
Agriculture and forestry	41	38	51	45	42	44	53	100	123	135	13
Mining and quarrying	34	40	60	66	59	83	83	133	94	89	8
Manufacturing	105	115	77	49	44	50	123	201	169	163	15
Electricity and water	27	36	36	19	18	14	26	47	133	136	15
Construction	11	9	8	4	3	6	12	17	28	28	3
Finance and Insurance	5	5	7	9	9	32	15	34	38	41	4
Real estate	47	57	44	48	36	30	34	53	58	55	5
Distribution, hotels and restaurants	17	17	19	17	19	24	44	50	47	27	3
Transport and communications	52	60	43	36	33	37	48	60	159	136	13
Public administration	11	12	9	18	21	18	21	26	33	52	5
Education services	11	12	13	13	11	10	8	18	24	26	3
Health services	6	6	8	7	8	8	7	7	8	11	1
Other services and unallocable	7	8	9	9	7	7	13	37	40	37	3
General purpose Investment by government	47	53	43	39	31	32	41	47	76	95	9
Total	421	468	427	379	341	395	528	830	1 030	1 051	100%

34

TABLE 23: Gross Fixed Capital Formation: 1974-83 (at constant prices)

	1974	1975	1976	1977	1978	1979	1980	1981	1982	1983	%
Agriculture and forestry	91	73	86	65	55	49	53	91	98	87	13
Mining and quarrying	75	77	102	97	76	92	83	114	72	54	8
Manufacturing	242	226	133	71	56	54	123	179	135	102	15
Electricity and Water	58	69	60	27	22	15	26	40	94	93	15
Construction	26	19	14	6	3	6	12	16	23	19	3
Finance and Insurance	11	9	12	13	12	38	15	28	27	24	4
Real estate	103	109	77	74	50	36	34	43	40	33	5
Distribution, hotels and restaurants	40	35	32	25	24	28	44	45	37	17	3
Transport and communications	116	114	72	54	40	40	48	54	123	87	13
Public administration	24	23	16	26	27	20	21	22	25	32	5
Education services	25	23	23	20	15	11	8	15	17	16	3
Health services	13	12	14	11	11	9	8	6	6	6	1
Other services and unallocable	16	16	16	13	9	8	14	31	29	23	3
General purpose investment by government	98	94	71	57	42	37	41	39	54	56	9
Total	938	899	728	559	442	443	528	723	780	649	100%

35

Manufacturing, electricity and water, agriculture and forestry, and transport and communication accounted for almost 60% of the total investment in 1983. Health and education, on the other hand, account for a surprisingly small proportion (1% and 3% respectively). The most noticeable increases in money terms (Table 22) over the ten year period and in particular, 1980-83 have been in finance and insurance, electricity and water, and public administration.

In real terms, most categories show a decline in spending over the ten year period (Table 23). Electricity and water, finance and insurance and public administration have been noticeable exceptions. Of the above three sectors only public administration employs a significant sector of the workforce (8,7%). All the productive sectors of the economy (excluding finance and insurance, and electricity and water) experienced declines in investment in real terms with manufacturing, the largest sector and second largest employer, experiencing a decline in investment of almost 60% over the period. Despite the rapid expansion of education and health since 1980 real investment in both these areas is well below the 1974 levels. This indicates that the expansion in these services has largely been in the area of recurrent expenditure (running costs) rather than capital expenditure.

Overall, the trend in investment spending has been one of falling levels of real investment in the years 1974-78 with the recovery beginning in 1979. The 1979-82 period was one of recovery with a sudden drop in 1983. The post-Independence boom was severely curtailed by the drought and the effects of falling commodity prices internationally (see Chapter 7).

The Relationship between Consumption and Investment
Table 24 deals with the relationship between consumption and investment spending. The figures indicate a rising trend in consumption spending in 1974-83 and a consequent falling trend in investment. The TNDP set targets of 80,9% for consumption spending and 25,6% for investment. The average over the plan period was 88,4% and 18,2% respectively. Changing the ratio of consumption to investment spending would require either a reduction in consumption spending (government and/or private consumption spending) in order to release more funds for investment purposes, or an increase in investment through higher levels of external borrowing.

TABLE 24: Components of National Expenditure for selected Years (per cent): 1974-83

Item	1974	1978	1980	1981	1982	1983
	At Constant prices (1980)					
1. Private consumption	57,8	62,0	66,6	64,3	66,1	69,8
2. Consumption of non-profit making bodies	1,2	1,3	1,0	0,8	0,7	0,7
3. Net government current consumption	9,3	20,9	19,7	19,4	20,9	22,5
4. Total consumption expenditure	68,3	84,4	87,3	84,5	87,7	93,0
5. Gross fixed capital formation	27,7	14,6	13,3	18,2	19,7	16,8
6. Increase in stocks	4,7	- 3,3	0,3	5,5	0,6	- 4,7
7. Net exports of goods and services	- 0,7	4,3	3,0	- 8,2	- 7,9	- 4,4
Total expenditure on gross domestic product	100,0	100,0	100,0	100,0	100,0	100,0

36

Reducing private consumption expenditure would affect the level of economic activity, thereby discouraging further investment. A reduction in government recurrent spending is more feasible, although has not materialized in practice. Relying on external finance to support investment has also proved to be difficult.

In the long run the level of investment will rise only in a stable economic environment which has potential for growth and development. Where the export market acts as a constraint of further development, internal sources of growth need to be identified and developed. In the period under review many of the conditions which are prerequisites for private sector investment were absent. If these conditions continue to prevent such investment in the future then increased levels of public sector investment are the only alternative.

Investment and Employment
The level of investment is, of course, directly related to the level of employment. As the population increases, thereby expanding the labour force, so too does the level of employment have to increase. Between 1974 and 1983 the population grew by approximately 2,2m people. In the same period real investment was dropping continually (particularly between 1974 and 1979) and even after the post-Independence resurgence of investment (as shown in Table 17), the level did not reach the 1974 peak. In 1983 real investment was $289m less than it was in 1974 (i.e. a 31% drop) despite a 36% rise in population.

In his 1985 budget speech the Minister of Finance, Economic Planning and Development reported that since 1980 a net average of only 7 000 jobs per year have been created in the formal sector. Bearing in mind that over 80 000 school-leavers enter the job market each year, it is clear that the current levels of investment are not adequate to employ the large numbers of school-leavers, and that the present levels of investment are not geared towards job creation. (Note that despite a doubling in the level of investment at current prices between 1980 and 1983 the size of the work-force increased by only 23 500, i.e. by 2% — see Table 14).

GNP — a Standard for Comparison

The use of GNP as an indicator of growth and development and as a standard of comparison between nations has come under considerable criticism in recent years . However, it remains one of the most widely used measures for both development and international comparison. Box 4 enables us to rank Zimbabwe (no. 81 on the Table) in terms of GDP per capita.

The question that needs to be asked is, "Does growth mean development?" On average the developing countries have achieved high rates of 'growth' (measured by GNP), yet the fruits of this growth have not reached the mass of the population. On the contrary, the gap between the standard of living of the rich and the poor, the educated and the illiterate, the employed and the unemployed, and in the urban and rural areas, has widened considerably. Evidence of this growing disparity, particularly in the developing world, is given by the following statistics: about 1 000 million people in the word are under-nourished in the sense of suffering from extensive deficiencies of calories and protein; 1 000 million people are inadequately housed; 1 000 million are illiterate; 1 300 million earn less than the equivalent of 90 dollars (US$) per year; 1 500 million people have no access to medical care; 1 700 million no access to clean drinking water; and for about 1 700 million people life expectancy is less than 60 years.[1]

The above statistics point to the fact that although economic growth has taken place (as evidenced by a growth of GNP per capita) the fruits of this growth do not seem to have reached the mass of the people. In order to understand why, we need to address the question of the distribution of wealth in the developing countries. A joint study undertaken by the Institute of Development Studies in Sussex, England, and the Development Research Centre of the World Bank highlighted the need for an index of development which incorporated both growth and distribution. The need for such an index was highlighted by the actual pattern of distribution of GNP in the developing countries as a whole (see Table 25 below)

TABLE 25: Income Distribution in Developing Countries

Proportion of Population	20%	20%	20%	20%	20%
Share of national income	53%	22%	13%	7%	5%

37

From Table 25 we can see that the richest 20% of the population in developing countries earn 53% of the total income; the upper two-fifths of the population earn 75% of the nation's income, whereas the poorest 60% earn only 25%. The growth in GNP in developing countries is, therefore, essentially only a measure of the increase in income of the upper two-fifths of the population. A measure of welfare (as opposed to growth) would therefore have to examine not only the increase in income, but how that increase was distributed.

The Development of Alternative Standards of Measurement

In an effort to move away from the purely economic bias of GNP, the United Nations Research Institut   for Social Development developed the Level of Living index, which is essentially an index of the state of welfare of the population. This index makes use of nine separate components divided into three separate groups. The first group measures the living level based on (1) nutrition, (2) clothing, (3) shelter, (4) health, and (5) education. Underlying the second group is the need people have for protection and safety; protection from over-work which may be harmful to health, security against social hazards such as a breakdown of law and order, unemployment, sickness, etc. The components of the second group are (6) leisure, and (7) security. The third group relates to the environment in which the members of that society live; the components are (8) social environment, which includes the conditions at work and the availability of recreational facilities, and (9) the physical environment (cleanliness, quietness and beauty). (See Box 3 for computation table of the Level of Living index).

McHale and McHale, *Basic Human Needs: A Framework for Action*, New Brunswick, 1979.

BOX 3: Level of Living Index — Computation Table

			"O"	"100" "M"	"A"
	Critical points of indicators		"O"	"100" "M"	"A"
	Designation of Sub-ranges of cardinal indicators expressing respective levels of need satisfaction		Intolerable	Inadequate	Adequate	Affluent
	Corresponding grades of ordinal indicators		IV	III	II	I
	Intermediate indicator index values for cardinal indicators		0	0 0<1'<100	100 100<1'< 1'A1'A	1'A
	Intermediate conventional index		0	0 50	100 150	200 200

| Components | Indicators | | Units of Measurement | | | |

Determination of cardinal indicators sub-ranges and ordinal indicator grades

Components	Indicators		Units of Measurement	Intolerable	Inadequate	Adequate	Affluent
1. Nutrition (food intake)	(a)	Calories intake	Calories intake per day per head as percentage of norm	Below 60% of norm	60% and more but less than 100% of norm	100% and more but less than 133% or norm	133% and more of norm
	(b)	Protein intake	Protein intake per day per head as percentage of norm	Below 60% of norm	60% and more but less than 100% of norm	100% and more but less than 200% of norm	200% and more of norm
	(c)	Percent of non-starchy calories	Percent of non-starchy calories in food intake	Less than 10%	10% and more 40%	40% and more but	60% and more
2. Clothing (use of clothes)	(a)	Cloth consumers and	Cloth used for sumption twined into ready-to-wear garments per year per head	None clothing sold to	Less than 15m²	15m² and more but less than 50m²	50m² and more
	(b)	Footwear consumption	Footwear pairs sold to consumers per year per head	None	Less than 3 pairs	3 pairs and more but less than 6 pairs	6 pairs and more
	(c)	Quality of	Ord. ind.	Most primitive	Poor	Satisfactory	Sumptuous
3. Shelter (occupancy of dwellings)	(a)	Services of dwellings	Ord. ind.	No permanent dwelling	Rustic or unfit for habitation	Conventional fit for habitation	Conventional with all amenities
	(b)	Density of occupancy	Rooms per inhabitant	Less than ¼	¼ and more but less than one	1 and more but less than ½	1½ and more
	(c)	Independent use of dwellings	Housing units per household	Housing unit unidentifiable or less than ½ housing unit per household	Less than one but more than ½ housing unit per household	One housing unit per household	More than one housing unit per household
4. Health (health services received)	(a)	Access to medical care	Ord. ind.	No access whatsoever	Access limited	Access adequate	All needs for medical care fully satisfied 99% and more
	(b)	Prevention of infection and parasitic disease	Percentage of deaths not due to infection or parasitic disease	Below 66%	66% and more but less than 96%	96% and more but less than 99%	99% and more
	(c)	Proportional mortality ratio	Percentage of deaths which occur at the age of 50 years and over to the total number of deaths	0%	Less than 80%	80% and more, but less than 90%	90% and over

5.							
5. Education (education received)	(a)	School enrolment ratio	Enrolment as percentage of norm	No enrolment	Less than 100%	100% or more but less than 150%	150% and more
	(b)	School output ratio	Not dropped out as percentage of enrolled	All dropped out	Less than 90%	90% and more but less than 100%	100%
	(c)	Teacher/pupil ratio	Teacher/pupil ratio as percentage of norm	Tuition not received	Teacher/pupil ratio below 100% of norm	Teacher/pupil ratio at or above 100% of norm but below 200% of norm	Teacher/pupil ratio at or above 200% of norm
6. Lesiure (protection from over-work)	(a)	Leisure time	Hours free from work per year	Less than 3 640 hours free from work per year (Badly over-worked)	3 640 hrs. and more but less than 6 336 hours from work per year (Overworked)	6 336 hrs. or more but less than 6 816 hrs. free from work per year (Not overworked)	6 816 hrs. or more free from work per year (Comfortable)
7. Security (security assured)	(a)	Security of the person	Ord. ind.	Law and order broken down (war, civil war, regime of terror	Law and order badly maintained (riots, gangsterism, hooliganism	Law and order adequately maintained	Law and order well maintained
	(c)	Security of the way of life	Ord. ind.	Economic chaos	No employment or sickness insurance, no pension schemes, not sufficient savings	Unemployment and sickness insurance, pension schemes and/or savings sufficient to maintain a minimum level of living	Complete coverage by insurance or pension schemes and/or savings sufficient to maintain the present way of life
8. Social environment (social contacts and recreation)	(a)	Labour relations	Ord. ind.	Riots. Repeated strikes and lock-outs	Tension in labour relations	Labour relations satisfactory	Labour relations good
	(b)	Conditions for social economic activity	Ord. ind.	Political oppression Social prejudice rampant	Occasional strikes. Difficult conditions for social and political activity	Satisfactory conditions for social and political activity	Good conditions for social and political activity
	(c)	Information and Communication	Ord. ind.	Isolation within a village community	Information and communication restricted	Information and communication satisfactory	Information and communication ample
	(d)	Recreation: cultural activities (music, theatre, cinema, visual arts, book reading)	Ord. ind.	Lack of cultural activities	Rudiments of cultural activities. Participation limited	Cultural activities adequately developed. Participation popular	Cultural activities well-developed. Participation enthusiastic and active
	(e)	Recreation: travel	Ord. ind.	Immobility	Travel occasional with a limited perimeter	Frequent travel by various means mostly within the home country	Frequent travel of distinct educational and cultural value witnin the home country and abroad
	(f)	Recreation: sport and physical exercise	Ord. ind.	No participation whatsoever	Occasional participation	Systematic practice of one type of exercise	Systematic many-sided practice of physical exercise
9. Physical environment	(a)	Cleanness and and quietness	Ord. ind.	Conditions unbearable	Conditions unsatisfactory	Conditions satisfactory	Conditions good
	(b)	Public amenities in the neighbourhood	Ord. ind.	No amenities	Amenities.inadequate	Amenities adequate	Amenities good
	(c)	Beauty of the environment	Ord. ind.	Depressing ugliness	Mediocre	Acceptable	Inspiring

BOX 4: Rank order of countries in terms of GDP per capita an P.Q.L.I.

Rank Country	GNP per Capita ($)	Physical Quality of Life Index	Rank Country	GNP per Capital ($)	Physical Quality of Life Index	Rank Country	Physical Quality of Life Index
1 Kuwait	15,480	76	54 Panama	1,310	81	108 Egypt	280 — 46
2 United Arab Emirates	13,900	34	55 Fiji	1,150	83	109 South Yemen	280 — 27
3 Qatar	11,400	32	56 Brazil	1,140	68	110 Togo	260 — 28
4 Switzerland	8,880	98	57 Mexico	1,090	75	111 Yemen Arab Republic	250 — 27
5 Sweden	8,670	100	58 Taiwan	1,070	88	112 Indonesia	240 — 50
6 United States	7,890	96	59 Jamaica	1,070	87	113 Kenya	240 — 40
7 Canada	7,510	97	60 Chile	1,060	77	114 Uganda	240 — 33
8 Denmark	7,450	98	61 Costa Rica	1,040	87	115 Central African Empire	230 — 18
9 Norway	7,420	99	62 Algeria	990	42	116 Haiti	200 — 31
10 West Germany	7,380	95	63 Turkey	990	54	117 Madagascar	200 — 44
			64 Cuba	860	86	118 Sierra Leone	200 — 29
UPPER MIDDLE			65 Malaysia	860	59	119 Sri Lanka	200 — 83
			66 Mongolia	860		120 Comoros	180 — 40
11 Belgium	6,780	95	67 Tunisia	840	44	121 Gambia	180 — 22
12 France	6,550	97	68 Peru	800	58	122 Tanzania	180 — 33
13 Luxembourg	6,460	96	69 Dominican Republic	780	64	123 Lesotho	170 — 50
14 Libya	6,310	42	70 Syria	780	52	124 Mozambique	170 — 23
15 Netherlands	6,200	99	71 Nicaragua	750	53	125 Pakistan	170 — 37
16 Australia	6,100	96	72 Mauritius	680	75	126 Afghanistan	160 — 19
17 Iceland	6,100	99	73 South Korea	670	80	127 Niger	160 — 14
18 Finland	5,620	95	74 Ecuador	640	68	128 Guinea	150 — 20
19 Austria	5,330	95	75 Paraguay	640	74	129 India	150 — 41
20 Japan	4,910	98	76 Colombia	630	71	130 Guinea-Bissau	140 — 10
21 Saudi Arabia	4,480	29	77 Guatemala	630	53	131 Malawi	140 — 29
22 New Zealand	4,250	96	78 Ivory Coast	610	28	132 Zaire	140 — 28
23 East Germany	4,220	96	79 Jordan	610	48	133 Benin	130 — 23
24 United Kingdom	4,020	97	80 Ghana	580	31		
25 Israel	3,920	90	81 Zimbabwe	550	42	**BOTTOM 12**	
26 Czechoslovakia	3,840	95	82 Albania	540	76		
27 Bahamas	3,310	87	83 Guyana	540	84	134 Burma	120 — 51
28 Italy	3,050	94	84 Morocco	540	40	135 Burundi	120 — 23
29 Spain	2,920	94	85 Congo	520	25	136 Chad	120 — 20
30 Poland	2,860	94				137 Nepal	120 — 25
31 Soviet Union	2,760	94	**LOWER MIDDLE**			138 Bangladesh	110 — 33
32 Singapore	2,700		86 El Salvador	490	67	139 Rwanda	110 — 27
33 Oman	2,680		87 Papua New Guinea	490	34	140 Somalia	110 — 27
34 Gabon	2,590	21	88 Sao Tome & Principe	490		141 Upper Volta	110 — 17
35 Greece	2,590	91	89 North Korea	479		142 Ethiopia	100 — 16
36 Venezuela	2,570	80	90 Swaziland	470	36	143 Mali	100 — 15
37 Ireland	2,560	96	91 Liberia	450	26	144 Laos	90 — 32
38 Puerto Rico	2,430	92	92 Zambia	440	28	145 Bhutan	70
39 Bahrain	2,410	60	93 Grenada	420	80		
40 Bulgaria	2,310	94	94 Botswana	410	38		
41 Hungary	2,280	92	95 China	410	59		
42 Trinidad & Tobago	2,240	88	96 Philippines	410	73		
43 Hong Kong	2,110	88	97 Bolivia	390	45		
44 Iran	1,930	38	98 Honduras	390	50		
45 Portugal	1,690	79	99 Senegal	390	22		
46 Yugoslavia	1,680	85	100 Nigeria	380	25		
47 Argentina	1,550	84	101 Thailand	380	70		
48 Barbados	1,550	88	102 Western Samoa	350	86		
49 Cyprus	1,480	87	103 Mauritania	340	15		
50 Rumania	1,450	92	104 Angola	330	15		
51 Iraq	1,390	46	105 Equatorial Guinea	330	28		
52 Uruguay	1,390	88	106 Cameroon	290	28		
53 South Africa	1,390	48	107 Sudan	290	33		

In order to calculate the level of living, the different components of the indicator system are valued and weighted on the basis of the framework of points given in the computation table opposite (see Box 3).

The Physical Quality of Life index (PQLI) makes use of far fewer indicators but it is certainly a lot easier to construct and to understand. Morris, who developed the model, felt that an indicator which anyone with five years of schooling could not understand within five minutes was not an indicator but a measure of control. The components for the PQLI index are (1) life expectancy, (2) infant mortality, and (3) reading and writing ability (literacy). The first two indicators express the sum of the effects of nutrition, health, income and environment, whereas the rate of literacy indicates the extent to which people can participate in the social and development process.

References

1. All figures from; *Quarterly Digest of Statistics*, CSO publications, Harare, September 1986.
2. *ibid* p.1.
3. *ibid.*, p.1.
4. Central Statistical Office, *Population Projections of Zimbabwe: 1982 to 2032*, A CSO publication, Harare, January 1986.
5. Central Statistical Office, *Statistical Yearbook 1985*, A CSO publication, Sweden, 1985, p.43.
6. Figures drawn from *Quarterly Digest of Statistics*, Harare, September 1986.
7. *ibid.*, p. 10.
8. *ibid.*, p. 10.
9. *ibid.*, p. 10.
10. Ministry of Finance, Economic Planning and Development, *Socio-Economic Review of Zimbabwe: 1980-85*, Harare, 1986, p. 20.
11. Figures for graph drawn from the *Socio-Economic Review of Zimbabwe: 1980-85*.
12. *ibid.*, p. 18.
13. Central Statistical Office, *Quarterly Digest of Statistics*, September 1986, Harare, p. 6.
14. *ibid.*, p. 6.
15. ibid., p. 10.
16. Figures drawn from the September 1986 *Quarterly Digest of Statistics*, Harare.
17. *ibid.*
18. *ibid.*
19. Figures derived from Table 11.
20. Figures derived from Table 11.
21. Figures derived from *Quarterly Digest of Statistics*, Harare, September 1986, op. cit.
22. *ibid.*
23. The basic date for the construction of the pie chart is from the *Digest of Statistics*, Harare, September 1986, p., 10.
24. Central Statistics Office, *National Income and Expenditure Report*, Harare, October 1985, p. 13-16.
25. *ibid.*, pp. 13-16.
26. Figures derived from *Quarterly Digest of Statistics*, September 1986, p. 11, *op. cit.*
27. *ibid.*, p. 11.
28. Figures for the diagrams derived from Table 17.
29. Central Statistical Office, *Statistical Year Book of Zimbabwe*, 1985, op. cit. p. 97 for 1977-84 figures. Central Statistical Office, *Quarterly Digest of Statistics*, op. cit. for '83-84 to '86-87 figures.
30. Central Statistical Office, *Quarterly Digest of Statistics*, September 1986, op. cit. p. 16.
31. Central Statistical Office, *Quarterly Digest of Statistics*, op. cit. p. 62.
32. Ministry of Finance, Economic Planning and Development, *Socio-Economic Review of Zimbabwe*, op. cit. p. 30.
33. Central Statistical Office, *Quarterly Digest of Statistics*, op. cit. p. 10.
34. *ibid.*, p. 10.
35. Figures derived from *Quarterly Digest of Statistics*, ibid., p. 11.
36. *ibid.*,
37. Drewnowski, J. *On Measuring the Quality of Life*, Paris, 1974.

Chapter 3

AGRICULTURE IN ZIMBABWE

Background to the Agricultural Sector

Having introduced the economy at a macro level (through National Income analysis and broad government policy directions) we can now turn to an examination of the first of the productive sectors of the economy, the agricultural sector.

Agriculture derives its importance from its ability to feed the nation; its contribution to foreign exchange earnings (generally in the region of 40%); its employment of 25% of the labour force (it is the largest single employer in the economy); its provision of raw materials for the economy as a whole; and its contribution to the food security of the entire Southern African Development Co-ordination Conference (SADCC) region. In addition it is estimated that at least 70% of the population live off the land in Zimbabwe.

TABLE 1: Agriculture's Contribution to Gross Domestic Products: 1954-84

Year	Agriculture	GDP	%
1954	76,6	336	23
1955	79,4	372	21
1956	92,2	425	22
1957	94,0	477	20
1958	93,4	500	19
1959	101,4	530	19
1960	105,4	562	19
1961	127,8	592	22
1962	128,0	600	21
1963	126,7	612	21
1964	125,7	630	20
1965	118,7	679	17
1966	138,4	681	20
1967	154,9	744	21
1968	124,2	782	16
1969	169,5	930	18
1970	153,0	989	15
1971	199,7	1137	18
1972	232,9	1299	18
1973	214,8	1430	15
1974	314,8	1791	18
1975	322,0	1902	17
1976	350,0	2064	17
1977	334,0	2069	16
1978	292,0	2166	13
1979	325,0	2539	13
1980	458,0	3226	14
1981	649,0	4049	16
1982	662,0	4609	14
1983	592,0	5081	12
1984	783,0	5699	14

1

Note: All figures in above table in Z$ millions.

The contribution of agriculture and forestry to the GDP has been in the region of 18% p.a. over the past 20 years, having fallen from 27% in 1948 (see Table 1).

The agricultural sector produces inputs for other sectors of the economy as well as being a major consumer of outputs from other sectors. Manufacturing outputs consumed by the agricultural sector include seed, chemicals and fertilizer, stock-feed, machinery and spares and liquid fuels. Of these inputs most are produced locally with the exception of tractors (although there is now a certain amount of local assembly of imported tractor kits) combine harvesters and other sophisticated machinery.

TABLE 2 : Inputs into the Agricultural Products Manufacturing Industry

Product	Manufacturing use
Maize	Milling industry, livestock feeds, cooking oil, beer and starch manufacture.
Sorghum	Traditional opaque beer production
Groundnuts	Cooking oil and livestock feed
Soyabeans	Oil, fishmeal and fodder production
Sugar-cane	Sugar processing, molasses, ethanol, carbon dioxide
Sunflower	Vegetable oil
Livestock	Meat processing, dairy products
Cotton	Cotton ginning, textile and clothing industry, oil expressors and livestock feed production.

2

Table 2 gives an indication of the agricultural inputs into the manufacturing industry.

The value of agricultural output in monetary terms is shown in Graph 1. This has increased by over 300% over the past six years., The most significant increase being in cotton which increased from less than $100m in 1980 to over $300m in 1986.

GRAPH 1: Value of Agricultural Output

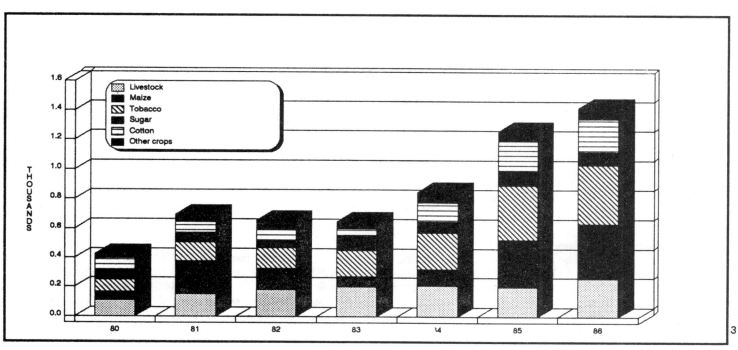

3

The level of employment in agriculture in the past nine years has declined from 363 800 in 1975 to 263 500 in 1983 (see Table 3). The lay-off of workers and the shift to more capital-intensive methods and away from labour-intensive crops is closely related to the rise in minimum wages in the agricultural sector. This underlies the need for both a closer examination of the minimum wage strategy as a means of moving towards equity, and the need for policies which support the employment generating agricultural sectors, i.e., the resettlement, communal and small-scale farming sectors.

TABLE 3: Employees in Agriculture: 1975-84

1975	364
1976	356
1977	348
1979	335
1980	327
1981	294
1982	274
1983	264
1984	266

4

Note: All figures in thousands
1984 figures as at June 1984.

Stratification of the Farming Sector

The agricultural sector in Zimbabwe can be divided into four distinct groupings:
— the large-scale commercial farmers;   — the small-scale commercial farmers;
— the communal farmers;   — the resettlement farmers.

Historically the commercial farming areas were located in the natural regions best suited to specialized and diversified farming. The quality of the land and the high rainfall made intensive farming possible in the areas.

The Commercial Farming Sector

The large-scale farmers, who all have freehold title, reside in the former commercial farming areas. The number of farmers in this sector has declined from 7 116 in 1970 to 5 481 in 1983 (figures from MFEP&D.) The average farm size in this sector has also decreased from 9 072 hectares to 8 653 hectares. The commercial farmers represent the modern, technologically advanced% side of agriculture. Although occupying approximately 14 million hectares of land, this sector only cultivated 692 000 hectares in 1983. The total number of people living and working in the commercial farming area is in the region of 1,7 million (including farm workers and their families).

54

The small-scale commercial farmers, whilst having different historical origins to the former grouping, also have freehold title and are essentially commercial farmers. This sector of the farming community resides in the former 'African Purchase Areas' and comprise some 8 500 farmers living on about 1,5 million hectares of land.

The Communal Farming Sector

Communal farmers do not have freehold title but instead have traditional rights to the land. They reside in the communal areas, which were formerly known as Tribal Trust Lands (TTLS). There are presently about 800 000 farm families totalling some four million people on about 16 million hectares in the communal lands.

About 36 000 people have, in the past five years, left the communal areas and been resettled on about two million hectares of land previously occupied by large-scale commercial farmers.

Resettlement Farmers

The decision to resettle farmers from the communal areas on land purchased by the government from the commercial farmers (on a willing seller — willing buyer basis) was an effort on government's part to redress the inequitable land distribution pattern inherited from the previous regime. Government had originally planned to resettle 162 000 peasant families (see Transitional National Development Plan), but due largely to financial constraints only 36 000 families have been resettled to date.

The Land Acquisition Bill, passed in 1985, was designed to speed up the process of resettlement by giving government the right of first refusal on any private land that was put up for sale, and the right to designate blocks of farms as land that the state would like to use for public purposes, in order to ensure that farmers in the designated blocks sell their land to the government.

Four different models of resettlement have been implemented by government, which vary in the degree of individual or communal ownership of land and property. Model A resettlement consists of individual plots; model B of collective and co-operative forms of organization; model C is a combination of individual resettlement and a co-operatively owned core-estate; model D does not entail any resettlement of people, but simply provides communally-owned grazing land to groups of communal area farmers.

Problems faced by the resettlement scheme include:
  i)   the shortage of funds both for the purchase and the development of the land;
  ii) the difficulty of obtaining land on a willing seller — willing buyer basis;
  iii) the difficulty (when land was made available) of acquiring large enough blocks of land for a resettlement scheme;
  iv) the problem of providing adequate water to the resettlement areas.

The majority of the land that has been acquired for the resettlement programme has been in natural regions 3 – 5 i.e. amongst the driest and least fertile in the country. The lack of development funds has also meant that government has not been able to provide the necessary assistance to ensure the viability of these areas.

The variations in resettlement have their roots in the historical development of the agricultural sector. In chapter 1 we saw that the early settlers only turned to farming when their hopes of establishing a 'second Rand' were dashed. The peasant farmers, on the other hand, had reacted positively to the creation of a new market and had increased their production in order to supply it. This meant that the European farmers were not able to establish themselves as easily as the BSAC had hoped, due to competition from the peasant farmers and their unwillingness to become workers on white farms. Peasant farmers were entitled to buy land until the Land Apportionment Act was passed in 1930. However, as they were rarely able to find either the money or willing sellers, very few peasant farmers managed to purchase land. After the act was passed, segregation was formalized and Africans could only 'own' land in the designated (TTL) areas. In addition, approximately 1,5 million hectares of land was set aside as 'Purchase Area Land' in which peasant farmers could own land on freehold title.

By 1978, black ownership of land was 3,4 hectares per person; for whites it was 423 hectares per person. Furthermore the black areas were about 3,5 times as densely populated as the white areas. One estimate[1] suggests that the black areas were over-populated by 85% in relation to their safe carrying capacity. Associated with this, 17 times as much land in the communal areas was being cultivated (as opposed to being used for grazing) as should have been.

It is not, therefore, surprising to note that the Chavanduka inquiry into the agricultural industry reported that 80% — 90% of black children in the rural areas of Zimbabwe are malnourished.,(The report states that it is not clear whether this malnutrition results from lack of food or incorrect knowledge of diet).

Geographical Factors

The type and distribution of rainfall in Zimbabwe is a major limitation to agricultural development. Much of Zimbabwe has a dry climate which, interspersed with heavy storms, tends to cause severe erosion. Rainfall patterns in the north and south of the country vary considerably, with the south being far more susceptible to drought. This, in turn, affects the nature of farming operations in these areas.

Zimbabwe has been classified into five main agro-industrial regions which indicate the agricultural potential of each region. These are:

Natural Region 1: (Specialized and diversified farming region). With a rainfall of over 1 000 mm per year. This area is particularly suitable for forestry, fruit and intensive livestock production.

Natural Region 2: (Intensive farming region). Slightly lower rainfalls of 750-1 000mm (confined mainly to summer) make this region suitable for intensive crop and/or livestock production.

Natural Region 3: (Semi-intensive farming region). This zone has 650-800mm of rain per year which comes in infrequent heavy falls. There are fairly severe mid-season dry spells making this region marginal as far as maize, tobacco and cotton are concerned.

Natural Region 4: (Semi-extensive farming region). Rainfall in this region drops to 450-650mm per year. Thus the land is mainly suitable for livestock production.

Natural Region 5: (Extensive farming region). The low erratic rainfall in this area means that this land is only suitable for extensive cattle and game ranching.

Historically the large-scale (commercial) farming areas were located mainly in natural regions 1, 2 and 3 (i.e. those with the most agricultural potential) whereas the small-scale communal farmers were located mainly in regions 3, 4 and 5. This is clearly illustrated through Maps 1 and 2 (following). By correlating the natural regions with the land distribution, we can see that the small-scale farmers were severely disadvantaged by the land allocation system.

The Dual Nature of Agriculture

Zimbabwe is a classic example of an economy in which a modern monetized sector co-exists and interlinks with a rural subsistence economy. The commercial farming sector, with its reliance on modern technology and commercial back-up is very much a part of the modernized sector of the economy; the traditional communal sub-sector, on the other hand, using few modern inputs and (in the past) forced when expanding output, to rely heavily on increasing its cultivated area, represents the other side of the coin.

[1]*Report of the Commission of Inquiry into the Agricultural Industry, Chaired by G.L. Chavunduka, Harare 1982.*

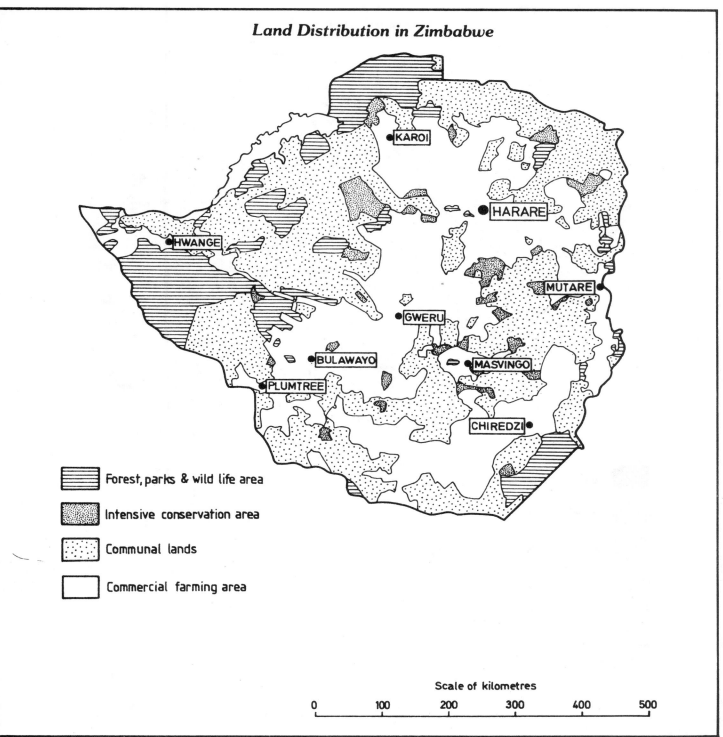

Land Distribution in Zimbabwe

KAROI

HARARE

HWANGE

MUTARE

GWERU

BULAWAYO

MASVINGO

PLUMTREE

CHIREDZI

Forest, parks & wild life area

Intensive conservation area

Communal lands

Commercial farming area

Scale of kilometres

0   100   200   300   400   500

57

Natural Farming Regions

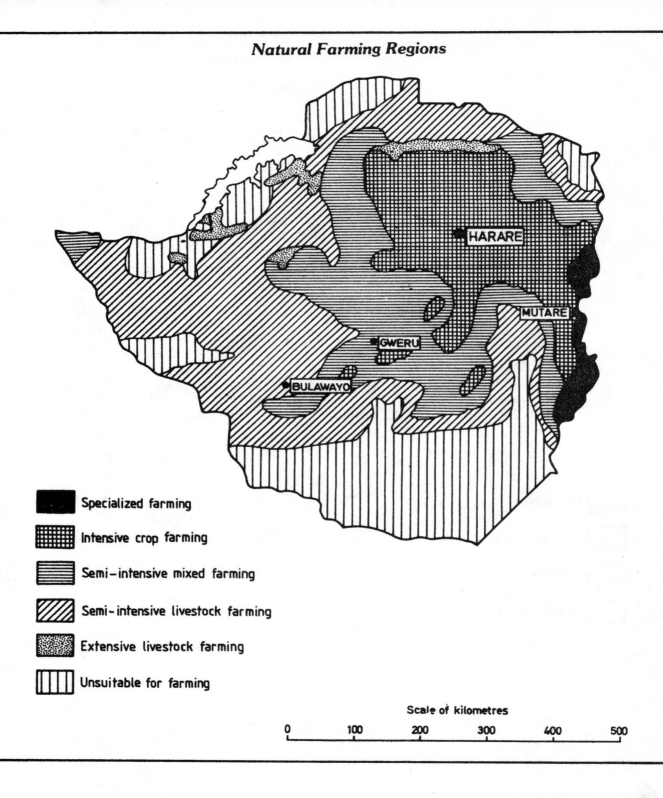

Legend:
- **Specialized farming**
- **Intensive crop farming**
- **Semi-intensive mixed farming**
- **Semi-intensive livestock farming**
- **Extensive livestock farming**
- **Unsuitable for farming**

Scale of kilometres

0   100   200   300   400   500

The unequal distribution of land and the concentration of peasant commercial farmers in the agricultural land has led to large disparities in income between the two major sectors of the agricultural community.

The communal areas have, until now, acted as labour pools, siphoning off the unemployed from the urban areas and intensifying the population pressure on the communal areas. It is estimated that some 21% of the black population live in the towns; 22% in the large-scale farming areas, and 54% in the communal areas; yet, at any one time, some 65-70% of all households are reliant on the rural areas for support. Although remunerative employment is really only possible in the urban areas, two-thirds of the black population survive by supplementing their wage earnings with food and income from the rural areas.

The dualistic nature of agriculture is perhaps best illustrated through a comparison of income in the two areas; the net average income of large-scale commercial farmers (after depreciation and interest payments) was $12 250 in 1979. Average net income in the communal areas in 1978 has been estimated at $250. The ratio is 49 : 1.

These disparities, however, tend to obscure the successes and potential of the communal areas. Despite all their disadvantages (limited land, land of poor agricultural quality, population pressure, traditional farming methods, etc.) the communal farmers managed not only to feed themselves, but sold a surplus of 850 000 tonnes of maize to the Grain Marketing Board (GMB) in the 1984-85 agricultural season and are expected to produce almost 60% of the total maize harvest in the 1986-87 agricultural season.

Table 4 gives production figures for individual crops in the commercial and communal areas over the 1980-83 period. Tobacco, wheat, tea, coffee, sugar and soya beans are clearly the domain of the commercial farmer, while the communal farmers dominate the production of sorghum and groundnuts and produce substantial (and increasing) volumes of maize and cotton.

TABLE 4: Commercial and Communal Farming : Production, Area planted and Yield: 1980 and 1983

	Area planted (hectares)		Production (tonnes)		Yield (kg/ha)	
	Commercial	Communal	Commercial	Communal	Commercial	Communal
Maize:						
1980	227 733	900 000	910 739	600 000	3 999	667
1983	283 880	1 050 000	624 786	285 000	2 201	271
Tobacco:						
1980	63 703	365	119 818	231	1 881	633
1983	46 327	1 439	93 331	655	2 015	455
Cotton:						
1980	74 924	15 000	145 533	12 000	1 943	800
1983	67 976	65 000	114 021	32 500	1 677	500
Wheat						
1980	32 556	-	154 593	-	4 749	-
1983	21 547	-	110 990	-	5 151	-
Soya beans:						
1980	40 783	12 000	89 405	8 000	2 192	667
1983	54 909	4 000	78 626	2 000	1 432	500
Groundnuts						
1980	3 841	175 000	10 675	67 000	2 779	383
1983	10 703	180 000	9 152	22 500	855	125
Sorghum						
1980	6 766	120 000	16 299	66 000	2 409	550
1983	7 672	280 000	7 536	44 000	982	157
Tea:						
1980	4 143	-	9 661	-	2 332	-
1983	4 476	-	10 551	-	2 357	-
Coffee:						
1980	4 098	-	5 261	-	1 284	-
1983	6 986	-	8 234	-	1 179	-
Sugar:						
1980	24 515	-	2 528 000	-	-	-
1983	33 833	-	3 438 000	-	-	-

5

Communal farmers have, since 1979, been producing an increasing share of the total agricultural output. In 1978 communal farmers produced 15% of the total output, rising to 25% by 1982; the drought in 1983 disrupted this trend.

The proportion of output retained for own consumption by communal farmers has also been declining (the 1983 figures indicate that communal farmers retained 58% of their output for own consumption in that year).

The productivity of the two agricultural sectors is usually compared by their respective output figures. The problem with this standard of comparison, as Table 5 shows, is that the input ratios are not taken into account. Large-scale commercial production is high-cost production (in terms of input costs per unit of land) whereas communal farming is low-cost production. On comparing the average outputs for the years 1974-80, we find that the commercial farmers produced over four times as much as the communal farmers, but when input costs are taken into account, we find that the difference in value added(as a measure of productivity) is only just over 2:1. Bearing in mind the added advantages that commercial farmers have because of the land quality, we find that the difference in productivity of the two sectors is even lower than 2:1. (On the other hand, however, the input ratio of the communal farmers is understated to the extent that family/unpaid labour is used for production purposes).

TABLE 5: Input/Output Accounts Commercial Farm and Communal Farm Sector: 1974-80 (Z$ million)

Year	Commercial			Communal		
	Total Outputs	Total Inputs	Total Value Added	Total Outputs	Total Inputs	Total Value Added
74	369	145	224	108	7	101
75	385	165	220	106	8	98
76	415	178	237	107	8	99
77	404	197	207	108	9	99
78	430	210	220	75	8	67
79	452	231	221	104	8	96
80	607	298	309	147	11	136
Average	437	203	234	108	8	99

6

Note: Estimates of output include own account capital formation, which is excluded in CSO estimates published in the Monthly Digest of Statistics.

The importance of commercial farming to the Zimbabwean economy far exceeds its total food production. Firstly, it purchases a large quantity of non-labour inputs which are locally produced. Secondly, it contributes raw materials to the manufacturing sector of the economy which are locally processed. Thirdly, it generates far more foreign exchange than it uses, thus subsidizing the import-dependent sectors of the economy. We can, thus, conclude that the commercial farming sector underpins a large domestic non-farm economy.

Government and Agriculture

We have introduced the agricultural sector by placing it in the context of its contribution to the national economy. Its development and success has, since the turn of the century, been closely connected with the assistance and participation of government. The following section will examine the structures through which government assistance is rendered, and the nature and extent of that assistance.

Government Structures

Government participation in agriculture has extended from the provision of inputs through to the final marketing of the product. The government agencies involved in this process include:
— the Ministry of Lands, Agriculture and Rural Resettlement (MLAR&R)
— the Ministry of Energy, Water Resources and Development
— the Agricultural Finance Corporation (AFC)

The contribution of the Ministry of Lands, Agriculture and Rural Resettlement is largely through Agritex (Agricultural Technical Services and Extension), the Department of Research and Specialist Services (R&SS), and the Department of Veterinary Services. Agritex is essentially concerned with providing agricultural advice to farmers through its 2 000 extension workers. The Research and Specialist Services concentrate on research into agricultural science and crop and pastoral production, and the Department of Veterinary Services is responsible for the prevention and control of animal disease.

The MLARR has responsibility for resettlement, small irrigation schemes, squatter control, and the Agricultural and Rural Development Authority (ARDA). The resettlement schemes are run in conjunction with Agritex which is responsible for pre-settlement policy; the Ministry then takes over at the point of resettlement. ARDA is an amalgamation of the Tribal Trust Lands Delopment Corporation (TILCOR), the Sabi-Limpopo Authority (SLA) and the Agricultural Development Authority (ADA). ARDA's role is to undertake planning for agricultural development throughout the country.

The Agricultural Finance Corporation is the only significant government-owned channel of agricultural credit in Zimbabwe. It is an autonomous parastatal body run by the Agricultural Finance Board, the members of which are appointed by the Minister of

Lands, Agriculture and Rural Resettlement, and include representation of all three Farming Unions. Whereas in the past the AFC directed 99% of its finance towards commercial farmers, today the AFC has a commercial farming scheme, a resettlement scheme, and a small farm credit scheme (see Box 1).

Box 1: The Agricultural Finance Corporation (AFC)

The AFC is a parastatal set up by Parliament in order to make credit available to all sections of the farming community in Zimbabwe. The AFC lends money on short-, medium- and long-term bases (see Table 1 below).

Table 1B: Categories of Farm Credit available through the AFC

Long Term (6-30 years)	Medium Term (3-5 years	Short Term (up to 2 years)
Farm purchase Dam construction Breeding stock Other capital development	Irrigation equipment Dairy stock Machinery Implements Boreholes Fencing Farm buildings	Seed Fertilizer Chemicals Land preparation Labour Living expenses

In 1979 the AFC act was amended in order to enable it to provide credit to communal farmers. In 1982, following a request from government the AFC began to assist the farmers in the resettlement areas. The present major thrust of the AFC is the provision of assistance to the small-scale farmer (see Graph 2).

The Impact of Agricultural Credit

Through services such as the provision of credit the output of the small-scale farming sector (including small-scale commercial farmers, communal farmers and resettlement farmers) has increased dramatically in both maize and cotton (see Table 2B).

Table 2B: The Production and Financing of Small-scale Commercial, Communal and Resettlement Farmers. 1979 - 1985

Crop Produced	1979/80 period		1984/85 period	
	tonnes prod.	% of Nat. Total	tonnes prod.	% of Nat. Total
Cotton	36 000	20%	115 000	45%
Maize	38 184	7%	389 664	41%
Volume of Credit	$1,6m/4345 loans		$53,9m/95 214 loans	

The AFC also administers the National Irrigation Fund which was established to promote the growing of winter wheat and other cash crops. The fund became operational in the 1985-86 financial year. In addition, the AFC has been asked to administer the Zimbabwe Agricultural Assistance Programme Fund which extends credit to co-operative unions. These loans will be guaranteed by the government.

Government Policies

The major policy areas that this section will deal with are input policy, extension and research, financial services, pricing and marketing and the transport infrastructure.

1. **Input policy:** While the commercial farmers have always enjoyed easy access to the manufacturers and wholesalers of agricultural inputs (fertilizers, seed, stock-feeds, machinery, chemicals, etc.) the position of the communal farmers has always been, and remains, quite different. For most farmers in the communal areas the lack of a distributive network is a major constraint. Anyone wishing to buy fertilizer and chemicals from the companies must pick them up at the factory and organize their own transport. The government's current approach of using the co-operative unions to assist in the distribution process in the communal area is a step in the right direction. What is still lacking is the managerial ability to deal with the organization required in such an exercise. Direct government participation in the distribution of inputs may well be necessary in order to overcome this constraint.

A separate problem in the area of inputs is that of the shortage of foreign exchange for imports. The national tractor fleet is becoming increasingly old. To keep the fleet and other agricultural machinery operative, the allocation of foreign exchange for replacement and spares requires the highest priority.

The Chavunduka report highlighted the difficulty small-scale farmers experience in servicing their tractors and machinery and recommended the establishment of tractor servicing stations in remote areas.

2. **Research and Extension policy:** Agricultural extension services provided through Agritex are now primarily oriented towards the small-scale farmers, and only provide advice on demand to the commercial farmers.

Agritex is an amalgamation of two separate institutions which existed prior to 1981: the Conservation and Extension Department (CONEX), formerly operating in commercial areas, and the Department of Agricultural Development (DEVAG) which operated in the communal areas. The role of Agritex includes advising farmers on the selection of suitable crops and better arable holding, and encouraging the adoption of moisture conservation tillage practices. Problems in this area include the lack of trained staff, the need for more training centres, the need for more female extension workers (much of the farming in the communal areas is done by the women), and the lack of adequately trained village extension workers.

The Department of Research and Specialist Services is now beginning to devote a major portion of its work to the specific problems confronting the small-holder while maintaining its basic research programme in plant and animal breeding and disease control.

R&SS is also involved in the development of appropriate machinery and equipment, through the department of Agricultural Engineering, for use in communal areas. On-farm testing is carried out through Agritex's extension network.

3. **Financial services:** The financial needs of the commercial and communal farmers are very different. The commercial farmers have, in the past, been well looked after by the AFC and the commercial banks. Their present needs are more in the area of foreign exchange in order to replace worn-out machinery. If the commercial farmers are to maintain past productvity trends, government will have to make large amounts of foreign exchange available.

The present demands of the communal farmers are for loans from the AFC, largely for fertilizer and seed inputs. Although the AFC has directed far more of its resources into this sector (see Table 2 Graph 2), the whole array of financial services is very under-developed in the communal lands. A highly centralized body such as the AFC is not ideal for providing finance to the large

TABLE 6: Loans granted by the AFC from 1975-86

Year	Large Scale Commercial % of total loans	Large Scale Commercial Value ($m)	Small Scale Commercial % of total loans	Small Scale Commercial Value ($m)	Resettlement Credit Scheme % of total loans	Resettlement Credit Scheme Value ($m)	Communal Farmers % of total loans	Communal Farmers Value ($m)	Total Loans $m
1975	100%	39,30	0	-	0	-	0	-	39,3
1976	100%	43,70	0	-	0	-	0	-	43,7
1977	100%	53,20	0	-	0	-	0	-	53,2
1978	100%	57,50	0	-	0	-	0	-	57,5
1979	98,5%	67,90	1,5%	1,02	0	-	0	-	68,9
1980	91,6%	86,90	4%	3,70	0	-	4,4%	4,20	94,8
1981	85,4%	88,80	4,4%	4,60	0,5%	0,50	9,7%	10,10	104
1982	82,2%	88,70	4,2%	4,50	1,4%	1,50	12,2%	13,20	107,4
1983	72,4%	110,20	5,3%	8,10	6,9%	10,60	15,4	23,40	152,3
1984	68,2%	110,30	5,4%	8,70	6,6%	10,70	19,8%	32,00	161,7
1985	65,8%	113,00	6,7%	11,50	4,9%	8,50	15,4%	38,80	171,8
*1986	52,5%	91,19	8,1%	14,08	5%	8,62	34,4%	59,89	173,78

NB. The value of loans granted to the resettlement sector dropped due to applications being withdrawn

* The 1986 loan Statistics are only up to the 31st December 1986. The financial year runs from 1st April to 31 March the following year.

7

number of small, geographically dispersed and relatively inaccessible communal farmers. The AFC has strongly supported the idea of granting 'group credit' to the co-operative unions which would then handle the task of distributing and collecting the funds from the individual farmers. This scheme has not, however, yet taken shape.

GRAPH 2: Loans granted by the AFC: 1975-86

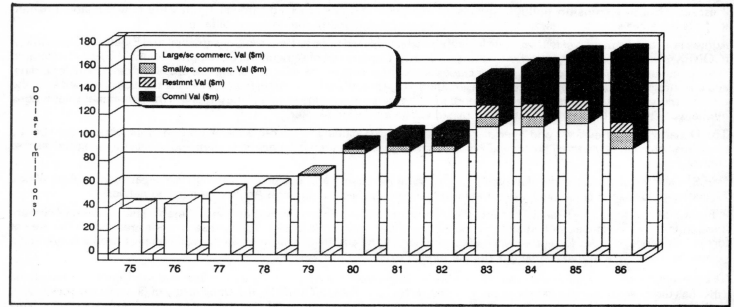

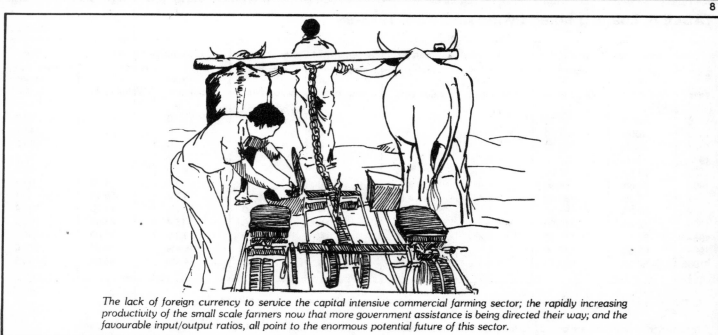

The lack of foreign currency to service the capital intensive commercial farming sector; the rapidly increasing productivity of the small scale farmers now that more government assistance is being directed their way; and the favourable input/output ratios, all point to the enormous potential future of this sector.

At present the AFC runs a Small Farm Credit Scheme designed to extend AFC facilities to small-scale farmers; loans, guaranteed by government, are extended to communal and resettlement farmers and money is provided to augment irrigation facilities in rural areas through the Irrigation Fund. All these facilities are, in addition to loans, granted to the large-scale commercial farmers. (See Box [1] for more details on the AFC).

4. Pricing policy: The seven most important agricultural products on which the government sets the price are beef, milk, maize, wheat, cotton, soya beans and groundnuts.

Other controlled crops include sorghum, sunflower, mhunga, rapoko and coffee (although coffee does not have a set producer price; the GMB buys it at a set floor price and then pays the farmers whatever additional profits are made from the sale of the crop). The procedure with the controlled crops is that the farmers in the commercial farming areas have no option but to sell all controlled crops to the GMB. They are not allowed to sell to each other or to any commercial outlet. The farmers in the communal areas, on the other hand, are allowed to sell to each other, but are not allowed to sell either to the commercial farmers or to any commercial outlet.

Government policy in the pricing of agricultural products has aimed at setting high producer prices (pre-planting prices) in order to maintain food self-sufficiency. In addition, government has, through the use of subsidies, maintained low food prices in order to subsidize the consumer. The dramatic increases in agricultural production in the 1980-81, 1981-82 and 1985-86 seasons have illustrated the responsiveness of all farmers in Zimbabwe, both large- and small-scale, to price incentives. The maintenance of uneconomic consumer food prices put added strain on a budget already in deficit and ultimately led the government to re-evaluate its cheap food policy in 1983, when much higher consumer prices were announced. Since 1983 food prices have continued to be adjusted upwards but the deficits of the GMB have continued to grow. (See Table 7 for the cost of subsidies).

TABLE 7: Budgetary Subsidies for Agricultural Products (Z$ thousand): 1974-83

Year	Maize	Maize Meal	Wheat	Flour	Soya-beans	Edible Oil	Beef	Dairy	Cheese	Total
1974/75									12	12
1975/76	272		2 191					1 875	1	4 339
1976/77	568		2 020		532		6 338			9 458
1977/78	420		2 798				11 265			14 483
1979/80	4 270	1 400	925	3 300	1 379		12 920	2 108		26 302
1980/81	9 662	14 439		5 607	1 919	4 822	9 619	4 500		30 568
1981/82	5 110	64 800		8 500	956	6 200	25 730	10 354		121 650
1982/83										140 000

9

Note: The maize, wheat and soyabeans subsidies are paid to the Grain Marketing Board; the beef subsidy to the Cold Storage Commission, the dairy and cheese subsidy to the Dairy Marketing Board, the flour maize meal subsidy to the millers, and the edible oils to the oil expressors. In the government budget, these subsidies are arbitrarily divided between the Ministry of Agriculture and the Ministry of Trade and Commerce. Flour, maize meal and edible oils go under the head of the Ministry of Trade and Commerce; the remainder to the Ministry of Agriculture.

In order to maximize the benefits of producer prices, they need to be set on time and in a manner that is understandable to all farmers. The Chavunduka Commission recommended that the price announcements for beef and dairy products be made in February/March, and those for crop prices (other than wheat) in May/June. Producer prices need to take the increased costs of production into account if agricultural development is to continue to take place. The decrease in agricultural employment from 275,4 thousand in 1975 (35% of total labour force) to 206 thousand in 1983 (25% of the labour force) has been one of the consequences of rising costs of agricultural production.

Pricing policy has, in the past, produced anomalous results. In the case of maize, the high producer price has led to an over-supply which is costly to store and not financially viable to export. Table 8 shows the position of small grains:

TABLE 8: Intakes, Sales and Stocks of small grain Crops
(all figures in tonnes)

	Intake*	Local Sales**	Stocks***
Sorghum	68 599	11 075	112 051
Mhunga	19 738	157	68 002
Rapoko	7 549	421	20 680

10

* Year ended 10 November 1986
** Year ended September 1986
*** Year ended 7 November 1986

The high producer price of mhunga was the only reason communal area farmers were persuaded to move out of maize production and into the production of a far more drought-resistant crop. From the point of view of the communal farmer there was no risk attached, as the GMB was compelled to purchase all they produced at the controlled price. The problem was how to dispose of the crop once it had been bought. From the above table it is evident that the GMB has been able to dispose of very little of the mhunga they bought.

The present stocks are estimated to be a 212 years supply for Zimbabwe at present rates of consumption.

The benefits of the low consumer prices, although intended to subsidize the standard of living of the poor, have not directly benefited the poorest sections of the population who live in the rural areas (and who produce their own food rather than buy the subsidized food). It was this last factor that led the government to re-evaluate its cheap food policy in 1983.

5. **Marketing policy:** The present system of agricultural marketing in Zimbabwe depends heavily on the following legally established parastatal marketing monopolies:
— the Grain Marketing Board (GMB)
— the Cotton Marketing Board (CMB)
— the Cold Storage Commission (CSC)
— the Dairy Marketing Board (DMB)

The GMB is the exclusive buyer of maize, sorghum, groundnuts, soya beans, wheat, sunflower and coffee. The CMB is the exclusive buyer of cotton and also operates seven ginneries around the country. The CMB has been taking steps to expand its ginning capacity to meet increasing levels of output, especially from the communal areas. The DMB has a monopoly in the purchasing, processing and distribution of milk and butterfat and the CSC acts as a residual buyer for cattle and livestock, and is engaged in the processing of meat products. The CSC also has a monopoly of the marketing of meat products on the export market. The role of the Tobacco Marketing Board (TMB) is somewhat different to the other parastatal marketing agencies in that it does not buy crops but acts as a regulatory agency whose main function is to ensure that the private trade in tobacco meets government standards. The Agricultural Marketing Authority (AMA) is responsible for co-ordinating the operations of the above boards, with the exception of the TMB. Each of these four agencies has an established AMA committee as its head; in the case of the CSC, the AMA's beef and livestock committee is made up of AMA board members, a representative of the ministry of Lands, Agriculture and Rural Resettlement, the CSC general manager and representatives from the three farmers' unions. In recent years the primary task of the AMA has been borrowing on behalf of the marketing boards in order to cover their growing deficits.

Although the marketing system applies to the whole country it has, in practice, mainly served the commercial areas where farmers are close together, there are good transport and communication links and the marketing authorities can maintain an extensive network. The strong representation of the commercial farmers on the management committees of all the parastatals has also been instrumental in ensuring this. The position in the communal areas is quite different. One survey showed that crop marketing costs for the average commercial producer comprise 5% of total variable operating costs; for the average communal farmer they comprise 25%. This underlies the fact that the marketing board system provides a relatively inadequate, costly and unreliable service in the communal areas. Government, in recent years, has made some inroads into solving this problem but a lot remains to be done. Essentially the parastatal depot system needs to be extended and the transport network into the communal areas should be further developed.

State Farming

The state participates in direct production in agriculture through the Agricultural and Rural Development Authority and to some extent through the DMB, the CSC and the CMB, all of which are involved in the processing of agricultural products. Total state ownership of land (through ARDA) amounted to 499 007 hectares by the end of 1984, of which 225 537 hectares were purchased after 1980. By the end of 1984, ARDA was operating 18 separate units which produced cotton, tea, coffee, rice, onions, carrots, tomatoes, wheat, pineapples, proteas, maize, groundnuts, soya beans, tobacco, sorghum, sunhemp, lucerne, beans, sunflower, rye grass, milk and beef. In some areas of production, for example wheat and cotton, ARDA compares favourably with the commercial farming sector. ARDA is also one of the single biggest employers in the rural areas, employing over 5 000 permanent staff and 16 000 casuals.

One may say that government participation in the agricultural industry has served to boost agricultural production in the commercial areas and has significantly increased communal area production. The close co-operation between government and the commercial farmers has served to maintain a degree of flexibility and responsiveness in the government's handling of this sector, a relationship which can only improve if the communal farmers begin to play a more important role in the parastatal agencies concerned with the agricultural industry.

The government committed itself to investigating the traditional system with a view to promoting greater equality between men and women.

Government Planning in the Agricultural Sector

1. The Transitional National Development Plan (1982-85)
The three-year Transitional National Development Plan includes the first major policy directives published by the new government for the agricultural sector.

These included:
— an intention to resettle 162 000 families on commercial farmland, though not all within the period of the plan;
— a proposed investigation of the traditional communal system with a view to reforming its potential for attracting investment, preventing over-exploitation, promoting equality between men and women, and improving the management of common assets;

— the need to strengthen the co-operative movement through the establishment of a co-operative bank, a credit league, consumer and housing co-operatives, the granting of assistance in areas such as cattle management, market societies, research and training, etc.;
— the need to bring market outlets closer to small farmers;
— ensuring that producer prices approximate market prices more closely in the future and the announcement of the former early enough to influence production. The food subsidy policy was thought to be too heavy a burden on the treasury and

to have neglected the communal areas. In future, the plan noted the intention to target food subsidies towards the poorest groups.;
— increasing the availability of credit and energy resources in the communal areas, and improving the system of foreign exchange allocation in recognition of the import requirements of agriculture.

Although many of the measures of the TNDP were not instituted due to the effects of the drought and the international recession on the expected growth rates (and hence expected revenues), they do give an indication of the direction of government's thinking.

2. The First Five Year National Development Plan (FFYNDP) 1986-90

The major issues raised in the 1986-90 FFYNDP include:
— an expected growth rate of 5% p.a. for the agricultural sector. The communal and resettlement sectors are expected to grow at an average rate of 7 — 8%, small-scale commercial farmers at 5 — 6% and large-scale commercial farmers at 3 — 4%. Given a projected population growth of 2,8% this still leaves room for export;
— a growth in employment in the sector of 2,2% p.a. which is mainly expected to occur in areas such as horticulture;
— the resettlement of 15 000 families per year; in addition, government aims to provide back-up services such as credit and specialist advice to the resettled peasants in order to ensure that agricultural production is improved;
— the introduction of public works schemes such as the construction of roads, bridges, schools, clinics, irrigation schemes, etc. as components of an integrated rural development programme;
— the strengthening of the infrastructure for the distribution of agricultural inputs and the marketing of crops in the communal and resettlement areas:
— an investment programme of $998 million to achieve the above goals, of which $880 million is to come from the Public Sector Investor Programme, and the balance from the private sector.

Successes and Failures: Although far from complete, the government's attempts to integrate the peasant farming sector more fully into the agricultural industry have shown marked successes. The volume of marketed output from this previously ignored sector has increased dramatically (see Table 4, page 60) as a result of increased producer prices and improved marketing

The public works' programme was an attempt to instil a sense of self-reliance at the same time as providing drought relief under the programme, the receipt of drought relief was linked to involvement in work on defined projects in the rural areas, and participants received $2 per day to assist them in buying of food. The projects include work in hospitals, roads and bridges.

facilities. The increase in credit facilities provided by the AFC and the progress of the resettlement exercise (albeit slower than envisaged) can also be seen as a success story.

On the negative side lies the lack of progress in developing a viable co-operative movement which could absorb some of the unemployed and relieve the land pressure in the communal areas. The declining share of total employment in the agricultural sector intensifies the problem of unemployment, which is felt most acutely in the rural areas.

The proposed public works scheme is clearly a step in the right direction, although it must be said that the FFYNDP is characteristically vague on the specifics of this vital project. A failure to come to grips with the problem of unemployment and its rural counterpart, increased land pressure in the communal areas, and the continuous rise in the price of agricultural inputs, could threaten the tenuous viability achieved thus far in the peasant farming sector.

Major Agricultural Products

Table 9 lists the nine major crops produced in Zimbabwe over the 1975-84 period (note that flue-cured and Burley tobacco have been combined) and gives their contribution to total crop production. The relative importance of crop and livestock production has also been listed.

Maize: Under normal conditions maize is the most important crop in both volume and value terms. Persistent droughts have, however, drastically reduced maize production in recent years and have necessitated maize imports. This has led farmers to switch to more drought-resistant crops causing a 68% drop in the production of maize from 1981 to 1983. Zimbabwe's total maize consumption is in the region of 1,6 million tonnes per annum.

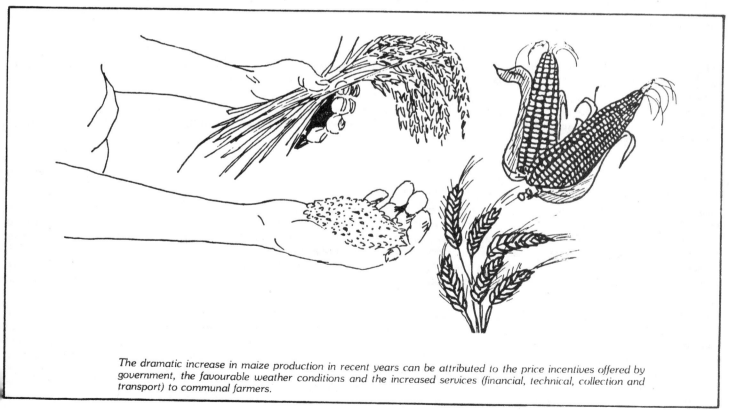

The dramatic increase in maize production in recent years can be attributed to the price incentives offered by government, the favourable weather conditions and the increased services (financial, technical, collection and transport) to communal farmers.

Although maize is grown throughout Zimbabwe the highest yields are in the wetter north-eastern districts where almost five tonnes per hectare are produced, compared to less than half a tonne per hectare in Matabeleland (Regions iv and v). Only about 6% of the land devoted to maize production is under irrigation, the rest relies on rainfall for good harvests.

TABLE 9: Summary of Sales of principal Crops and Livestock per cent shares: 1975-84

	1975	1979	1980	1981	1982	1983	1984
Livestock	25,2	30,6	24,5	18,5	27,0	30,5	25,8
Crops:	74,8	69,4	75,5	81,5	73,0	69,5	74,2
of which:							
Maize*	19,5	11,8	19,4	41,2	30,3	14,9	18,8
	(25,1)	(22,7)	(26,6)	(41,6)	(32,7)	(17,7)	-
Tobacco	25,0	36,0	26,8	22,5	27,6	37,1	36,4
Sugar	22,8	12,8	20,6	14,2	14,2	18,9	16,3
Cotton	14,9	21,0	18,9	13,2	14,4	16,8	19,7
Wheat	6,0	6,9	5,9	6,0	7,3	5,6	3,5
Soyabeans	1,2	4,4	4,0	1,9	3,1	3,8	3,7
Coffee	1,4	4,1	3,3	1,3	2,2	3,7	2,5
Groundnuts	2,6	1,3	1,2	0,9	0,8	0,5	0,2
Sorghum	0,0	0,6	0,5	0,5	0,4	0,1	0,4

11

* Since a substantial proportion of maize is produced for own consumption, the percentage in brackets has been computed as a proportion of estimated value of production, including production for own consumption, to the value of total agricultural output, in order to get an estimate for the share of maize in total agricultural output.
 = Not yet available.

Tobacco: This is the second most important crop in terms of the value of production but it is the single most important foreign exchange earner. Between 1979 and 1983, tobacco earned, on average, 46,5% of Zimbabwe's foreign exchange. It is a more drought-resistant crop than maize, but has the problem of being relatively labour-intensive in a time of continually rising wages. Tobacco's labour-intensive nature is illustrated by its employment of close on 100 000 males in 1982. Favourable tobacco prices and increased productivity ratios have enabled farmers to increase yields in recent years although the crop remains sensitive to increased input costs.

Most of the tobacco grown in Zimbabwe is concentrated in the north and north-east of the country. Despite the importance of tobacco in the pre-colonial period, most of the country's crop is presently grown by the commercial farmers. Most tobacco grown is of the Virginia flue-cured variety with Burley tobacco making up only 2 — 3% of total production.

Sugar-cane: The growing of sugar-cane (from which we get our sugar) is almost entirely carried out on irrigated land in the lowveld by large multi-national companies (primarily the Triangle and Hippo Valley Estates). Zimbabwe exports sugar mainly to the European Economic Community (EEC) where it has a guaranteed quota, and to the USA, thereby earning valuable foreign exchange. Some sugar is also used locally for the production of ethanol at the Triangle ethanol plant which opened in 1980. The plant produces 40 million litres of ethanol a year which is blended with petrol and accounts for over 15% of the country's petrol requirements. Approximately 50% of the sugar produced is now consumed locally (approximately 200 000 tonnes) with the rest being exported.

Cotton: This crop has only been produced on a large scale in Zimbabwe over the past 20 years. This is largely due to the efforts of the state-sponsored Kadoma (formerly Gatooma) Cotton Research Station which produced a variety of cotton suitable for local conditions. Sales rose from under 7 000 tonnes in the 1964-65 season to almost 300 000 tonnes in the 1985-86 season, making cotton the second most important crop (see Table 9) and an important contributor to foreign exchange earnings. Commercial area production of cotton has been declining in recent years due to the labour-intensive nature of its production, whereas communal area production has been on the increase, largely because of its drought-resistant qualities. The labour-intensive nature of cotton production is because 90 to 95% of Zimbabwe's cotton is hand-picked which makes it very attractive on the international market.

Cotton does best when grown in areas below 1 200m (i.e. low altitude areas), because low temperatures at higher altitudes restrict growth.

Wheat: This is a winter crop usually grown in rotation with soya beans and cotton (as summer crops). Because of the summer rainfall pattern, wheat has to be grown under irrigation which has been a limiting factor in the past. Production of the crop is capital intensive and 95% is grown by the commercial farmers, the rest by ARDA on state farms. Prior to 1980, Zimbabwe was self-sufficient in wheat production, but rising demand for wheat products has outstripped production. Domestic demand for wheat is estimated to be in the region of 220 000 tonnes p.a.; production in the 1985-86 season (a good year for wheat) was 205 528 tonnes. Wheat grows best under conditions of cool temperatures and moderate moisture in the growing season, with a warmer and drier period for harvest. These conditions are found in the highveld areas where most of the country's wheat is now grown. An irrigation fund was established through the AFC in 1985 in order to promote the growing of winter wheat and a return to self-sufficiency.

Soya beans: The production of soya beans is capital intensive and, as such, they are almost entirely produced by the commercial farmers. However, the rise in minimum wages and other input costs, have driven many farmers out of maize and into soya bean production. Since 1980, production has averaged 80 000 tonnes p.a., almost all of which is consumed locally. Small quantities are being used for fodder, but the major demand is for oil and meal products. Another major advantage of soya bean production (besides the labour-saving nature of the crop) is the short growing season and the minimal fertilizer requirements of the crop.

Coffee: This is a fairly new crop which is grown primarily under irrigation in the Eastern Highlands. Coffee production requires high capital costs to begin production but, thereafter, is a labour-intensive crop which, under irrigation, could be grown in the communal areas (over two-thirds of the area under coffee is now irrigated). The value of coffee production has increased dramatically in recent years from $10 565 000 in the 1979-80 season to $43 914 000 in the 1985-86 season. Around 85% of the coffee produced is exported, making coffee the fifth largest agricultural export of Zimbabwe (coffee contributes approximately 7% of total agricultural exports).

Groundnuts: These are grown almost exclusively by communal farmers, and form an important protein source in the communal areas. The production of groundnuts began in the pre-colonial era and is to-day one of the most important of the communal area crops, together with maize and sorghum. The marketed sale of groundnuts ($3 582 000 in 1985-86) represents only a small proportion of the groundnuts grown, as most of the crop is used for home consumption.

Sorghum: This is a relatively minor commercial crop but it is of major importance to communal farmers as a subsistence crop. Its main commercial use is in the brewing of opaque beer but it is sometimes used for feed. Government has recently increased the producer price of sorghum to $180,00 per tonne in an effort to shift communal farmers out of maize production and into the production of the more drought-resistant sorghum. The delivery of over 80 000 tonnes of the crop to the marketing authorities in 1986 (a four-fold increase over the previous year) illustrates the success of this policy. However, this in itself has presented the marketing boards with a different set of problems, i.e. how to get rid of its current large stock of sorghum. On the 1st May, 1986, the GMB held 56 000 tonnes of sorghum; in the subsequent year to mid-February 1987, a further 69 658 tonnes were delivered to the GMB while only 20 529 tonnes were sold in that period (of which 208 tonnes were exported). At the end of February 1987 the GMB, therefore, held 103 181 tonnes of sorghum in stock.

Livestock: This important agricultural product accounted for almost 26% of total agricultural production in 1984 (see Table 9). Cattle are the most important livestock in Zimbabwe and account for 70% of all livestock slaughterings; pigs account for another 23% and sheep the remaining 7%. The national livestock herd was at its peak in 1977 at 6 614 000 head and declined to around 5 318 000 in 1984. Approximately 58% of the herd was in the hands of the communal farmers in 1984 although it is the commercial farmers who account for 80 — 90% of the country's marketed beef supply. Cattle in the communal lands are kept for a number of reasons including draught power, social security and milk for home consumption. Although there are some very big cattle ranches in Zimbabwe with herds numbering over 60 000 head, the majority of the cattle are owned in smaller herds. Cattle native to Zimbabwe are the Nkone, Mashona and Tuli but a number of different breeds have been introduced including Sussex, Hereford, Simmentaler, Charolais, Afrikander and Brahman. The largest cattle buyer in the country is the CSC which also operates two programmes to support the rebuilding of the national herd, the Cattle Finance Scheme which provides credit to farmers to help them acquire breeder-stock and cattle for feeding, and the Breeder Finance Scheme which provides for the purchase of female cattle at equivalent slaughter value.

Large-scale farmers produce nearly all the marketed milk with communal farmers mainly producing for their own consumption. Dairy farmers are concentrated around the major urban centres with 48% of the dairy herd located in the Mashonaland South province.

Poultry: This is currently the fastest growing livestock industry in Zimbabwe and has the potential to capture a far greater share of the meat market than its present 10%. Poultry production is controlled by a few large producers but hundreds of unregistered small producers have sprung up in the urban areas in response to the beef shortages, and holdings of poultry in the communal areas, largely for subsistence purposes, are extensive.

Central Issues for the Future Development of the Agricultural Industry

1. Population Growth versus Food Production: The Malthusian Problem

The Chavunduka Commission of Inquiry into the Agricultural Industry stated that the demand for food will probably increase by 3,8% to 5% p.a. in the 1980s. The rate of growth in the past five years has averaged 2% p.a. (at 1980 prices) while the average annual growth in the production of food has, in the past, averaged 2,6% p.a.

In order to meet the expected rise in demand, food production will have to increase to at least 5% growth p.a. The Commission went on to estimate that at the current levels of population growth, the agricultural industry will have to feed 10,6 million people in 1990 and 15 million people in the year 2000. Based on a planned resettlement of up to one million people, a population drift of 3% per decade into the urban areas and a population growth rate of 2,8% p.a., the Commission estimated that by 1990, 7 916 000 people will be living in the rural areas of Zimbabwe. Of this figure, 4,2 million will be living in the communal areas, giving a population density of 3,88 ha/capita after resettlement. The land holding per capita is below (i.e. worse, because there is less land available per person) that of the 1980 crisis level of 4.04 ha/capita.

Assuming the full resettlement of 1,37m people, the communal lands will require a minimum increase in productivity of 5% p.a. if they are to maintain incomes at the 1980 levels of approximately $259 per capita p.a. (the crisis levels). If the level of resettlement is any lower, then the land per person will fall still further and productivity gains will, accordingly, have to be higher. (Note that by all indications the levels of resettlement will be considerably lower than the projected targets.) By November, 1984, only 36 000 families (180 000 to 200 000 people) had been resettled; the FFYNDP planned a further resettlement of 15 000 families p.a., i.e. another 410 000 people. So if the government meets its projected target, still only 600 000 people will have been resettled by the year 1990.

The high growth rate in Zimbabwe has meant that areas which were sparcely populated some 50 years ago are today over-crowded. If this high rate of population growth continues it could spell future disaster.

2. Wages, Productivity and Employment

The relationship between rising labour costs and unemployment is perhaps one of the most important issues facing the agricultural sector and the Zimbabwean Government at the moment. Since 1980, productivity in commercial agriculture grew at an annual rate of 9%; at the same time real wages are estimated to have risen by 7% p.a. In so far as wage costs are concerned, agriculture appears to have improved its position; the question that remains is exactly how the commercial farmers have managed to increase their competitiveness in the face of rising statutory minimum wages.

The truth of the matter is that commercial agriculture has lost its crucial role as a generator of jobs; between 1974 and 1984, 100 000 jobs were lost in agriculture (about 27% of the farm labour force — see Table 3, page54).During this same period the volume of commercial agricultural output remained virtually unchanged. In order to remain profitable in the face of rising wages, commercial farmers have made increasing use of capital intensive technology. The productivity of the remaining workers increased by some 50% at constant 1980 prices over the past few years (see Graph 3 below)

GRAPH 3: Index of Employment, average earnings and production in the agricultural sector: 1974 - 84

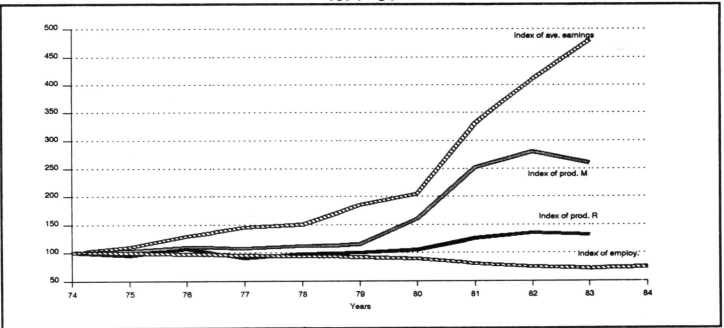

12

Graph 3 shows the falling rate of employment plotted against average earnings and productivity in the industry. All figures have been reduced to indices using 1974 as the base year in order to simplify comparison. The falling index of employment (from 100 in 1974 to 72 in 1983) shows a decline in employment in the industry of 28% over the ten year period. One of the contributing factors leading to this high rate of unemployment has been the rise in wages. The period 1974-80 shows a fairly steep rise in the 'average earnings' curve, the period after 1980 showing a dramatic rise in wages which is met by an increasingly high rate of unemployment. The steep rise in the 'Index of Productivity' curve is partly due to the declining size of the work-force. The Productivity (M) curve reflects the money value of agricultural output in the period, while the Productivity (R) curve makes use of real (deflated) values for total output. The difference between the two curves is a reflection of the high rate of inflation, especially in the post-Independence period. The significant gap between the 'Index of Average Earnings' (M) and the 'Index of Average Earnings (R)' once again highlights the effects of inflation. Once we have deflated the figures (working with the (R) curves) we can see that wages have consistently been above the productivity levels in this sector. As minimum wages rose sharply (both in money and real terms) after 1980, the gap between productivity and wages widened, causing the farmers to increase the lay-off of workers. Since 1982, real wages in the sector have actually declined, lay-offs have increased and productivity has fallen.

The largest single drop in employment was in 1980-81 when over 17 000 agricultural jobs were lost. This was also the period in which the minimum wage was established and wages rose from an average of $25 per month in 1979 to $53 per month by the end of 1981. The policy of implementing statutory minimum wages (SMW) was part of the government's drive for growth with equity.

On the positive side, minimum wages have increased the level of domestic demand and, therefore, the size of the domestic market. Low per capita incomes have, in the past, meant that the size of the domestic market remained small. The only opportunity for expansion was, formerly, through the export market. Rising minimum wages could change that.

On the other hand, rising minimum wages have meant that, in the past ten years, over 100 000 people have lost their jobs. In 1975 some 275 thousand people were employed in the agricultural sector, earning an average wage of $17 per month, representing a monthly demand of some $4,675m (i.e. $17 × $275 000); in 1983 only 206 thousand people were employed, earning an average wage of $80, which represented a monthly demand of $16,480m. Clearly demand has risen and the potential exists for the productive sectors of the domestic economy to increase output, and therefore employment, accordingly. The export nature of the economy and, in particular, agriculture, acts as a strong brake on this potential expansion.

If agriculture is to remain competitive in the international market, costs have to be minimized. Labour costs, representing the major component of production costs have, therefore, to be kept at a minimum. If wages are rising, then the number of workers employed has to fall in order to keep costs under control.

While First World countries which have traditionally suffered from labour shortages during periods of expansion, may be able to afford the replacement of labour with machinery, Third World countries such as Zimbabwe which have an over-abundance of labour, clearly cannot afford such strategies. If competing in the international economy demands that Zimbabwe use the same production techniques as the First World (and therefore replace labour with machinery) then we need to seriously question whether we can afford this pattern of export-led growth. The shortage of foreign exchange with which to purchase additional inputs of machinery has meant that many commercial farmers have switched to the production of less labour-intensive crops — which has the same effect as replacing labour with machinery.

Alternatively, if we are to remain on our present export-led path, then government needs to devise other means of redistributing income towards the poor than through increases in the SMW.

Despite the lack of capital equipment and the often out-dated farming methods used, the communal farming sector has managed to generate a sizeable and increasing proportion of the national harvest in recent years.

3. Dualism in Zimbabwean Agriculture

The Zimbabwean Government inherited an agricultural system characterized by a division between commercial and communal farmers. Its possible options were to either consolidate the communal areas into large-scale commercial farms, or to divide the commercial farms into small-scale communal-type plots. The present government has adopted neither policy. It has chosen instead to maintain the dualism it inherited, and on land which came up for sale, resettle the peasant farmers drawn from the overcrowded communal lands. The resettlement policy was inspired more by the desire to achieve a more equitable distribution of land than by an attempt to develop a coherent agricultural policy.

The competing demands for land between the overcrowded communal areas and the landless peasants on the one hand, and the under-utilized commercial farms (see page 54) on the other, is an inevitable consequence of government's pragmatic compromise in this area.

At present both the commercial and the communal sectors play vitally important roles in the economy as a whole. The commercial sector's strategic importance lies in its role as a major food exporter providing close to 40% of total exports in 1984. It remains the largest employer in the economy, being responsible for one-quarter of total employment in March 1985, it functions as the main supplier of raw materials to the manufacturing sector, and it is the largest purchaser of industrial consumer goods and input items in the economy.

The communal sector's importance lies in the number of people who manage both to feed themselves and their families, and to provide an increasing share of total marketed output. At present some 4,5 million people live in the communal areas and although many of the adults may spend at least some period of the year in wage employment in the formal sector, their existence depends in part on the output of their land.

4. The Foreign Exchange Constraints

The problem of foreign exchange affects mainly the large-scale commercial farmer due to the degree of mechanization in this sector (all farmers would of course need crop chemicals, etc. which would make use of foreign exchange). The increasing cut-backs in forex could well be one of the future constraints limiting the growth of the commercial farming sector.

In the recent past, the commercial farmers accounted for well over 90% of farm exports. Any move towards the production of crops (e.g. groundnuts or Virginia tobacco) which require relatively few foreign inputs, and away from the large foreign exchange consumers (e.g. maize) would have to compensate for the corresponding loss in foreign exchange earnings.

Generally speaking, this constraint might in the future lead towards a development programme based on the conservation of foreign exchange which would tend to favour the development of small-scale farming.

5. Land Allocation

If the small-scale sector is to be able to absorb larger numbers of the unemployed it will need access to better land in the long term. Up to now over 70% of the resettlement has been on land falling into natural regions III — V, and only 1,27% on land from natural region I. This prejudices the performance of these resettlement models from the start.

Given the capital resources, managerial skills and mechanical equipment of the commercial farmers, they would seem relatively more suited to the natural regions III — V than the small-scale farmers with their smaller tolerance to risk and lack of a supporting infrastructure.

6. Diversification

Zimbabwean agriculture is in danger of becoming a victim of its own success. The large maize surpluses of 1985 and 1986 (leaving the GMB with an opening stock of close to two million tonnes of maize in March 1987) is tying up nearly $400 million in bank credit and imposing large interest and storage costs on the GMB.

Although stockpiles of maize act as an insurance against food shortages in drought years, the interest and storage costs incurred in maintaining the stockpile need to be seriously assessed.

Reports from the AMA indicate that both local and export sales of maize have been lower than expected, raising fears that it may be difficult to dispose of the maize stockpile. In response to this situation of over-production and declining consumption, government announced measures which were designed to limit maize production in the 1986/87 growing season. Small commercial farmers who produced and delivered 1 000 bags or less would receive the full producer price of $180 per tonne, and large commercial farmers would be permitted deliveries of 50% of last year's deliveries plus a further 1 000 bags, for which they would receive $180 per tonne. Deliveries in excess of this quantity would be paid for at the rate of $100 per tonne.

As is evident from these measures they only affect the commercial farmer despite the fact that communal farmers delivered over 45% of the total GMB intake of maize in the 1985-86 season. A further complaint from farmers was that the measures were announced after they had completed their planning and purchases for the 1986-87 season.

The cost of such disincentives over and above the costs sustained in the actual production and storage of the surplus (subsidies, loans to farmers, agricultural services, etc.) and the fact that maize exports are not financially viable, all point to the urgent need for diversification out of maize production. The problem, however, is in the direction of diversification. The world market for agricultural goods is fiercely competitive, and being landlocked, Zimbabwe is at a distinct disadvantage. The problem is essentially one of demand: international demand for commodities has been sluggish, and while domestic demand has been rising it has not been rising as fast as production.

There are to possible solutions to this dilemma of overproduction and underconsumption. If Zimbabwe is to attempt to maximize agricultural exports then it is imperative that agriculture maintains and increases its competitiveness internationally. The foreign exchange earnings from the agricultural sector will be vital for the capital regeneration that is needed to maintain and enhance competitiveness in agriculture, and to provide the necessary inputs for manufacturing. Ways will have to be found to decrease inflation and rising input costs, which may well necessitate a major reversal in the government's minimum wage and social spending policies.

The alternative would be to concentrate more on the domestic market and to look for opportunities for further import substitution. Diversification would be essential as the agricultural sector already produces far more maize than the domestic market can absorb, but not enough rice, wheat, oil, etc. Employment generation schemes and rising minimum wages would then contribute to expanding the size of the domestic market rather than simply reducing the competitiveness of our products abroad.

References

1. UNCTAD, *Zimbabwe: Towards a New Economic Order*, Statistical Annex, United Nations, 1980.
2. RAL Merchant Bank Ltd, *Executive Guide to the Economy*, Harare, December, 1986.
3. Ministry of Finance, Economic Planning and Development, *Socio-Economic Review of Zimbabwe 1980-85*, Harare, 1986, p. 114.
4. RAL Merchant Bank Ltd, *Executive Guide to the Economy*, Harare, December 1986, p. 4.
5. Central Statistical Office, *Statistical Yearbook, 1985*, A CSO publication, Sweden, 1985, p. 52.
6. Ministry of Finance, Economic Planning and Development, *Socio-Economic Review of Zimbabwe 1980-85*, p. 115.
7. Ministry of Agriculture, Harare.
8. Compiled from *Agricultural Finance Corporation Quarterly, Digest of Statistics*, Volume 1 No. 2, 1986, Harare.
9. Compiled from figures given in table 6, see note 7 above.
10. Agricultural Finance Corporation, *An Introduction to the AFC*, Spectrum Public Relations Consultants, Harare, 1985, p. 4.
11. Agricultural Finance Corporation, Annual Report, 1985, Harare.
12. Jansen, Doris J, *Agricultural prices and subsidies in Zimbabwe: benefits, costs and trade-offs*, Harare 1982.

THE MAIZE DILEMMA

1

Government increases the price of maize to $180 per tonne in order to stimulate increased production of maize.

2

At the same time government increases minimum wages as part of its policy of growth with equity. Wages in agriculture

increase from $75 pm to $85 pm. In agro-industries government wants workers to be paid the same wages as industrial workers.

3

Farmers claim that they cannot afford the wage increases as costs are too high and lay off farm workers. In the years since independence (since the introduction of the minimum wage policy) over 50 000 agricultural workers have been retrenched.

4 MEANWHILE

In the meantime the price of mealie meal goes up in accordance with the rise in the price of maize. The increase in the cost of living (which comes about due to price increases such as the increase in the price of mealie meal) exceeds the increase in wages for the fortunate workers who are still employed. For the unemployed the situation becomes desperate. Those who still have jobs now find that they are expected to support the ever increasing number of unemployed relatives.

5

The increase in the maize price generated bumper harvests in the years in which there was no drought. Government however finds that it cannot sell all the maize produced domestically or internationally. Domestically a lot of people cannot afford to buy the maize as the price is too high; internationally there is an oversupply of maize and the overvalued Zimbabwe dollar prices our maize out of the market. In the meantime the GMB is incurring very high storage and interest costs as a result of the huge maize stockpile.

THE DILEMMA

* farmers demand a high producer price and low wages;
* workers demand high wages and low food prices.
* if the producer price is high then workers cannot afford to buy food, and the price is too high for the international market;
* if wages are too high, and the producer price low, then producers will not produce.
* one possible alternative would be for government to pay high producer prices to farmers and subsidise food prices for consumers. The questions is: who would subsidise government?
* Government has opted for a policy mix which supports producer prices in order to generate food security; restraint on the rise of wages, which has in practice meant that prices rise faster than wages thereby eroding living standards; and a reduction of food subsidies, which further erodes living standards (the price of maize meal has increased from about $90 per tonne in 1982 to $349 per tonne on 1986).

Chapter 4

THE MANUFACTURING SECTOR

Introduction

Zimbabwe's manufacturing sector plays a vital role in the domestic economy; it provides a substantial share of the GNP, it contributes more than a quarter of all government revenue, and it generates almost a fifth of total employment (see Pie graphs for details). Traditionally, the manufacturing sector has been a net consumer of foreign exchange, although its contribution to exports has been rising. Unlike most others in Africa, the manufacturing sector in Zimbabwe produces over 6 000 different products spanning virtually all the consumer products demanded locally as well as many producer goods. Chemicals, primary metals, metal products and machinery and equipment together account for more than 40% of total manufacturing output.

FIGURE 1: The Contribution of the Manufacturing Sector to the Domestic Economy (1985 figures)

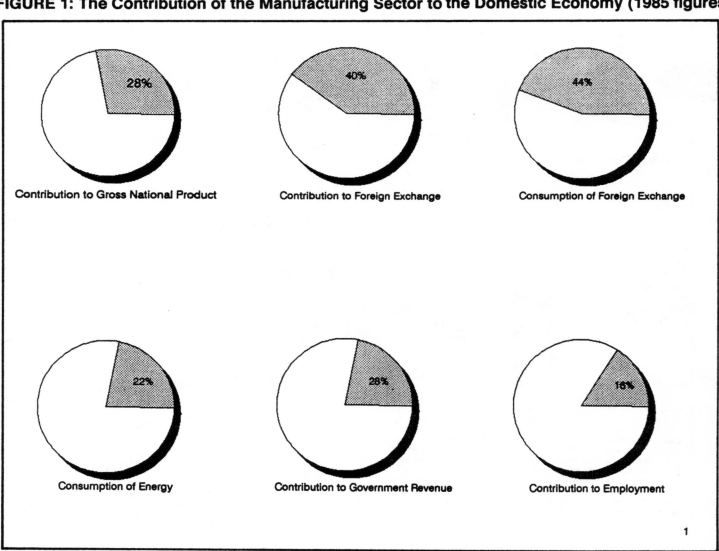

| Contribution to Gross National Product | Contribution to Foreign Exchange | Consumption of Foreign Exchange |
| Consumption of Energy | Contribution to Government Revenue | Contribution to Employment |

1

Although the manufacturing sector in Zimbabwe combines almost 10% of the GNP, the structure of the industry is similar to that of most Third World countries, i.e. the highly paid research and development work takes place in First World countries while the former merely assemble the components.

Zimbabwe's uniqueness in Africa is clearly portrayed by the contribution of the domestic manufacturing sector to total value added on the continent. In the mid-seventies Zimbabwe's share of African iron and steel production was about 30%; the corresponding figure for industrial chemicals was 12%, for clothing, 11%, for plastic products, 11%, and for machinery, 16%.

Historical Development of the Sector

The process of industrialisation began at the turn of the century. Initially it played a support role for the agricultural and mining sectors, being largely dominated by their input needs. By the late 1930s the sector was well established and in a position to respond to the major political developments which placed increased demands on it. The first of these political developments was the outbreak of the Second World War. The resultant transport problems made it difficult to import industrial products, and local production was therefore boosted. The accession to power of the Nationalist Government in South Africa in 1948 was also a significant political development in the region as it created uncertainty in South Africa and caused an outflow of capital into Rhodesia. The establishment of the Federation of Rhodesia and Nyasaland in 1953 more than doubled the size of the domestic market and placed Southern Rhodesia, as the only country in the Federation with a developed manufacturing sector, in a prime position to exploit this new market.

By 1965, the share of the manufacturing sector in GDP had already reached 19% and, at that point, roughly 20% of the sector's output was exported. The fourth significant political development was the declaration of UDI by the Smith government. The international community responded with the imposition of sanctions which restricted the access of local firms to external markets, cheap sources of imports and foreign investment. The Smith government retaliated by introducing various policy and institutional measures, including fuel rationing, the extension of price controls, rules prohibiting firms affected by sanctions from laying-off workers and, most importantly, strict rationing of foreign exchange and import licensing. The effect of these measures was to induce a strong domestic growth of the sector with a heavy orientation towards import substitution. The boom lasted until the mid-seventies when the developing liberation war began to take its toll. By that time, exports had fallen below 10% of the sector's output.

The effects of the liberation war and the tightening of sanctions were, however, not the only factors which impeded growth after 1974. Import substitution had gone beyond the first easy stages and the small size of the market was beginning to impose limits to further growth in this direction. The 1973 oil price rise also affected the local economy. It led to a huge increase in the fuel import bill and reduced export earnings and foreign exchange allocations. Thirdly, the closure of the border with Mozambique in 1976 increased transport costs substantially, further aggravating the balance of payments problem.

An important feature of the industrialization process during UDI was the re-orientation of the industrial sector towards the production of capital goods and heavy industry. This was reflected in the rapidly rising share of these industries in total output and employment.

After Independence the volume of manufacturing output increased for the first two years, and then changed dramatically in 1982 (see Table 1). This weak performance continued until 1984, for the following reasons:

— increasing shortages of foreign exchange due to rapidly rising imports and increased service charges (particularly interest charges);

— drastically reduced import allocations due to the shortage of foreign exchange;

— recession in the industrial countries which caused falling demand for some sectors, e.g. mining;

— drought in Zimbabwe (1982-84) which caused falling real incomes and hence a decline in domestic demand.

In contrast to the rapid growth in the 'heavy industries' during the UDI period, industrial growth in the post-Independence period mainly comprised expansion of output in the consumer goods sectors. (These same sectors, i.e. food processing, textiles, clothing and footwear, wood and furniture, paper, etc. had grown slowly after UDI). The recovery of the consumer goods industries was clearly linked to the expansion of domestic demand which resulted from the easing of restrictions on the import of intermediate goods, to an expansionary government policy, and to the increased consumer spending brought about by the introduction of minimum wages. Defence spending continued at high levels after Independence because of the security situation in the region. This meant that there was only a small decline in the defence budget. In addition there was a significant expansion in the provision of social services, including free primary education and free health care for all those earning less than $150 per month.

TABLE 1: Index of Volume of Manufacturing

Year	Index
1970	66,5
1971	72,6
1973	81,4
1974	93,8
1975	91,6
1976	86,0
1977	81,2
1978	79,2
1979	87,2
1980	100,0
1981	109,4
1982	108,7
1983	105,8
1984	100,7
1985	112,2
1986	*114,1

2

* For the first 10 months only.

These additions raised the level of government expenditure by more than 17% in current terms over the 1979-80 financial year. Moreover, very little of the increase in government spending in this period was directed at investment spending (Gross Fixed Capital Formation). The increase in demand was not therefore met by an increase in the economy's ability to supply. Having said this, it is also important to point out that the government had a moral responsibility to the electorate to redress some of the imbalances which resulted from 90 years of colonial rule. Fulfilling this whilst maintaining security in the region, often left government with little choice as to its spending patterns.

TABLE 2: Gross Fixed Capital Formation (GFCF) (at current prices)

Year	By Industry/ Manufacturing	By type of asset/ equipment, plant and machinery
1974	105	135
1975	115	121
1976	77	154
1978	44	144
1979	50	145
1980	123	194
1981	201	295
1982	169	244
1983	196	411
1984	234	599
1985*	—	857
1986*	—	883

3

* Estimate

Characteristics of the Manufacturing Sector

1. Monopolization

The recently published UNIDO (United Nations Industrial Development Organization) report on the manufacturing sector stated that of the 6 000 different products produced by the manufacturing sector in Zimbabwe, 50% of them are each manufactured by *only* one firm, 80% by one, two or three firms. According to the Monopolies and Mergers Commission of the UK, a firm which controls more than 25% of the market share for a product is a monopoly. By this definition 80% of Zimbabwe's manufacturing sector is monopolized. Of the remaining 20% in which some form of competition exists, only 50 products of the 6 000 produced by the whole sector (i.e. 0,8%) are produced by 20 or more firms.

The second major aspects of the monopolization of the sector is indicated in Table 3 (below), which shows the number of firms classified according to people employed and contribution to total output. From this we can see that relatively few firms contribute to the bulk of the sector's output: 52% of the firms produce only 8% of total output, and employ only 8% of the total labour force. At the other end of the scale, 8% of the firms produce 41% of total output and employ 44% of the total work-force (these are the largest firms in the country). These figures indicate a high degree of concentration in the manufacturing sector with a few large firms (approximately 105) producing over 40% of total output. The degree of concentration has increased noticeably in the past five years with the largest 8% of the firms having increased their share of net output from 36% in 1977 to 41% in 1982.

Geographically one also notices a degree of concentration with Harare being responsible for 50% of manufacturing output and 46% of manufacturing employment despite having only 8% of the country's population. The three major industrial centres, Harare, Bulawayo and the Kwekwe/Redcliff area, together account for 82% of total manufacturing output and 79% of manufacturing employment but only 14,2% of the population currently lives in these three centres.

Over the five year period 1977-82 the volume of manufacturing production increased by 136%. The greatest percentage increases were recorded in Harare (155% increase) and Bulawayo (150% increase) thereby intensifying the concentration of industry in these two centres.

TABLE 3: Trends in the Size and Contribution of manufacturing Units by Numbers of Employees for 1977 and 1982

Item	Numbers employed					
	Up to 50	51 to 100	101 to 500	501 to 750	Over 750	Total
Number of units, 1977	759	194	260	91	51	1,355
Number of units 1982	703	205	288	43	105	1,344
Percentage change 1977 to 1982	- 7	+ 6	+ 11	- 53	+ 106	- 1
Numbers employed 1977	14,319	12,877	45,870	30,829	37,356	141,233
Percentage of total 1977	10	9	32	22	26	100
Numbers employed 1982	13,773	13,997	55,315	16,718	76,460	176,223
Percentage of total 1982	8	8	31	9	43	100
Percentage change 1977 to 1982	- 4	+ 9	+ 21	- 46	+ 105	+ 25
Share of net output 1977 (%)	9	8	31	15	36	100
Share of net output 1982 (%)	8	8	31	12	41	100

4

2. Industrial Groups (sub-sectors) within Manufacturing

(See Box 1 for list of sub-sectors and sub-categories within each sub-sector).

(i) Foodstuffs (sub-sector 1) is the largest sub-sector, and its contribution to the gross manufacturing output has increased from 22% in 1980 to 25,5% in 1985. It outstripped the metals and metal-products sector (sub-sector 9: see Table 4) in 1983 to become the largest contributor to manufacturing output. Table 4 gives figures for 1982 (the most recent available at time of publication) which indicate that the foodstuffs sub-sector contained 11% of all the firms in the manufacturing sector in that year, generated 7,4% of the sector's total exports, employed 26 334 workers and held 15,3% of the sector's capital stock.

The index of production (which measures the volume of output) of the foodstuffs sub-sector rose to a peak of 126,9 in 1983 and fell back to 121,8 by October 1986. Foodstuffs is one of the sub-sectors which has grown steadily since 1980, for the following reasons:

a) increased wages for people in the low income categories has stimulated local demand for foodstuffs (note that although the proportion of total income spent on food has declined — see Chapter 2, page 37, total spending on food at current prices has increased);

b) this sector requires relatively few imported inputs and has, therefore, not been affected by the foreign exchange cutbacks (with the exception of the canning and preserving sub-category which is dependent on foreign exchange for the import of the tin plate used in the production of tin cans).

(ii) The metal and metal products sub-sector is the second largest in the manufacturing sector after foodstuffs. It reached its peak in 1984 (the index of production was 114,7 in 1984 using 1980 as the base year) but had declined to 94,6 by October 1986 (the fastest period of growth in this sub-sector was during the years of UDI when import substitution generated dramatic growth). This sub-sector is the most diversified in terms of both the range of commodities produced and the varieties of end-users of the products. The sector contains 30% of all manufacturing firms, produces 18,7% of net output, generates 53% of manufacturing exports, employs 24% of all employees in the sector, and accounts for 32% of the capital stock. The sector also has extensive backward and forward linkages with other sectors in the manufacturing industry.

Of the output in the metal and metal products sub-sector, 47% comes from the metal products, machinery and equipment sub-category (excluding electrical equipment), which includes the heavy engineering firms involved in design and production of machine equipment and the production of spares for other industries. Another 39% of the output of this sub-sector comes from the non-ferrous metal and iron and steel industries which is dominated by Zimbabwe Iron and Steel Corporation (Zisco).

(iii) The chemical and petroleum products sub-sector (sub-sector 7), together with the two sub-sectors mentioned above, generates 60% of the total output of the manufacturing sector.

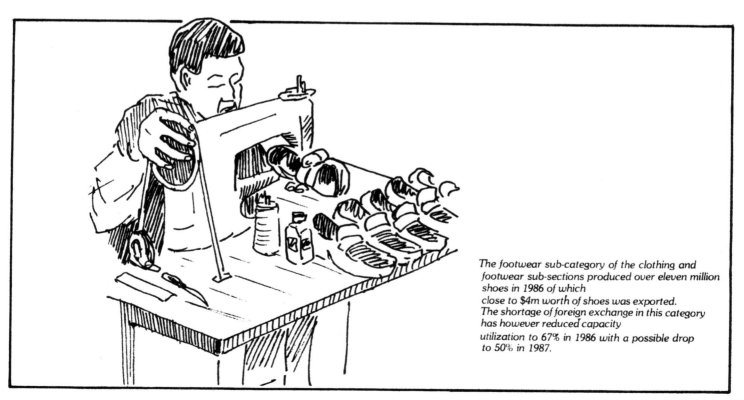

The footwear sub-category of the clothing and footwear sub-sections produced over eleven million shoes in 1986 of which close to $4m worth of shoes was exported. The shortage of foreign exchange in this category has however reduced capacity utilization to 67% in 1986 with a possible drop to 50% in 1987.

TABLE 4: Some key Characteristics of manufacturing Industry by broad Sector: 1982*

Sectors	Export (4)	Percentage of exports	Number of employees (5)	Percentage of employees	Capital stock (6)	Percentage of capital stock
Foodstuffs	20,435	7,4	26,334	14,9	573,100	15,3
Drink and Tobacco	2,481	0,9	13,206	7,5	341,200	9,1
Textiles including ginning	57,861	20,9	20,789	11,8	362,900	9,7
Clothing and Footwear	10,774	3,9	21,879	12,4	119,900	3,2
Wood and Furniture	9,060	3,3	12,914	7,3	83,600	2,2
Paper, Printing and Publishing	2,445	0,9	9,445	5,4	189,300	5,0
Chemical & Petroleum Products	15,096	5,4	12,945	7,3	507,400	13,5
Non-Metallic Mineral Products	1,717	0,6	7,818	4,4	243,200	0,5
Metal and Metal Products	147,295	53,1	42,237	24,0	1,218,900	32,4
Transport Equipment	3,507	1,3	5,245	3,0	86,000	2,3
Other Manufactured Products	6,545	2,4	3,411	1,9	30,800	0,8
	277,216	100%	176,223	100%	3,756,300	100%

Sectors	Number of units (1)	Percentage number of units	Gross output (2)	Percentage of gross output	Net output (3)	Percentage of net output
Foodstuffs	152	11,1	788,273	25,9	198,320	15,9
Drink and Tobacco	53	3,9	229,831	7,5	136,367	10,9
Textiles including ginning	67	4,9	302,415	9,9	107,311	8,6
Clothing and Footwear	148	10,9	211,259	6,9	111,256	8,9
Wood and Furniture	98	7,2	93,964	3,1	49,098	3,9
Paper, Printing and Publishing	114	8,4	163,489	5,4	84,131	6,7
Chemical and Petroleum Products	126	9,2	395,246	13,0	159,131	12,7
Non-Metallic Mineral Products	58	4,3	94,361	3,1	56,749	4,5
Metal and Metal Products	408	29,9	639,137	21,0	290,963	23,3
Transport Equipment	46	3,4	93,836	3,1	36,486	2,9
Other Manufactured Products	94	6,9	37,195	1,2	18,880	1,5
	1,364	100%	3,049,006	100%	1,248,692	100%

5

* All figures in thousands of dollars.

The volume index of chemical and petroleum production remained fairly constant between 1981 and 1986, at approximately 115 (1980 = 100). Of the chemical group's output, 33% came from the fertilizer, insecticides and pesticides sub-category (based on 1982 figures). Currently there are only four firms in production, namely Zimbabwe Phosphates (Zimphos), Sable Chemicals, Zimbabwe Fertilizer Corporation (ZFC) and Windmill. A further 24,5% of production comes from the soaps and detergents sub-category.

(iv) The drink and tobacco, textiles, and clothing and footwear sub-sectors (sub-sectors 2, 3 and 4) are next three largest sub-sectors, jointly comprising 25,4% of total manufacturing production.

3. Export Ratio

The ratio of exports to gross output in the manufacturing sector is only 13%, indicating that the sector is primarily geared towards serving the needs of the domestic economy rather than generating exports (although when taken as a proportion of net output rather than gross output the ratio of exports rises to 22%).

The transport and equipment sub-category plays a vital role in the production of trucks and rolling stock which is used to transport our exports to the harbours at Beira, Maputo and Durban. This sub-sector's share in gross output of the manufacturing sector was 3.8% in 1985, having risen from 2.5% in 1980.

4. **Relative Efficiency of the Sector**

Table 5 gives an indication of the relative efficiency of different sectors. As indicated above, sub-sectors 1, 2, 3 and 7 are dominated by large firms. This is born out by the evidence in column 1. The amount of capital employed per worker indicates the degree of capital and/or labour intensity in the sector. From these figures it would appear that the chemical and petroleum sector is by far the most capital intensive, followed by the non-metallic mineral products, the metals and metal products and the drink and tobacco sectors. At the other end of the scale the clothing and footwear and the wood and furniture sectors are the most labour intensive. Columns 2 and 4 which deal with gross and net output per employee give an indication of the degree of labour productivity in each sector. Based on the net output figures, the most productive section of the labour force is in the chemical and petroleum products sector — which is also the most capital intensive sector. The print, paper and publishing sector is interesting in that it has the third highest net output per employee despite having a relatively low degree of capital intensity.

The difference between net and gross output reflects the value of the inputs. Total purchases plus changes in stocks should give the value of inputs. Gross output less inputs equals net output. The relationship between net output and gross output gives the value added (value added being the value generated by the industry in question). Column 6 of Table 5 gives an indication of the value added per industry. Relatively high scores for net output as a percentage of gross output indicates a relatively high level of value added in the production process. Sectors 2 and 8 (drink and tobacco, and non-metallic minerals) have high levels of value added. Sectors 1,3 and 10 (foodstuffs, textiles, and transport) have low levels of value added. Column 5 gives an indication of the export effectiveness of each sector. From this column we can see that it is only the textile and the metal and metal products sectors which have relatively high proportions of exports. Column 7 shows that the most labour intensive sectors of the economy are clothing and footwear', wood and furniture, and 'other' (sector 11). This indicates that these sectors are able to achieve higher value added with lower amounts of capital inputs.

5. **Manufacturing Inputs**

A closer examination of the inputs into the manufacturing sector is necessary in order to be able to devise an appropriate development strategy for the industrial sector. Table 6 deals with the three major elements of input cost: material purchases, wages and salaries, and services. Material purchases include energy costs (fuel, water, coal, etc.) as well as the costs of raw

BOX 1: The Sectoral Classification of the manufacturing Industry in Zimbabwe

1. *Foodstuffs* including slaughtering and processing of meat; canning and preserving fruit and vegetables; grain mill products and animal feeds; bakery products; chocolate and sugar confectionery; dairy and other food products.

2. *Drink and Tobacco* including beer, wine and spirits; soft drinks and carbonated waters; tobacco products including post-auction grading and packing.

3. *Textiles and Ginning* including spinning, weaving, finishing textiles and carpets; knitted products, rope and cordage; and other textile products.

4. *Clothing and Footwear* including wearing apparel and footwear.

5. *Wood and Furniture* including saw-milling and wooden products; furniture and wooden fixtures.

6. *Paper, Printing and Publishing* including pulp, paper, paperboard and products, printing, publishing and allied industries.

7. *Chemical and Petroleum Products* including fertilizers, insecticides and pesticides; paints, varnishes and filling materials; soaps, detergents, toilet preparations and pharmaceuticals; matches, inks, candles, glues and polishes; basic chemical products and gases; rubber products; plastic products.

8. *Non-Metallic Mineral Products* including structural clay products and bricks; glass, cement and other associated and non-metallic mineral products.

9. *Metals and Metal Products* including non-ferrous metal and iron and steel basic industries including smelting and refining but excluding these products when manufactured at mine-sites; metal products, machinery and equipment including electrical; radio and all communication equipment.

10. *Transport Equipment* including motor vehicles and reconditioning; and other vehicles.

11. *Other Manufactured Products* including leather products and substitutes; pens; watches; jewellery; toys; photographic and optical instruments.

materials. Service costs include repair and maintenance, advertising, hire or rent of machinery, insurance costs and any payments made to the head office abroad.

From the Table we can see that for the foodstuffs, textiles, chemicals and transport sectors, material purchases are in the region of 70 to 80% of total inputs. Expansion in these sectors will therefore depend on the availability of the material inputs.

TABLE 5: Some key Variables of the manufacturing Sector for 1982

Sector	Gross output per unit ($'000) (1)	Gross output per employee $ (2)	Capital per employee $ (3)	Net output per employee $ (4)	Exports as % of output (5)	Net output as % of output (6)	Net output as % of capital (7)
Foodstuffs	5,186	29,934	21,763	7,531	2,6	25,2	35
Drink and Tobacco	4,336	17,404	25,837	10,326	1,1	59,3	40
Textiles including ginning	4,514	14,547	17,456	5,162	19,1	35,5	30
Clothing and Footwear	1,427	9,636	5,480	5,085	5,1	52,7	93
Wood and Furniture	959	7,276	6,474	3,802	9,6	52,3	59
Paper, Printing and Publishing	1,434	17,310	20,042	8,907	1,5	51,5	44
Chemical Petroleum Products	3,137	30,533	39,197	12,293	3,8	40,3	31
Non-Metallic Mineral Products	1,627	12,070	31,108	7,259	1,8	60,1	23
Metal and Metal Products	1,567	15,132	28 859	6,889	23,0	45,5	24
Transport Equipment	2,040	17,891	16,397	6,956	3,7	38,9	42
Other Manufactured Products	396	10,904	9,030	5,535	17,6	50,8	61
Total	2,235	17,302	21,316	7,086	9,1	41,0	33

6

The clothing, printing, furniture and non-metallic sectors, by contrast, all have wage and salary expenditure in excess of 30% of total input costs. This indicates a higher degree of labour intensity, making these important sector in terms of employment generation as long as wage costs do not increase too rapidly.

TABLE 6: Manufacturing input Characteristics by Sector: 1982 (percentages)

Sector	Material purchases as percentage of total inputs (1)	Wages and salaries as percentage of total inputs (2)	Services payments as percentage of total inputs (3)	Totals (4)	Energy[1] inputs as percentage of material purchases (5)	Imported[2] inputs as percentage of raw material purchases (6)
Foodstuffs	81,5	12,5	6,0	100,0	2,3	2,4
Drink and Tobacco	51.3	28,2	20,5	100,0	6,7	24,0
Textiles including ginning	73,5	19,5	7,0	100,0	3,1	23,0
Clothing and Footwear	55,8	32,9	11,3	100,0	1,3	39,0
Wood and Furniture	51,0	32,0	17,0	100,0	6,1	14,0
Paper, Printing and Publishing	54,6	32,2	13,2	100,0	5,4	24,0
Chemical and Petroleum Products	68,9	19,9	11,2	100,0	6,5	52,0
Non-Metallic Mineral Products	54,6	35,8	9,6	100,0	21,3	16,0
Metal and Metal Products	60,8	29,6	9,6	100,0	15,4	41,0
Transport Equipment	68,9	24,5	6,6	100,0	1,8	60,0
Other Manufactured Products	56,1	30,6	13,3	100,0	2,8	25,3
Total	67,0	23,1	9,9	100,0	6,3	25,3

7

From the point of view of total energy consumption the requirements of the non-metallic mineral sector and the metal products sectors are far in excess of the needs of any of the other sectors. An industrial strategy which stressed the conservation of energy would have to take account of varying energy requirements.

The most important consideration, however, lies in the area of import dependency. Column 6 indicates the percentage of raw material inputs which are imported for each of the 11 sectors. Any development strategy formulated for Zimbabwe would have to take into account the shortage of foreign exchange. Those sectors which require minimal amounts of foreign exchange for material purchases would most likely be favoured as areas of potential expansion. The most import-dependent of the sectors is the transport equipment sector with 60% imported raw material purchases. At the other end of the scale is the foodstuffs sector in which only 2,4% of the raw material purchases are imported.

It is necessary to stress, however, that a development policy cannot be based on only one or two variables. Whilst it is correct to say that the metal products sector uses a large proportion of imported raw materials, this particular sector also generates 53% of all manufacturing exports, accounts for over 20% of the sector's output, and employs 24% of its labour. A comprehensive development strategy would, therefore, have to examine all the above variables.

6. Ownership and Control of the Manufacturing Sector

Recent estimates based on 1984 data judged that of the $2,8bn total capital in the manufacturing sector 85,5% was held by the private sector (84,5% by private companies and 1% by unincorporated enterprises), 4% by central government (IDC controlled companies), 10% by parastatals, and 0,5% by local authorities. Central government and/or parastatals have an influence in three major sectors: foodstuffs, textiles and the metals and metal products sectors. Together the Dairy Marketing Board and the Cold Storage Commission account for 25% of the total output in the foodstuffs sector. Government participation in the textiles sector is through the Cotton Marketing Board which contributes 38% of the output in this sector; government holdings in Zisco, Lancashire Steel and F. Issels contribute 17% of the output in the metals sector. In all the other sectors, private companies controlled over 90% of total turnover. IDC's largest investment is in the metal and metal products sector, while the only significant contribution by local authorities was in sector 2, drink and tobacco, through municipal beer production.

Estimates of the degree of foreign ownership of the manufacturing sector vary widely. The first set of figures published refer to a survey of companies carried out by the CSO in 1963 which estimated that 72% of the gross profits in the sector accrued to foreign companies while only 28% accrued to local companies. More recently, in June 1984, Colin Stoneman estimated that of a total capital of $2,4bn, 70% was foreign-owned and 30% locally owned.[1]

Table 7 below shows the results of two separate studies undertaken on the degree of foreign ownership in the manufacturing sector. Both studies conclude that the percentage of foreign ownership is in the region of 48% — 50%. The first study was based on information collected by the Department of Customs and Excise and separate information collected by the Confederation of Zimbabwe Industries (CZI) which was then put together by UNIDO. The second study was done by D. Jansen. Although the overall results of both surveys are similar, the degree of foreign ownership per sector varies widely in some cases (see columns 2 and 4). Sub-sectors in which there is a wide divergence include foodstuffs (the UNIDO study estimated 39,4% foreign ownership, while the Jansen study estimated only 8%); the clothing and footwear sector, and the transport equipment sector. Columns 3 and 5 indicate the size of the sample survey. In the case of the foodstuffs sector the size of the sample was 65,6% (UNIDO) and 70% (Jansen) and yet there was still a large difference in their findings. This would seem to indicate that more substantial analysis should be carried out in this area.

TABLE 7: Foreign/domestic Ownership Pattern of the manufacturing Sector: UNIDO and Jansen data compared

Sub-sector (1)	UNIDO study results 1981/84		Jansen study results 1980	
	percentage of foreign ownership (2)	based on percentage of foreign ownership (3)	percentage of foreign ownership (4)	based on percentage of foreign ownership (5)
Foodstuffs	39,4	65,6	8	70
Drink and Tobacco	60,9	23,6	61	67
Textiles and ginning	24.4	47.0	30	70
Clothing and Footwear	17.3	16.1	62	44
Wood and Furniture	37.0	22,4	85	46
Paper, Printing and Publishing	61,3	68,1	49	61
Chemical and Petroleum Products	62,7	70,1	74	77
Non-Metallic Mineral Products	54.1	72,2	65	77
Metal and Metal Products.	52,2	54,8	53	63
Transport Equipment	47,8	96,6	84	45
Other Manufactured Products	74,3	75,6	n.a.	0
Total	48,1	56,6	50	65

8

7. Development and Linkages of the Sector

The development of the manufacturing sector reflects the combination of import substitution and export promotion policies adopted in the past. Many of the locally produced products which were developed as a result of sanctions have been exported to other Southern African countries and further afield. Import substitution in Zimbabwe has passed the stage of replacing formerly imported consumer goods, i.e. only 15% of our consumer goods are imported at present. The manufacturing sector produces and exports capital equipment and intermediate goods. Examples of locally manufactured capital goods include agricultural machinery such as tillage, spraying, reaping and curing equipment; low temperature cryogenic vessels and stainless steel storage and cooling vessels used in food and drink processing industries; irrigation equipment and hollow-ware produced by the metal products sector; and items such as locally designed buses and railway rolling-stock produced by the transport equipment sector.

Manufacturing's input into the agricultural sector was in the region of $300 million in 1982, and $330 million in 1983. The largest single component was fertilizer, which accounted for approximately 14% of total output, followed by stock-feed (8%) and

UNIDO Study of the Manufacturing Industry in Zimbabwe, UNIDO, Vienna, 1985 p. 43.

Most of the material inputs into the construction sector - cement, bricks, steel, paint, glass, electrical materials, wood, asphalt, bitumen ore locally produced in the manufacturing sector with very little imported content. This acts as an important source of demand for manufactured goods as well as an important source of employment.

maintenance costs (5,5%). Purchases of inputs from the manufacturing sector represented 36% of agriculture's total output in 1982, and 39% in 1983.

In 1983, sales to the agricultural sector represented approximately 11% of manufacturing output.

Input figures for the mining sector are more difficult to compute because of the problems of defining where the mining sector ends and where the manufacturing sector begins (i.e. there are a number of mining firms in Zimbabwe which carry out processing activities and manufacturing firms which carry out mining activities, and the need to allocate these firms to one sector or another often gives rise to discrepancies). Estimated purchases of manufactured products by the mining sector vary from $105 million to $209 million depending on which definition of the mining sector is used. This means that somewhere between 24% and 47% of the gross output of the mining sector is made up of purchases from the manufacturing sector. These inputs into the mining sector represent between 4% and 7% of manufacturing output.

In 1981 the total of all manufacturing purchases by the construction sector amounted to $138,4 million, approximately 33% of the sector's gross output. The construction sector's input into the manufacturing sector is of two kinds: first, there is the repair and maintenance and, second, there is the construction of new buildings (factories, offices, etc). The total value of this input by the construction sector was $64,2 million (2,1% of manufacturing output) in 1981, and $53 million (1,7% of manufacturing output) in 1982.

8. Investment

The level of real investment in the manufacturing sector was practically the same in 1983 as it was in 1970. There is a desperate need for increased levels of investment from both local and foreign sources. The increased mobilization of domestic resources for investment is essential, but the foreign exchange costs of new investment cannot be met in this way. At present, the foreign debt of the manufacturing sector amounts to only 3% of the total foreign debt of the country. An increase in foreign borrowing would help to solve the investment needs of the sector but would not necessarily bring technological improvement or access to foreign markets. The UNIDO Report on the Manufacturing Sector (September 1985) strongly recommends the formation of joint ventures between Zimbabwean companies, the government and foreign companies, in proportions found suitable to government, as the main way in which direct foreign investment should be encouraged.

The extent to which foreign investment will be attracted depends on two sets of factors. Firstly, the "climate" needs to be that which attracts foreign investment; this is determined by the general health of the economy, its social and political stability, its attitude to private investment, etc. Secondly, specific measures such as tax concessions play a relatively small role in attracting investment compared to the importance placed on the correct economic and social climate.

As far as Zimbabwe is concerned the potential benefits of foreign investment include the possible improvement in the balance of payments both in the current account (due to increased exports generated by foreign investment) and in the capital account (due to the inflow of funds), the increase in employment, the opportunities for technological advances, and the acquisition of skills and marketing ability.

There are also some disadvantages to foreign investment which need to be considered:

— increasing the extent of foreign control in a country which is already dominated by foreign capital;

— the greater the capital inflow, the greater the resultant capital outflow will be, due to remittances;

— insufficient benefits may accrue to the local economy due to transfer pricing (i.e. the transfer of profits out of the country by illegal means such as under- and over-invoicing); (See Box 1, Ch. 5, p109)

— it could merely exploit advantages offered by the host country and then disappear when these are exhausted;

— the possible use of a low level of technology (such as assembly work) which adds little to the development of the manufacturing sector;

— lastly, even if high-technology is involved, no provision may be made for its diffusion and integration into the country as a whole.

Finally, the continued devaluation of the Zimbabwe dollar due to the sliding exchange rate has resulted in higher import costs in a sector which is highly import-dependent and has had a negative effect on the sector's expansion potential while not necessarily guaranteeing higher export receipts.

BOX 2: The Export Incentive Scheme

The Export Revolving Fund is intended to provide foreign exchange for inputs required for goods which are going to be exported. Any raw materials, machinery, or spare parts for machinery which is to be used for the manufacture of exports could be bought with money from the Export Revolving Fund. Prior to March 1983 the initial capital for the fund came only from the government. As part of a programme to promote manufactured exports from Zimbabwe, the World Bank contributed Z$83m to the fund in March 1983. Since that date the quarterly allocation of foreign exchange for the manufacturing sector and a proportion of the net export proceeds of manufactured goods are all paid into the fund.

Manufacturers can only draw from the fund if they are in possession of a valid export order. If raw materials bought with money from the Export Revolving Fund are used for goods produced and sold to the local market, strict penalties will be imposed including a possible permanent embargo on access to foreign exchange.

Finally, if the decision is made to encourage foreign investment, bearing in mind the constraints noted above, it would need to be directed into sectors which are in need of new investment and not into sectors which will simply generate large profits for foreign capital while putting local enterprises out of business. The food processing, clothing and textile, non-ferrous metals, and iron and steel sectors represent areas in which significant industrial capacity has already been built up. Future expansion in these sectors will depend on their ability to keep pace with international industrial restructuring, an area in which the participation of foreign capital, in the form of joint ventures, may prove to be vital.

Government Policy and Manufacturing Sector

1. Central issues outlined by the Transitional National Development Plan (TNDP)

Government, in the TNDP, has identified five key issues which are relevant for the future growth and development of the manufacturing sector. These are:

— the formation and implementation of an industrial strategy that would focus on the issue of employment generation through the promotion of small-scale, labour-intensive industry. Such a strategy would also have to look into the protective nature of import controls and their effect on the manufacturing sector (see section on the degree of monopolization of the sector, p 82).

— the heavy dependence of the sector on imported inputs which has meant that manufacturing in Zimbabwe has remained a net user of foreign exchange. The present need to replace worn out and out-moded equipment (the legacy of the UDI period) has intensified the import dependency of the sector. The failure to promote raw-material processing industries and/or labour-intensive production methods adds to the above problem.

— the past over-reliance on imported manpower plus the out-flow of local skills which, in the past five years, has created a serious shortage of skilled manpower, limiting the potential for growth in the sector.

— the high degree of concentration in the industry, both in terms of geographical concentration and the degree of monopolization.

— the sector is under considerable foreign ownership and control.

2. Underlying Assumptions in the Plan

The TNDP recognizes the pivotal role that the manufacturing sector occupies in the national economy, and therefore stresses that whatever industrial strategy is decided upon, cannot be implemented in isolation from the rest of the economy. The high degree of linkage between the manufacturing and other sectors of the economy means that whatever policies are implemented will have wide repercussions.

The Plan also makes provision for an increasing degree of government intervention in the manufacturing sector which will take the form of direct investment through the IDC, loans through the Small Enterprises Development Corporation (SEDCO) and/or investment through the newly formed Development Bank.

The realization that the twin objectives of growth and equity might well be contradictory in the short-term, indicates that an industrial strategy will have to highlight these potential contradictions and indicate priorities. Employment creation might, for example, contradict the policy of international competitiveness in the short-term, just as the rapid expansion of exports may limit the economy's ability to satisfy all aspects of domestic demand. (Note that the problem at the moment (1986-87) is somewhat different in that most firms are operating far below capacity due to the shortage of foreign exchange).

3. Future Objectives (as laid out in the TNDP)

In order to overcome the import dependency of the manufacturing sector, government hopes to promote the processing of raw materials in Zimbabwe and the production of many of the components which are, at present, being imported. The establishment of small- and medium-scale industries in the rural areas is intended to alleviate the high degree of rural unemployment.

In the long-term it is hoped that import controls can be removed due to the increased competitiveness of Zimbabwean products. At the same time, government hopes to increase the export competitiveness of the sector's products. Without granting more protection to the manufacturing sector, government plans to encourage further import substitution in areas such as energy, fertilizer production, heavy industrial machinery, light machine tools and electronics. This would mean a further saving in foreign exchange. Where new industries are being developed in order to serve the local market, labour-intensive technologies will be used, thereby enhancing the economy's capacity to generate jobs.

The problems of concentration of industry, lack of skilled personnel, and foreign ownership, will also be tackled by government, by promoting staff training at all levels, encouraging more local participation and ownership of industries by Zimbabweans and implementing policies aimed at the decentralization of industry.

The plan outlines "The fundamental and ultimate goal as the development of a democratic and egalitarian and socialist society set in a dynamic framework of a developing economy."

The criteria for the allocation of foreign exchange were to be reviewed with the introduction of export incentives, export promotion institutions and mechanisms, tax incentives, industrial licensing and advisory services, all of which were to be aimed at the expansion of the export market.

The problems experienced with the private sector were to be addressed by government committing itself to the creation of a climate conducive to meaningful consulation, co-operation and, where appropriate, co-determination on matters of mutual interest.

4. Evaluation of the TNDP's Implementation

Only in the area of export promotion and in the related field of increased foreign exchange allocations has government had any measure of success; a range of policies has been implemented that have successfully increased the manufacturing sector's exports (see Chapter 7 — export incentives). In addition, new export incentives have been introduced, export promotion through the Ministry of Trade and Commerce has been improved, and advisory services now form a constituent part of SEDCO's activities.

On the negative side, little progress has been made in the formation of a comprehensive industrial strategy; in encouraging the growth of more labour-intensive industries, labour-intensive technologies or employment generation; in accelerating state participation in the economy; in assisting small- and medium-scale enterprises to process and manufacture in the rural areas; or in giving preference to technologies using local inputs as opposed to those dependent on imports.

One of the reasons for the rather low level of policy implementation was the relative inexperience of government in the field of macro-planning evidenced in the excessive optimism of the Plan's projections (which were no doubt influenced by the 1981 boom). A second important reason for the Plan's 'failure' was the rapid change in Zimbabwe's economic fortunes that would have been difficult if not impossible to predict, i.e. the combined effects of the drought and the international recession that resulted in the rapid drop in the real growth rate from 13% in 1981 to zero growth in 1982, and negative growth in 1983 (see Table 1, page 1)

5. Government Objectives in the First Five Year National Development Plan (FFYNDP)

The FFYNDP published in April 1986 and covering the period 1986-90 emphasized the following objectives:

— increased government participation in the manufacturing industry, especially in areas deemed strategic to socio-economic development. Government participation will be in the form of joint ventures with local or foreign partners, or directly through the IDC;

— a move towards decentralization in view of both the monopolization of the sector and the degree of geographic concentration. To this end small-scale industries capable of using locally available raw materials, local technology, and labour-intensive production processes will be encouraged in the rural areas;

— emphasis on the mastery and adaptation of imported technology. The proposed Council for Industrial Research should assist in the co-ordination of all industrial research and development and in determining how best the manufacturing industry can develop an indigenous technology.

— the intention to revamp the Standards Association of Central African in an attempt to improve the quality of industrial production for both the local and export markets and, thereby, improve the competitiveness of locally produced products.

The large degree of overlap in the objectives of the TNDP and FFYNDP indicate that many of the government's objectives in the TNDP were not successfully implemented. The overlap also indicates that its objectives have not substantially changed at all. Thus, it is hoped that while the unfavourable international and domestic economic environment prevented the implementation of the objectives of the TNDP, more favourable economic conditions over the next five years will lead to improvement.

Effects of Government Participation in the Manufacturing Sphere

Government participation in the manufacturing sector has been in the areas of export promotion, direct investment and financial assistance, the control of prices and wages, and labour regulations.

Government, in its attempts at making exports more competitive, has devalued the Zimbabwe dollar, introduced the Export Incentive Scheme and operated an Export Revolving Fund (for details on the Export Incentive Scheme and the Export Revolving Fund see Boxes 2 and 3; the effects of devaluation are dealt with in Chapter 7, page 165). The various Commodity Import Programmes negotiated by government have also been used for the importation of materials and equipment for the sector, alleviating the effects of the shortage of foreign exchange.

BOX 3: The Export Revolving Fund

The present export incentive scheme was first introduced in 1982 in an effort to encourage the export of manufactured goods. In order to qualify for the scheme the goods exported must have at least 25% local content. The scheme is in effect a subsidy for the manufacturer calculated as a percentage of the export value of the goods, which then allows the manufacturer to sell the goods at a lower price on the world market. At present some 800 local firms are registered under the scheme and claimed in the region of $18m in the 1985-86 fiscal year.

The effectiveness of the export incentive scheme in increasing the level of exports depends on the elasticity of our exports. If lowering the price increases the demand for our goods (i.e. if they are elastic in demand) then the scheme should achieve the desired effects. If a drop in price does not affect demand (i.e. if demand is inelastic) then the scheme will only serve to reduce the costs of production of the manufacturer and will have little or no effect on the level of exports.

Through the Industrial Development Corporation the government has undertaken direct investment in the manufacturing sector, primarily in the metals and metal products sector. Government is also involved in the processing of agricultural commodities (which falls under manufacturing, not agriculture) through the Cold Storage Commission, the Dairy Marking Board and the cotton ginnery.

Since 1980 the government has also acquired equity in a number of companies under its programme of participation in the private sector. Government has acquired a majority share in National Printing and Packaging, in Astra Corporation (chemicals), in CAPS Holdings Ltd. (pharmaceuticals); in Olivine Holdings (foodstuffs), etc.

In terms of labour regulations, government introduced a policy of statutory minimum wages in 1980 and has been steadily increasing the wage level ever since. Although this policy has had some negative effects in that it increased production costs, its overall effect was one of boosting domestic demand for manufactured goods. The wage freeze at the other end of the scale has had a detrimental effect on both the acquisition and retention of skills, and on production levels. Government controls on the hiring of foreign labour to overcome the skills shortage has intensified that shortage, and further depressed skills and production levels. The contradiction between the growth and the equity policies is very clear in these examples as well as in the area of labour dismissals. Because firms now have to seek special permission to dismiss labour, firms are reticent to hire new labour, and they steer clear of labour-intensive technology.

The control of prices by government has meant that prices can no longer automatically increase in order to compensate for increased costs of production. Business people now have to apply for a price increase which often takes a very long time to come through. This has lowered profit margins and directly affected their desire to reinvest. The lack of new investment in the face of outmoded and deteriorating machinery has become a major problem for the manufacturing sector. Without investment there can be no growth, and without growth an increase in equity is impossible.

Also in the area of prices, government has dramatically increased electricity charges which have had a significant effect on costs and have lessened the competitiveness of key manufactured exports such as ferrochrome and steel. The increase in the import surcharge has had the direct effect of raising the cost of capital and of all imported inputs into the manufacturing sector. Government's decision not to limit price increases for the National Railways of Zimbabwe and air-carriers has, on the other hand, helped to keep costs down and so has helped to maintain domestic demand and export competitiveness.

References

1. United Nations Industrial Development Organization (UNIDO), *Study of the Manufacturing Sector in Zimbabwe*, Geneva 1985.
2. Central Statistical Office, *Statistical Yearbook, 1985*, A CSO publication, Sweden, 1985.
3. Central Statistical Office, *Update on National Accounts*, A CSO publication, Harare, February, 1987.
4. UNIDO report., ibid, p. 30.
5. UNIDO report., ibid, p. 34 & 36.
6. UNIDO report., ibid, p. 37.
7. UNIDO report., ibid, p. 49
8. UNIDO report., ibid, p. 53

Chapter 5
ZIMBABWE'S MINING SECTOR
The Development of the Mining Sector

The industrial development of Zimbabwe owes much of its progress to the exploitation of the mineral deposits found beneath the soils. Mining has, however, played a role for at least the past 1 000 years in the region now called Zimbabwe. By the end of the nineteenth century there was evidence of some 4 000 different sites which were mined.

Gold, silver, copper, iron and tin had all been worked prior to the arrival of the settlers. The majority of the mines established by them were located on the 'old workings'. Examination of these sites has led people to believe that the local inhabitants not only undertook alluvial mining, but rock mining (deep level) as well. The average depth of these mines was 40 metres, or as deep as the water level. Estimates made in 1890 of the value of gold mined prior to that date were in the region of £60m showing that the mining process used, although somewhat slower than methods used elsewhere (as the quantity of gold mined indicates) was every bit as effective. The rocks were broken by heating them with fire and then cooling them rapidly with water. The ore was thus easy to remove. Once extracted the ore was treated in the same way so as to make it easier to crush and extract the gold.

The period after 1890 was marked by the rule of the British South Africa Company which had been attracted to Zimbabwe by the tales of the early explorers who mistakenly believed there to be as much gold in Zimbabwe as there was on the reef in Johannesburg. During the period up to 1903 the Company (which was administering the territory) prohibited the mining of gold

TABLE 1: The Development of Zimbabwean Towns

Town/City	Mine	Mineral
Harare	Jumbo Mine (est. 1903)	Gold
	Arcturus Mine (est. 1910)	Gold
Bindura	Trojan Mine (later also smelter and refinery	Nickel
Shamva	Shamva Mine (est. 1906)	Gold
Banket	Mtoroshanga	Chromite deposits
Chinhoyi	Alaska Mine (and later smelter)	Copper
Karoi	Miami Mine	Pegmatite
Hwange	Wankie Mine	Coal
Mashaba	Lennox Mine	Chrystalite
Shabane	Sabi Mine	Asbestcs
Bulawayo	Old Nick; How 3; Dawn Mine	Gold
Mutare	Redwing and Old West Mines	Gold
Filabusi		Nickel
Gwanda	Banket, Vubachikwe and Freda Mines	Gold
Colleen Bawn		Limestone
Eiffel Flats	Cam and Motor Mine (est. 1910) (Later a Nickel and copper-cobalt refinery were established in the area).	Gold
Kadoma &	Golden Valley (est. 1903)	Gold
Chegutu	Dalny Gold Mines (est. 1910)	Gold
	Patchway Mine (est. 1906)	Gold
	Pickstones Mine	Gold
Kwe-Kwe	Gaika, Globe and Phoenix Gold Mines (later the development of Zisco, and the production of high-carbon ferro-chrome alloys by Union Carbide).	Gold
Shurugwe	Wander (est. 1902, Camperdown and Tebekwe.	

1

by all except registered companies. This measure was aimed at destroying the indigenous trade in gold. The BSAC was further to receive the first 50% of the proceeds of any mining company.

After 1903 individuals and syndicates were allowed to own and operate mines. The normal procedure was for prospectors to hire a local inhabitant to point out a site where gold had been mined in the past. The prospector would then sink a vertical shaft on one side of the old working to test whether it still contained gold.

By 1907 there were 254 mines providing under 1 000 ounces of gold p.a., and 75 producing between 1 000 ounces and 10 000 ounces p.a., and 14 mines producing over 10 000 ounces p.a. By 1933 the number of small mines had increased to 755, medium-sized mines had dropped to 71 and large ones to ten.

Most of the early mines in the region were gold mines which, upon discovery (or rediscovery), formed the centres of commercial activity around which permanent communities soon sprang up. Towns which did not develop as a result of mining activity are the exception in Zimbabwe, as is shown by Table 1.

The Role of Mining in the Economy

The contribution of mining to GDP (around 20% before the Second World War) has dropped from a fairly stable level of 8% during the seventies, to about 6% in the eighties, compared with 13,5% for agriculture and 27% for manufacturing.

Table 2 shows the development of the mining sector over the past ten years.

TABLE 2: Mining Output and Value Added over the period : 1974-86

Year	(1) Value Added Z$m	(2) % of GDP	(3) Volume Index	(4) Unit Value	(5) Output (Z$m)
1974	136	7,6	103	38,6	165
1975	131	6,9	104	41,1	178
1976	152	7,4	113	48,9	230
1977	149	7,2	108	52,8	237
1978	156	6,9	103	59,1	252
1979	226	8,5	102	73,4	315
1980	285	8,8	100	100,0	415
1981	250	6,2	96	99,9	394
1982	217	4,7	96	101,7	383
1983	284	5,6	93	130,0	470
1984	330	5,7	97	142,3	546
1985			969	162,3	*630
1986			96,9	168,2	**662

2

* Estimated   ** Projected

Column 2 in Table 2 shows the falling trend in the contribution of minerals to GDP. From the table it is clear that 1980 was a boom year for the mining industry: the gross value of mineral production (including ferro-alloys but excluding steel) was $502,3 million. The volume index (column 3) indicates that from 1976 there has been a consistent decline in levels of production; the steadily climbing value of production is largely due to domestic inflation and the falling value of the dollar. It was only during the years 1980-82 that the money value of mineral production did not rise; this was because of static unit prices (see column 4).

The total output figures in column 5 include the input costs which have been subtracted in order to arrive at the value added figure (column 1). It is the value added figure which is used in the calculation of Gross Domestic Output.

The ten years prior to the period dealt with in Table 2 showed a very different picture. The unit value index remained virtually static in the years 1964-72 (1964 = 23,3; 1972 = 26,8) while the volume index rose from 55 in 1964 to 102,9 in 1974. These rapid increases in output were largely due to a highly supportive domestic policy environment and a buoyant international market.

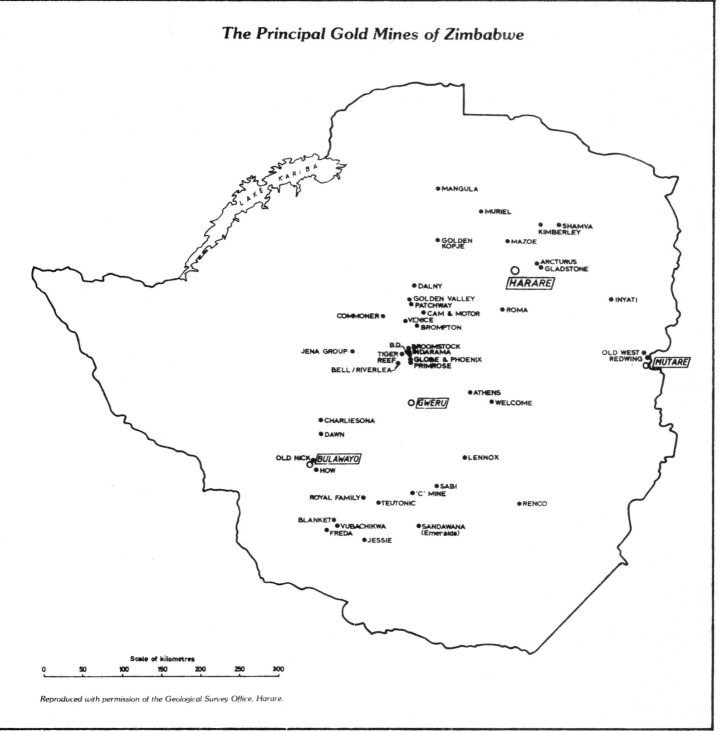

The Principal Gold Mines of Zimbabwe

LAKE KARIBA

• MANGULA

• MURIEL

• SHAMVA
KIMBERLEY
• GOLDEN   • MAZOE
KOPJE

○ • ARCTURUS
• GLADSTONE

☐ HARARE

• DALNY   • INYATI

• GOLDEN VALLEY
• PATCHWAY
COMMONER •   • CAM & MOTOR   • ROMA
• VENICE
• BROMPTON

B.D.
• BROOMSTOCK
JENA GROUP •   TIGER • NDARAMA   OLD WEST •   ☐ MUTARE
REEF   • GLOBE & PHOENIX   REDWING ○
BELL/RIVERLEA   • PRIMROSE

• ATHENS
○ ☐ GWERU   • WELCOME

• CHARLIESONA

• DAWN

OLD NICK • ☐ BULAWAYO   • LENNOX
○ • HOW

• SABI
ROYAL FAMILY •   • 'C' MINE   • RENCO
• TEUTONIC

BLANKET •   • SANDAWANA
• VUBACHIKWA   (Emeralds)
FREDA
• JESSIE

Scale of kilometres
0   50   100   150   200   250   300

Reproduced with permission of the Geological Survey Office, Harare.

97

Major Minerals mined in Zimbabwe

At present there are approximately 43 different minerals mined in Zimbabwe. Table 3 only gives the ten top producers; amongst the remainder are platinum, magnesite, tungsten, antimony, bauxite, graphite, lithium, and many others. From the table it is clear that the top ten producers accounted for 95% of all mineral production in 1984, and 93% in 1985; gold alone accounts for almost 40% of all mineral production. Graph 1 shows the contribution of the five major minerals over the 1979-85 period as a proportion of total mining output measured in Zimbabwe dollar terms.

Gold has been the most valuable of the minerals produced in Zimbabwe throughout the era of industrialization, except for a brief period in the sixties when it was overtaken by asbestos. Since 1979 gold has contributed an average of 35% to the mining sector's output value, rising to almost 40% in 1986. Earnings in the year October 1985 — October 1986 rose to $279,1 million. Concern over the unstable price of gold (which has been falling since 1981 — see Graph 2) led the government, in November 1984, through the Reserve Bank of Zimbabwe (RBZ), to introduce a gold Price Support Scheme aimed at maintaining a steady increase in the production of the metal. Under the scheme, producers are paid Z$500 per fine ounce when the market price falls below Z$500 and are expected to pay into the fund when the price rises above Z$500. Producers are expected to pay 25% of the proportion of the market price in excess of $500 back to the government until the value of the support given to producers has been repaid. The reason the government introduced the gold support price was to prevent small producers of this valuable foreign exchange generator from going out of business when the price dropped below the cost of production level. At the time of writing (May 1987) the gold price on the London Metal Exchange (LME) was US$470 per fine ounce, equivalent to Z$764,1.

TABLE 3: The top ten Minerals: 1984 and 1985 ($'000)

Mineral	1984 output	% of total	1985 output	% of total
1. Gold	214 120	39	241 312	38
2. Asbestos	80 778	15	84 544	13
3. Nickel	59 704	11	73 425	11,5
4. Coal	58 264	11	66 845	10
5. Copper	33 764	6	43 340	7
6. Chrome Ore	29 719	5	33 674	5
7. Tin Metal	18 510	3	22 594	4
8. Iron Ore	14 532	3	18 930	3
9. Silver	9 031	2	7 871	1
10. Cobalt	981	0,2	2 978	0,5
11. Other	27 064	5	45 499	7
Totals	546 467	100%	641 012	100%

3

Output of gold has varied between ten and 18 tonnes per year from 1964-86, with production in 1986 being 14,8 tonnes. There are about 200 mines in operation around the country with almost 70% of the output coming from the ten biggest mines. Known reserves of gold are estimated to be about 100 tonnes, which at the present rate of production is about eight years' supply.

Plans to establish facilities for Zimbabwe to refine its own gold were announced recently. At present it is being refined in Australia.

Zimbabwe is one of the world's largest producers of _asbestos_; other major producers are Italy, China and Canada. Adverse publicity has, however, led to the introduction of substitutes for asbestos products in developed countries leading to a drop in demand for the product worldwide. The chrysotile or white asbestos variety mined in Zimbabwe is reported to have no close substitute. The 1983 output of 153 000 tonnes is the lowest in more than 15 years; 1986 production figures (164 000 tonnes) showed a slight upturn although production was still substantially lower than in 1982. The expected increase in building activity in Zimbabwe, due to the post-1985 economic recovery, is likely to provide a sustantial domestic market for asbestos cement products. Known reserves of asbestos are estimated to be in the region of 100 million tonnes with most deposits concentrated around Zvishavane.

GRAPH 1: Value of Mineral Production 1979 - 85

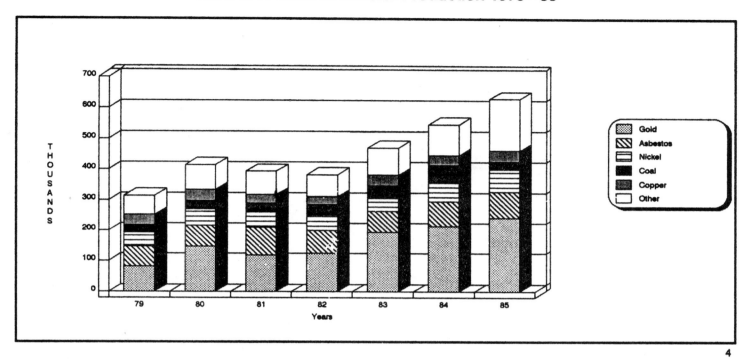

GRAPH 2: Average Price Index for Gold per fine Ounce on the London Market: 1975-86

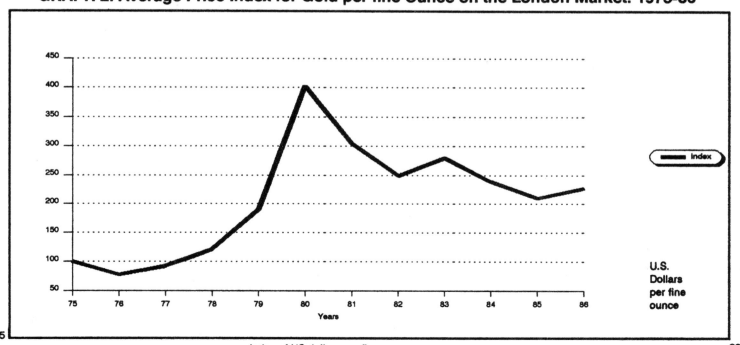

Index of US dollars per fine ounce

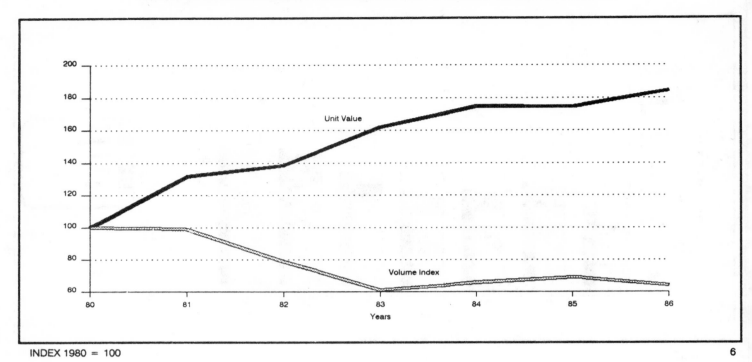

GRAPH 3: Asbestos — Unit Value and Volume Indices: 1980-86

INDEX 1980 = 100   6

Graph 3 indicates the difference in the volume and value indices. The declining popularity of asbestos is primarily responsible for the falling trend in the volume index; the rising trend in the unit value is largely as a result of the devaluation of the Zimbabwe dollar.

The price of *nickel* on the world market has been dropping steadily since 1980 when it fetched 195,68 US cents/pound, which was an all-time high. The price declined rapidly to 211,95 cents in 1983 and then recovered slightly to US$240 per pound in 1987 (May). Graph 4 indicates the price fluctuations in the market for nickel in both pound sterling and in Zimbabwe dollar terms. The sterling price shows a declining trend from early 1985 to the present; the Zimbabwe dollar price, although falling, shows brief periods of recovery as a result of the dollar devaluations.

Nickel production was at its peak in Zimbabwe in 1977 when almost 17 000 tonnes was produced. Since 1980 the level of production has fallen steadily from 15 074 tonnes to the present level of around 10 000 tonnes. Reasons for the decline in nickel production include the high labour costs and power charges (which form 50% of total costs), tax losses and substantial borrowing requirements which have resulted from the fall in nickel prices. Nickel production has also been affected by the declining ore grades at the major mines. The dollar devaluation has been an important factor in the continued survival of this sector of the mining industry.

At the current rate of output (around 10 000 tonnes p.a.) nickel deposits in Zimbabwe should last for another 50 years. Zimbabwe ranks tenth or eleventh in the production of nickel world-wide. The nickel mines are located near Bindura, Filabusi, and Shangani and are controlled mainly by British and South African companies.

The present low prices of *copper* are as a result of surplus stocks and falling international consumption. Graph 5 indicates the trend in the copper price on the London Metal Exchange and the effects of the dollar devaluation on the local price. Although copper output declined by 1,4% in 1985 the depreciation of the Zimbabwe dollar helped boost the value of production by 30,4%.

GRAPH 4: Fluctuations in the World Nickel Price: 1984-87

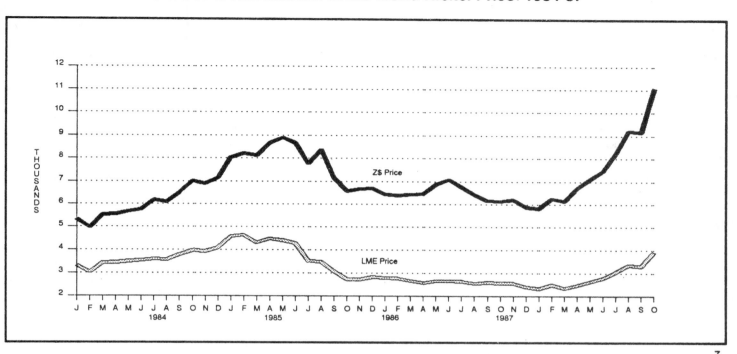

GRAPH 5: Fluctuations in the Copper Price: 1984-87

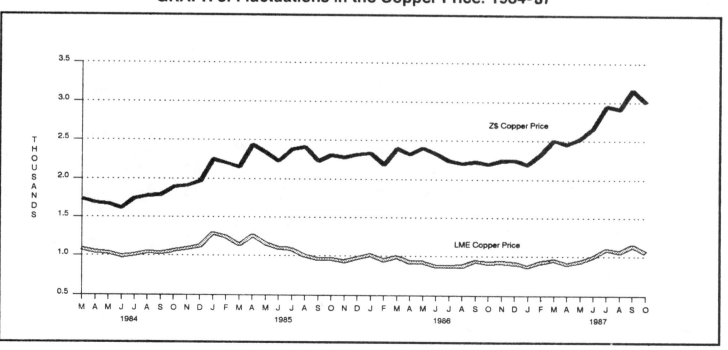

Zimbabwe is one of the world's largest producers of *asbestos*; other major producers are Italy, China and Canada. Adverse publicity has, however, led to the introduction of substitutes for asbestos products in developed countries leading to a drop in demand for the product worldwide. The chrysotile or white asbestos variety mined in Zimbabwe is reported to have no close substitute. The 1983 output of 153 000 tonnes is the lowest in more than 15 years; 1986 production figures (164 000 tonnes) showed a slight upturn although production was still substantially lower than in 1982. The expected increase in building activity in Zimbabwe, due to the post-1985 economic recovery, is likely to provide a substantial domestic market for asbestos cement products. Known reserves of asbestos are estimated to be in the region of 100 million tonnes with most deposits concentrated around Zvishavane.

The present annual output, 20 400 tonnes, represents a 43% decline in production since the 1979-80 period. Zimbabwe ranks among the top ten producers of copper in the world but its known reserves are only estimated to last another six years at capacity production.

Zimbabwe and South Africa together control over 90% of the western world's chrome deposits. Known reserves would last for about 100 years at the present rate of supply which is in the region of 500 tonnes p.a. The chrome industry is dominated by the American firm Union Carbide. Zimbabwean chrome has, in the past, been sold as an alloy (ferro-chrome) on world markets, which greatly increased its value.

Anglo American controls the only large-scale colliery in Zimbabwe at Hwange which produces over 3 million tonnes of coal p.a. In October 1982, government bought 40% of the shares in the colliery through the Zimbabwe Mining Development Corporation (ZMDC); the management of the colliery has, however, remained in the hands of Anglo American. Reserves of coal are estimated at 700 million tonnes, enough for a century or more. Coal is one of the few minerals mined in Zimbabwe that is mainly used for local consumption, with only about 10% being exported.

GRAPH 6: Mining Production 1975-86

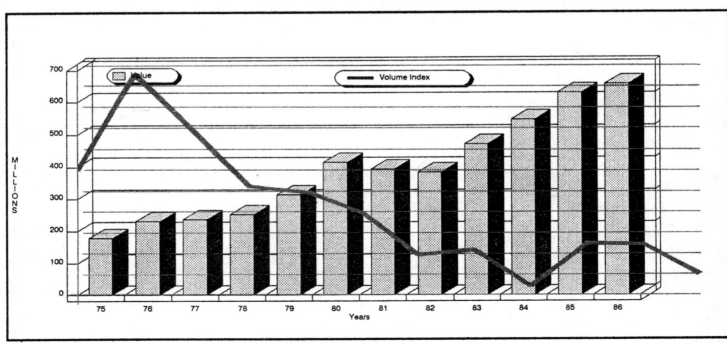

Overall Trends in Mineral Production

Graph 6 indicates that although the value of minerals mined in Zimbabwe is increasing every year, the volume of production has remained virtually unchanged since Independence. The major reason for this stagnation is the rising cost of production in the face of declining international commodity prices. The increasing value index reflects the continual devaluation of the dollar; this policy has meant that the mines get more Zimbabwe dollars for their minerals even though the US$ price may be static, or even falling.

The devaluation of the dollar, however, also has a negative effect on the mines in that it reduces the purchasing power of the import allocations given to the mining companies. Table 4 shows that import allocations have increased quite substantially in current prices since 1983. The input costs, however, have risen even faster so that in real terms the allocations have lagged behind requirements.

Breaking down the 1986 figure for the mining sector's import allocation we find that $9,6 million was for projects and $24,2 million was for spare parts. At current import prices (which are continually rising due to devaluation) it is estimated that the mining sector has a foreign exchange requirement of about $75 million a year.

So, although the currency devaluation has helped the competitiveness of the country's mineral exports and assisted in the depletion of the accumulated stockpile (as a result of the depressed demand during recession), the profitability of the sector was affected by the rapidly rising import costs and the inability of import allocations to keep pace.

TABLE 4: Foreign Exchange Allocation for Imports: 1983-86

1983	ZS13,66 million
1984	Z$18,88 million
1985	Z$24,94 million
1986	Z$33,86 million

10

Table 5 shows the number of Exclusive Prospecting Orders (EPOs) that have been issued in the past five years. The sharp reduction (from 53 in 1981 to six in 1985) shows that interest in the mining industry has fallen considerably in the past five years. The falling level of investment reflects the same trend.

TABLE 5: Exploration and Investment in the Mining Sector: 1981-85

	Number of EPOs	GFCF ($ million (1980 = 100)
1981	53	114
1982	36	72
1983	17	54
1984	15	*40
1985	6	*35

11

* Projections

In direct contradiction to this trend the ZMDC has increased its exploration expenditure from $750 000 in 1984-85 to $1 500 000 in 1985-86.

Costs, combined with poor world prices for many minerals, are the major factors constraining new investment in the industry. Other reasons for the downturn in the mining sector, are:
— high levels of taxation;
— inadequate foreign currency for imported inputs;
— interest rate increases that have caused financial costs to rise;
— low returns on investment;
— increased labour costs;
— delays on the part of government when approving projects;
— the unattractive investment code;
— the fear of increased socialization of the means of production

TABLE 6: Leading Exports 1983-84

Item	Z$m 1985	Z$m 1984
1. Tobacco	233	287
2. Gold	104	160
3. Ferrochrome	116	155
4. Cotton	75	117
5. Asbestos	69	74
6. Nickel	68	63
7. Steel	47	57
8. Sugar	52	56
9. Copper	48	43
10. Meat	18	37

12

Contribution to Export Earnings

Table 6 shows Zimbabwe's ten leading exports for the years 1983 and 1984, and demonstrate the central role of minerals in the generation of foreign exchange. Six of the top ten export earners are minerals; together, they contributed $552m (or 43%) to the total export earnings of $1 271m in 1984. (Note that some definitions of the mining sector exclude ferro-chrome and steel, classifying them as manufactured products.) When considering steel and ferro-chrome as manufactured products, the value of mining exports is $340m. Given that the mining sector generated only 6% of GDP, such foreign exchange earnings (26% of the total) are a significant achievement.

It must be remembered that the impressive growth and foreign exchange earnings of the mining sector are largely a result of currency movements. Graph 7 shows the value of mining output measured in Zimbabwe dollars and in Special Drawing Rights (SDRs — the IMF currency). The large devaluation of the Zimbabwe dollar in 1982 and its continued fall since then has resulted in large export earnings (in Zimbabwean dollar terms) for the mining sector.

The increase in production from 1980 (Z$414 760) to 1985 (Z$641 012) is 54% in Zimbabwe dollar terms; the SDR position is quite different, showing a fall of 20%.

Ownership of the Mining Sector

The First Five Year National Development Plan estimates that 80% of the mining sector is owned and controlled by foreign companies. The establishment of the ZMDC was meant to rectify this situation, but this is obviously a long-term strategy. The Ministry of Mines has committed itself to participating within the mining industry only on a 'willing buyer — willing seller' basis and to use the ZMDC to strengthen the industry as a whole.

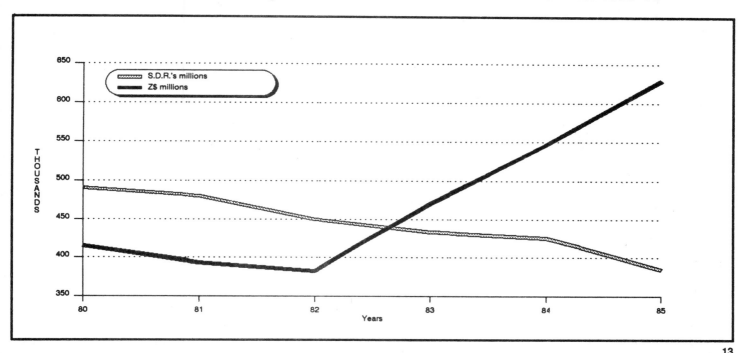

GRAPH 7: Value of Mining Production Zimbabwe Dollars and SDR's: 1980-85

S.D.R.'s millions
Z$ millions

THOUSANDS

Years

The extent of foreign domination is indicated below. The information groups the mines under the controlling company. The number of workers employed at each mine (1986 figures) is given as an indication of the size of the mine. The maps on pages 97, 108 and 118 show the locations of the mines.

American Interests

Union Carbide has extensive mining interests in Zimbabwe, mainly in chrome and nickel but also in gold.

Mines controlled by Union Carbide

1. Zimbabwe Mining and Smelting (previously known as African Chrome), which has a labour force of 710.
2. Lennox Gold mine, in Mashava, has a labour force of 238.
3. Peak and Railway Block are both chrome mines in Shurugwi. They have a combined labour force of 2 031 workers.
4. Mimosa Nickel, now closed, had a labour force of 184.

British Interests

Britain has the most extensive interests of any foreign country in mining in Zimbabwe. The four major British companies are Lonrho, Rio Tinto Zinc, Falcon mines and Turner & Newall. A fifth, smaller British company, is Selection Trust.

British Mines classified by Company

1. Lonrho is virtually the only significant producer of gold in Zimbabwe. It controls the following gold mines:

a) Arcturus — 807 workers
b) Athens (Mvuma) — 550 workers
c) How (Bulawayo) — 552 workers
d) Inyati (Headlands) — 824 workers
e) Mazoe — 620 workers

f)	Muriel (Chinhoyi)	— 652 workers
g)	Redwing (including Old West) (Penhalonga)	— 1247 workers (when in operation)
h)	Tiger Reef (Kwe kwe)	— 330 workers
i)	Shamva	— 670 workers

2. Rio Tinto Zinc is mainly involved in the production of gold. It controls the following mines:

3. Falcon mines are exclusively involved in gold production and control the biggest gold mine in the country (in terms of workers employed). Their interests include:

a)	Dalny gold mine (Chakari)	— 2226 workers
b)	Old Nic gold mine (Bulawayo)	— 295 workers

4. Turner & Newall dominate the production of asbestos in Zimbabwe. The company controls the following mines:

a)	Gaths asbestos mine (Mashaba)	— 2710 workers
a)	Brompton gold mine (Kadoma)	— 381 workers
b)	Patchway gold mine (Kadoma)	— 448 workers
c)	Renco gold mine (Triangle)	— 926 workers
d)	Sandawana emerald mine (West Nicholson)	— 226 workers
b)	Shabani asbestos mine (Zvishavane)	— 4423 workers

5. Selection Trust operates a lithium mine in Bikita which employs 274 workers.

South African Interests

After Britain, South Africa has the largest share of the mining industry. Their interests, however, are controlled almost exclusively by one company, the Anglo American Corporation. The only exception is the Dorowa phosphates mine which is owned by African Explosives and Chemical Industries (AECI), itself a subsidiary of the British ICI. The Dorowa mine employs 260 workers and supplies the Zimphos plant, also owned by AECI.

Anglo American Interests in the Mining Sector

a)	Caesar Chrome mine (Kildonan)	— 499 workers
b)	Epoch Nickel mine (Mbalabala)	— 615 workers
c)	Madziwa Nickel mine (Shamva)	— 768 workers
d)	Sutton Chrome mine (Kildonan)	— 192 workers
e)	Trojan Nickel mine (Bindura)	— 2080 workers
f)	Vanad Chrome mine (Mvurwi)	— 307 workers
g)	Wankie Coal mine and colliery (Hwange)	— 4719 workers
h)	The two Messina mines — Alaska and Mangula	—
i)	Shangani Nickel Mine (Nsiza)	— 1011 workers
j)	Netherburn Chrome mine (Gweru)	— 700 workers

Locally controlled Mining Companies

The most significant development in the locally controlled mining sector has been the establishment of the Zimbabwe Mining Development Corporation (see page 112 for more information on ZMDC).

Foreign companies own and control a major portion of the mining industry in Zimbabwe, leaving only a small 'piece of the cake' for local business people.

Important Industrial Mineral Deposits in Zimbabwe

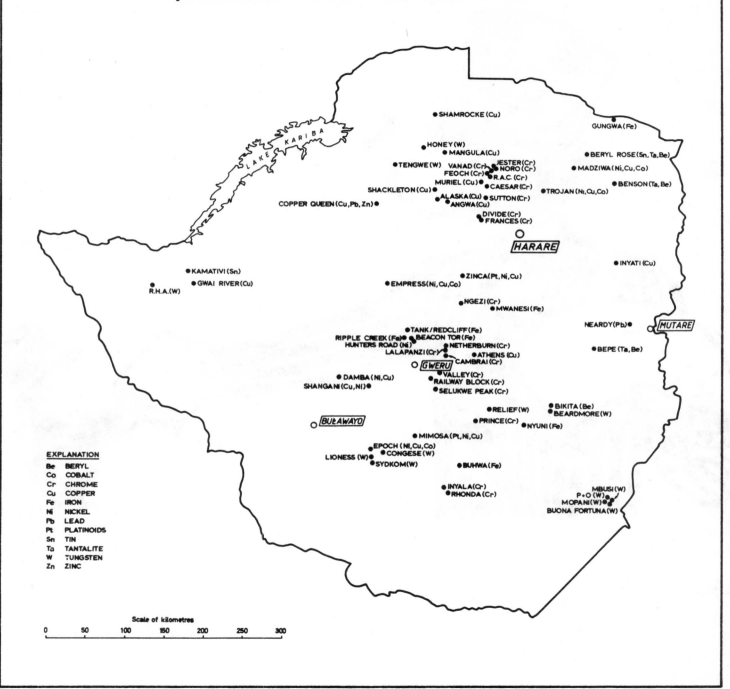

SHAMROCKE (Cu)

GUNGWA (Fe)

HONEY (W)

MANGULA (Cu)

BERYL ROSE (Sn, Ta, Be)

TENGWE (W) VANAD (Cr) JESTER (Cr)
NORO (Cr)

MADZIWA (Ni, Cu, Co)

FEOCH (Cr) R.A.C. (Cr)

MURIEL (Cu) CAESAR (Cr)

BENSON (Ta, Be)

SHACKLETON (Cu)

ALASKA (Cu) SUTTON (Cr) TROJAN (Ni, Cu, Co)

COPPER QUEEN (Cu, Pb, Zn) ANGWA (Cu)

DIVIDE (Cr)
FRANCES (Cr)

○ HARARE

INYATI (Cu)

KAMATIVI (Sn)

ZINCA (Pt, Ni, Cu)

GWAI RIVER (Cu)

EMPRESS (Ni, Cu, Co)

R.H.A. (W)

NGEZI (Cr)

MWANESI (Fe)

NEARDY (Pb) MUTARE

TANK/REDCLIFF (Fe)

BEACON TOR (Fe)

RIPPLE CREEK (Fe) NETHERBURN (Cr)

BEPE (Ta, Be)

HUNTERS ROAD (Ni)

LALAPANZI (Cr) ATHENS (Cu)

CAMBRAI (Cr)

○ GWERU

DAMBA (Ni, Cu) VALLEY (Cr)

SHANGANI (Cu, Ni) RAILWAY BLOCK (Cr)

SELUKWE PEAK (Cr)

BIKITA (Be)

RELIEF (W) BEARDMORE (W)

○ BULAWAYO

PRINCE (Cr) NYUNI (Fe)

MIMOSA (Pt, Ni, Cu)

EPOCH (Ni, Cu, Co)

LIONESS (W) CONGESE (W)

SYDKOM (W) BUHWA (Fe)

INYALA (Cr)

MBUSI (W)

RHONDA (Cr) P+O (W)

MOPANI (W)

BUONA FORTUNA (W)

EXPLANATION

Be	BERYL
Co	COBALT
Cr	CHROME
Cu	COPPER
Fe	IRON
Ni	NICKEL
Pb	LEAD
Pt	PLATINOIDS
Sn	TIN
Ta	TANTALITE
W	TUNGSTEN
Zn	ZINC

Scale of kilometres

0   50   100   150   200   250   300

ZMDC: Subsidiary Companies

1) MTD (Mangula) Limited: ZMDC owns 54,56% of the shares in this company, giving it the controlling interest. MTD operates two copper mines (Miriam and Norah) at Mhangura, a smelter and a refinery at Alaska. The company's primary product is copper, with silver, gold and precious metals being by-products of the copper refining process. The company realized a profit of $163m in 1985 despite experiencing problems with plant and equipment which affected production.

2) Merits Limited (65% owned by ZMDC): Merits own 100% of Lomagundi Smelting and Mining. Other shareholders of Merits are Anglo American (10%) and MTD (25%). Lomagundi Smelting and Mining operates two copper mines, Angwa and Avondale, which are both in Alaska. The company sells its copper to MTD. In 1985 it made a loss of $1,39m. At the time of purchase by the ZMDC the mines were already making a loss and their future life was estimated at two years; this can be extended for another two or three years if the low-grade copper is also mined. The policy of low-grading has now been adopted and financial assistance is being sought from government in order to undertake the necessary development work.

3) ZMDC Management Services: this subsidiary is a shareholder in the following gold mining operations: Bar 20 mine, Jena Mine, and Sabi Consolidated Gold Mines. ZMDC Management Services also provides accounting, financial and management services to the member companies. As a group, the ZMDC gold mining companies earned a profit of just over $1 million in 1985.

4) Peneast Mining Company (Pvt) Ltd (100% owned by ZMDC). This subsidiary owns a gold dump and although it was expected that production would commence in 1985, this has been delayed due to the shortage of foreign exchange to purchase essential parts.

Other locally controlled Mining Companies

1. *Forbes and Thompson* operates two mines in Zimbabwe:
    a) the Freda Gold mine, located outside Gwanda. The mine employs 389 workers.
    b) The Vubachikwe Gold mine, close to the Freda Gold mine, which employs 557 workers.
2. *RAN Mines* is the controlling company for Kimberly Gold mine, near Bindura, which employs 155 workers.
3. *J. Mack and Company* runs the Golden Valley Gold mine near Kadoma, employing 406 workers.
4. *Refractory Minerals* runs a magnesite mine which employs 109 workers.

BOX 1: Transfer pricing through over-invoicing and under-invoicing

The formation of the Chamber dates back to July 1895 when mining companies in Matabeleland came together to form an organization to represent their interests called the Rhodesia Chamber of Mines. The Salisbury Chamber of Mines was set up soon afterwards, followed by the formation of a number of regional associations set up to represent the interests of the mine owners. In 1931 the regional associations combined under the umbrella of the Rhodesian Mining Federation (RMF). In 1939 the two city based chambers, the Rhodesian Chamber of Mines (Bulawayo) and the Salisbury Chamber of Mines merged to form the Chamber of Mines of Rhodesia, which in turn merged with the RMF in 1957 leaving the Chamber as the only organ representing all sectors of the mining industry.

Members of the Chamber pay subscriptions according to the size of the labour force employed and the value of production.

The functions of the Chamber are to represent the interests of the mine owners in the field of labour negotiations with trade unions and more generally in the sphere of industrial relations. In this capacity the Chamber would negotiate on behalf of the mine owners with the trade unions; would give advice on industrial relations; would liaise with other employer organizations and the Ministry of Labour, Manpower Planning and Social Services.

Part of the Chamber's function as representative of the mining industry involves a degree of collaboration with the Ministry of Mines. The Chamber examines all new legislation pertaining to the mining industry and passes on its comments to the Ministry. The Chamber also comments on specific actions by Government which have a bearing on the industry. One of the major reasons for on-going contact with officials of the Ministry and statutory bodies is to ensure that they are aware of the views of the mining industry.

The Chamber is also involved in the provision of certain services to the industry; a training facility is offered through the School of Mines; the recruitment of labour for the whole industry is co-ordinated by the Chamber; sporting facilities and competitions are organized; an awareness of safety is generated through the work of the Safety and Prevention of Accidents Committee and through the organization of first aid competitions; the financial interests of the mine owners are looked after through the operations of sub-committees on purchasing, taxation, etc.; and finally, the provision of secretarial services for the Chamber and its various sub-committees.

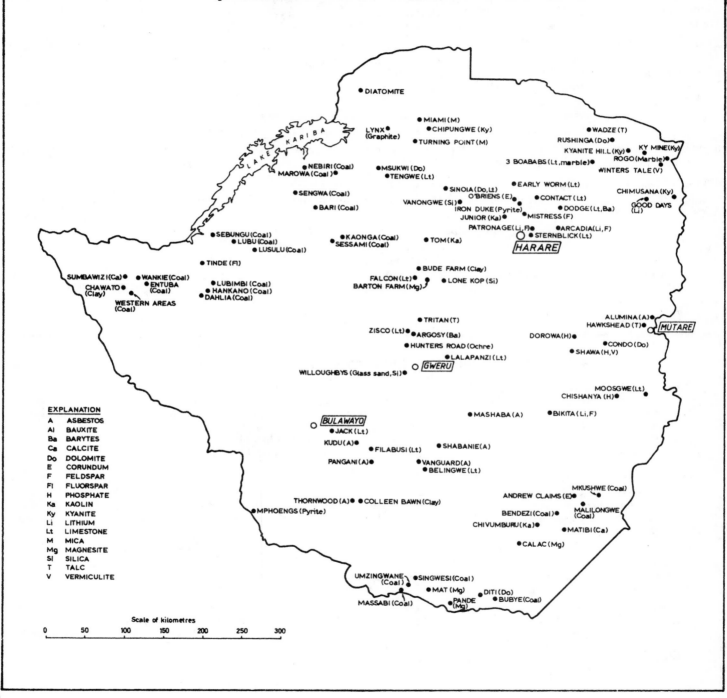

Important Base Mineral Deposits in Zimbabwe

DIATOMITE

MIAMI (M)
LYNX (Graphite)
CHIPUNGWE (Ky)
TURNING POINT (M)
WADZE (T)
RUSHINGA (Do)
KYANITE HILL (Ky)
KY MINE (Ky)
3 BOABABS (Lt, marble)
ROGO (Marble)
WINTERS TALE (V)

NEBIRI (Coal)
MAROWA (Coal)
MSUKWI (Do)
TENGWE (Lt)
SINOIA (Do, Lt)
EARLY WORM (Lt)
CHIMUSANA (Ky)
O'BRIENS (E)
VANONGWE (Si)
CONTACT (Lt)
SENGWA (Coal)
IRON DUKE (Pyrite)
DODGE (Lt, Ba)
GOOD DAYS (Li)
BARI (Coal)
JUNIOR (Ka)
MISTRESS (F)
PATRONAGE (Li, F)
ARCADIA (Li, F)
SEBUNGU (Coal)
STERNBLICK (Lt)
LUBU (Coal)
KAONGA (Coal)
HARARE
LUSULU (Coal)
SESSAMI (Coal)
TOM (Ka)

TINDE (Fl)
BUDE FARM (Clay)
SUMBAWIZI (Ca)
WANKIE (Coal)
LUBIMBI (Coal)
FALCON (Lt)
LONE KOP (Si)
CHAWATO (Clay)
ENTUBA (Coal)
HANKANO (Coal)
BARTON FARM (Mg)
WESTERN AREAS (Coal)
DAHLIA (Coal)

TRITAN (T)
ALUMINA (A)
HAWKSHEAD (T)
MUTARE
ZISCO (Lt)
ARGOSY (Ba)
DOROWA (H)
CONDO (Do)
HUNTERS ROAD (Ochre)
SHAWA (H, V)
LALAPANZI (Lt)
GWERU
WILLOUGHBYS (Glass sand, Si)
MOOSGWE (Lt)
CHISHANYA (H)

BULAWAYO
MASHABA (A)
BIKITA (Li, F)
JACK (Lt)
KUDU (A)
SHABANIE (A)
FILABUSI (Lt)
PANGANI (A)
VANGUARD (A)
BELINGWE (Lt)

MKUSHWE (Coal)
THORNWOOD (A)
COLLEEN BAWN (Clay)
ANDREW CLAIMS (E)
BENDEZI (Coal)
MALILONGWE (Coal)
MPHOENGS (Pyrite)
CHIVUMBURU (Ka)
MATIBI (Ca)
CALAC (Mg)

UMZINGWANE (Coal)
SINGWESI (Coal)
MAT (Mg)
DITI (Do)
BUBYE (Coal)
PANDE (Mg)
MASSABI (Coal)

EXPLANATION
A — ASBESTOS
Al — BAUXITE
Ba — BARYTES
Ca — CALCITE
Do — DOLOMITE
E — CORUNDUM
F — FELDSPAR
Fl — FLUORSPAR
H — PHOSPHATE
Ka — KAOLIN
Ky — KYANITE
Li — LITHIUM
Lt — LIMESTONE
M — MICA
Mg — MAGNESITE
Si — SILICA
T — TALC
V — VERMICULITE

LAKE KARIBA

Scale of kilometres
0 50 100 150 200 250 300

110

Mining Co-operatives

At the end of May 1986 the number of registered mining co-operatives was 34, of which 19 were mining chrome, and the remainder were in the prospecting stages. Although the ZMDC plays an advisory role in the mining co-operative movement, the technology used remains very low. The ZMDC posts resident advisors on the co-ops. The 19 chrome mining co-ops together account for 6,7% of national production.

Among the causes reported to have resulted in fluctuating output from mining co-operatives were frequent breakdowns of machinery, unreliable transport services, poor road conditions and work stoppages associated with the rainy season. Most co-operatives operate between five to eleven months per year. Average incomes are reported to have been $126 per member for the twelve months ended May 1986.

Summary

Of the 50 odd mines listed in the above tables approximately half are owned by Britain; one-fifth by South Africa; one-fifth by local companies (of which half are owned by the ZMDC); and the rest (approximately five mines) are owned by American interests. Lonrho — a British company, controls gold mining in Zimbabwe, while asbestos production is dominated by Turner and Newall and chrome is shared between Union Carbide and Anglo American. Mine owners in Zimbabwe came together as early as 1895 in order to secure an adequate supply of labour for the industry as a whole (see page109).Co-operation between the mine owners has since developed into areas such as research, training, joint negotiation with both labour and government, the production of journals for the whole industry, all of which are co-ordinated by the Chamber of Mines (see Box2).

Government Participation in Mining

The specific conditions which prevail in the mining industry in Southern Africa necessitated a high degree of government involvement from the early stages of the development of the industry. Most important amongst these conditions is the low grade of the ore mined which makes mining in Southern Africa far less profitable (and far more sensitive to cost increases) than mining in other parts of the world. The internationally controlled prices of minerals, and their decline in recent years, has also meant that the industry could not survive without special assistance from government.

Free Government Assistance to the Industry

Government assistance dates back to 1911 when the Ministry of Mines first set up a Department of Mining Engineering to give free technical advice to the mining industry and to ensure that the safety measures laid down by government were strictly adhered to. This department is also responsible for the testing and issuing of blasting licences, certificates of competency and Mine Managers' diplomas. The Plant Hire scheme also falls within it.

The Department of Metallurgy within the Ministry of Mines provides free services to the industry in the fields of extractive metallurgy, process evaluation, development investigation and rectification of routine plant problems. This department also operates a Carbon in Pulp pilot project, a mineral dressing section, a chemical laboratory, an assay section, a ceramics section and a minerology section.

The Minerals Development unit is a multi-disciplinary Unit within the Ministry charged with the following tasks:
— advising the Minister on the formulation of policies related to the overall development of the mining industry;
— formulating, co-ordinating and monitoring projects emanating from within the unit itself or from one of the other technical departments within the Ministry;
— following trends in the mining industry both at home and abroad including monitoring production and prices of our minerals, and
— assisting in the formulation and provision of assistance to mining co-operatives and small-scale miners (this particular function now falls under the ZMDC.

The Rhodesian government first established the School of Mines in 1936, which became part of the Bulawayo Technical College in 1970. Its function was to train mining and metallurgical technicians, mining surveyors, and run courses for learner mine officials.

The Mining Promotion Council (MPC) was first established as a subsidiary of the IDC in 1967. The MPC was to promote the exploration of old mines and prospects in which the private sector was not interested. With the formation of the Zimbabwe Mining Development Corporation (see below) the functions and the investments of the MPC, and the investments of the IDC, reverted to the ZMDC.

The Institute of Mining Research was established at the University in 1969 in order to carry out studies in economic geology and metallurgy. The institute also undertakes contract work for the mining companies.

The government also gives direct assistance to the mining industry through its loan scheme and cash grant scheme. The loan scheme came into operation in 1912 and initially supported prospectors as well as producers.

Today the Ministry provides ordinary loan assistance (based on the merits of the project) to purchase mines, develop mines, assist in the purchase of plant and equipment, for the construction of water and/or electricity supplies, establish extractive plants on gold mines, emergency loans, and speculative loans. In addition the plant hire scheme gives small miners the opportunity to hire machinery they cannot afford to buy, and gives them the option of buying at any point in the duration of the contract.

The scrapping of the gold standard in 1931 caused a rise in the gold price and led to a significant expansion of the industry (from 449 to 1 634 mines) in 1934. The government introduced a Gold Premium Tax in 1932 in order to tax large earnings. It lasted until 1945 when the depressed state of the industry necessitated its removal. In its place the government introduced a Gold Subsidy Act which was to assist potentially economic mines that were running at a loss due to the state of the industry and extend the lives of dying mines. Government financial assistance to the gold-mining sector has, in one form or another, continued ever since.

An export promotion scheme was briefly introduced between 1966 and 1973 (during UDI) when it was withdrawn. The scheme allowed for between two and four times the cost of developing the new markets to be deducted from taxable income. The scheme was withdrawn when Sterling, the US dollar and the Rand were all devalued by 20%.

In the 1982-83 and the 1983-84 periods government had to come to the assistance of the mining sector as a result of increasing electricity costs and rail tariffs in the wake of falling commodity prices. Government granted assistance to the tune of $6,7 million and $8,0 million in the two above periods in the form of loans to individual firms.

Government Participation in Direct Production

The depressed state of the mining industry in recent years and the lack of any exploration by the existing mines, coupled with government's desire to participate more in the economy, led to the formation of the Zimbabwe Mining Development Corporation in November 1983. The ZMDC is essentially the productive arm of government in the mining sector. Its functions, as stipulated in the Act, include total involvement in all facets of mining including the promotion of mining co-operatives.

The government's intention in establishing the ZMDC was not to take over existing mines (except on a 'willing buyer — willing seller' basis) but rather to develop new mines through exploration and thereby expand the mining sector.

The government provided an initial grant of $750 000 in order to enable the ZMDC to get established. Most of this was spent on administration, fixed assets and investment.

At the time of the formation of the ZMDC there was only one mining co-operative in operation (although there were 13 registered mining co-ops); this was the Ingezi Chrome Mining Co-operative. By the end of May 1986 the number of registered co-ops had risen to 34 (see page ...) The aim of the ZMDC is to station resident advisers at all mining co-ops (these advisers are ZMDC staff).

The Corporation received a further $1 million in Government grants and $6 million in interest-free loans in 1985. The grants were used for administrative expenses, while $5,5m of the loan was used to purchase Messina Mining's interests and $500 000 for plant and equipment.

In its second year of operation, 1985, the ZMDC made a net loss of $348 000, while the MTD (Mangula) Ltd group of companies — wholly owned by ZMDC — made a profit of $1,5 million. (A list of ZMDC investments to date is given on page111 and 109)

Government Participation in Marketing

The Minerals Marketing Corporation of Zimbabwe (MMCZ) was established in March 1983 by an Act of Parliament to handle the external selling and marketing of all minerals and metals (with the exception of gold and silver) and the selling of a few minor minerals.

The establishment of the corporation came as a result of government's concern over the possibility of irregularities in the marketing of minerals in the form of under-invoicing or under-pricing. (See Box 1 opposite for an explanation of how under-invoicing and under-pricing work). The centralized marketing provided by the MMCZ means that the private mining houses no longer play any role in the external sale of their products.

The functions, powers and duties of the MMCZ laid down in the act include:

— acting as the sole marketing and selling agent for all minerals;
— the investigation of marketing conditions inside and outside Zimbabwe;
— the purchase of any mineral on its own account and the sale of such minerals;
— advising the Minister on all matters connected with the marketing of minerals.

In the marketing of minerals the MMCZ can either act as an agent, purchase the goods for resale, or simply authorize a sale made directly between buyer and seller. The most common method of operation is acting as an agent on behalf of the producer. In such a case the MMCZ would find the buyer, arrange the transport and insurance, and collect the final payment for the minerals. The MMCZ only purchases minor minerals such as tantalite, beryl, tungsten ores, tin ore and uncut gemstones for resale. The MMCZ sells mainly to direct customers rather than to traders or merchants.

The present value of the MMCZ's business substantially exceeds $600m p.a. The volume of sales depends on the output of the mining industry and the state of the international economy, neither of which the MMCZ controls.

The revenue of the MMCZ is largely derived from its commission of 0,875% which it charges for its services. The establishment costs of the Corporation have long been recouped and the MMCZ is now completely self-financing.

TABLE 7: Summary of MMCZ Financial Transactions over the 1983-85 period

Transaction	1983	1984	1985
Sales as Agent	*73 000	459 000	560 000
Commissions earned from sales as agent	642	4 017	4 900
Sales on own Account	35	460	716
Operating Surplus /Deficit	(207)	2 097	2 791
*Note: All figures in thousands.			

14

In his capacity as Chairman of the MMCZ board, Cde Chris Ushewokunze noted that in its second full year of operation the corporation has been able to:

— expand and develop new markets for Zimbabwean minerals,
— develop new markets in Africa with sales of steel to Kenya and coal to Tanzania,
— pursue investigations into potential markets for new products (e.g. kyanite),
— begin investigations into the local cutting of emeralds which, at present, are being exported in rough form; and
— begin investigations into the possibility of expanding the domestic consumption of major metals such as steel, ferro-chrome, nickel, copper and tin.

Labour and Operating Costs in the Mining Sector

The low labour and operating costs were a vital feature in the development of the local mining sector as many of the base metal mines were developed from ores which elsewhere would be regarded as lean and therefore unprofitable to mine. The copper and nickel content of the ore, for example, was less than half the amount that was present in the copper mines of Zambia and the nickel mines of Ontario, Canada.

The mining sector is therefore dependent on low operating costs for its survival. The increases in average wages (wages now represent 43% of total costs) together with the increased cost of spares, freight and electricity (electricity charges have increased three-fold since 1980) have threatened the survival of the mining industry.

TABLE 8: Investment and Returns in the Mining Industry : 1979-82

	1979	1980	1981	1982
Funds Employed	370 731 764	413 916 044	429 367 554	425 695 689
Cost of all mining operations	520 570 925	599 809 873	630 342 995	702 204 860
Gross Profit	80 057 572	114 582 489	58 572 804	10 827 151
Net Profit	66 025 062	86 483 676	40 377 571	(16 226 102)
Gross value of Minerals Prod.	361 146 000	502 331 000	473 041 000	460 206 000

15

Table 8 shows that 1979 and 1980 were good years for the mining industry. In 1981 and 1982 the gross value of minerals produced dropped from the high 1980 level. The cost of mining operations, however, continued to rise despite the lower levels of production; production dropped by approximately 6% in 1981, yet the cost of production increased by 5%. The same pattern was repeated in the following year; production decreased by 3% over the 1981-82 period, yet the cost of production increased by 11%. The drop in Net Profit tells the whole story; over the 1980-81 period net profit dropped by 53%; over the 1981-82 period it dropped a further 115%.

From Table 9 we can see that the wage bill (total earnings) increased over the entire period despite the declining number of people employed in the 1982-83 periods. Labour costs as a proportion of the total value of minerals produced was 46,6% in 1982 compared to 35% in 1972 (see Table 10). The most rapid increase was in the 1980-82 period when the proportion of labour costs to total value increased from 28% to 46%.

Earnings in the mining sector over the 1980-85 period have risen from $116,3 to $221,3 million. In the same period the number of employees has fallen from 66 million to 54 million. This rise in wage costs to the industry, at a time of falling commodity prices, has resulted in a drastic fall in profitability.

114

TABLE 9: People employed and average Wages in the Mining Sector 1978-1984

Year	($) Average Wage	(Millions) Number Employed	(Millions) Total Earnings
1978	94	58,1	72,6
1979	105	59,5	85,4
1980	131	66,2	116,3
1981	177	68,2	157,3
1982	214	63,7	178,7
1983	236	60,4	186,0
1984	270	n.a.	n.a.

16

If labour costs have increased so, too, have electricity costs. Since 1980 the latter have doubled for asbestos producers; increased 2,4 times for nickel producers; and 1,7 times for ferro-alloy smelters. These increases were, however, overdue as there had been no increase in the cost of power in real terms for the previous two decades.

Declining Profitability

In order to calculate the profitability of the industry in the face of these rapidly rising costs, we compare the 'average value of labour' (i.e. the value generated per worker, which is calculated by dividing the number of employees by the gross value of output) with the 'average cost of labour' (total earnings divided by the number of people employed).

From Table 10 we can see that the average value of labour increased 4,5 times from 1970 to 1983, whereas the average cost of labour increased 4,9 times in the same period. This indicates that costs rise faster than productivity in the mining sector, thereby reducing profitability.

The replacement of skilled personnel presented some difficulties immediately after 1980 due to the outflow of people at that particular time and contributed to the general decline in profitability; since then, however, great strides have been made due to the in-service training schemes run by most of the mining companies.

TABLE 10: Output, Employment and Value over the 1970-84 period

Year	Total Output ($m)	Total Earnings ($m)	Proportion of labour payments to total value	Number Employed (000's)	Average value of labour ($ per worker)
1970	98 702	35,4	35,8%	157,2	1 726
1971	101 230	37,1	36,6%	58,0	1 745
1972	107 376	38,0	35,4%	58,4	1 839
1973	135 966	40,3	29,7%	58,1	2 340
1974	165 154	48,2	29,2%	62,0	2 664
1975	177 838	57,1	32,1%	62,6	2 841
1976	230 477	65,7	28,5%	63,8	3 613
1977	237 489	71,4	30,1%	61,6	3 855
1978	252 196	72,6	28,8%	58,1	4 341
1979	314 801	85,4	27,1%	59,5	5 291
1980	414 760	116,3	28,0%	66,2	6 265
1981	393 524	157,3	40,0%	68,2	5 770
1982	383 044	178,7	46,6%	63,7	6 013
1983	470 454	186,0	39,5%	60,3	7 802
1984	546 468	—	—	—	—

17

115

Falling Commodity Prices

The international prices of all metals in 1980-81 dropped by 14%. In the following period, 1981-82 prices dropped a further 9,2%. Over the 13 year period from 1970 to 1983 copper prices fell by 54% while nickel prices fell by 64%.

Relative to the export prices of manufactured goods sold by industrial countries, commodity prices are close to their post-1945 low. The sluggish growth of the industrialized countries who demand the bulk of Third World commodities; technological advances such as the introduction of plastics and synthetic fibres (and in recent years the falling oil price which has reduced the cost of producing these synthetic substitutes) and the trend towards miniaturization; high real interest prices which have reduced the speculative buying of commodities and the holding of stockpiles; and the improved supplies of agricultural products which has depressed world prices, have all contributed to the current weakness of commodity prices.

The most serious price movement from Zimbabwe's point of view over the past year (1985) has been the 32% drop in the cotton price. The 1985 price changes for some of Zimbabwe's leading exports are shown in Table 11 below:

TABLE 11: Price changes in selected Commodities over the 1984-85 period

Product	End 1985	1984/85
Gold: US $/oz	327	+ 6%
Copper: /tonne	973	- 14%
Nickel: US cents/lb	193	- 15%
Cotton: US cents/lb	49	- 32%
Maize: /tonne	142	- 3%
Sugar: US $/tonne	126	+ 17%

18

The outlook for the future couple of years remains bleak with the prediction of the Organization of Economic Co-operation and Development (OECD) countries that relative to the prices of manufactured goods, commodity prices will at best remain stable.

Transport Difficulties

Due to its landlocked position, Zimbabwe is dependent on the port facilities of either Mozambique or South Africa for the export of its mineral products. The deteriorating security situation in Mozambique and the threat of sanctions against South Africa has meant that the transport situation is particularly serious. Before 1975 (prior to Mozambiquan Independence) two-thirds of Zimbabwe's exports passed through its ports. The disruption caused by the Renamo bandits in recent years has forced Zimbabwean exporters to increasingly use the South African ports — an option which might no longer be possible with sanctions.

Raising new Capital

Raising new capital locally for investment purposes has proved to be difficult for the bulk of the mining sector which is foreign based (see section on Investment, p48). The local borrowings for the multi-national corporations is limited to 15% of the value of their share capital. If a local subsidiary wants to borrow more than the 15% limit, Reserve Bank approval is needed and the company loses its right to repatriate profits. An alternative strategy would be for the subsidiary to issue more shares locally in order to raise capital (rather than borrowing from the banks) but this means that the profits they can remit decrease proportionately (as more profits have to be paid to local shareholders in the form of dividends) and the holding of the parent company is diluted.

The present position in regard to the repatriation of profits is that companies can remit 50% of their after-tax profits. These remittances are subject to an additional non-resident's shareholders tax of 20%; effectively reducing the repatriation to 40% of after-tax profits. (Recent temporary cutbacks in this remittance of dividend earnings are contained in the section on Investment referred in Appendix 1).

Table 12 shows the extent of investment in the mining sector over the past ten years. Column 1 gives the investment figures in current prices while column 2 gives investment in real terms. The level of investment in real terms in 1983 ($54 million) was lower

TABLE 12: Gross Fixed Capital Formation in the Mining Sector: 1974-83

Year	G.F.C.F. at current prices (1)	*G.F.C.F. in real terms (2)
1974	34	75
1975	40	77
1976	60	102
1977	66	97
1978	59	76
1979	83	92
1980	83	83
1981	133	114
1982	94	72
1983	89	54

19

* Gross Fixed Capital Formation at constant (180) prices.

than it had ever been— almost 30% lower than real investment in 1975. One of the reasons for the low level of investment is the lack of foreign exchange made available to the mining sector in order to replace plant and machinery; another reason is the difficulty of raising capital

The mining sector currently employs 60 300 workers (1983 figures), which is 5,8% of the total labour force. In 1980 the mining sector employed 66 200 workers
which represents a reduction of 9% over a three year period.
The increase in minimum wages and the rising cost of electricity at a time when metal and mineral
prices are at their lowest internationally has meant that even major mines are having to turn to the government for assistance.

Beneficiation

Eighty per cent of the minerals mined in Zimbabwe are exported in their raw state. These minerals are then transformed into finished products some of which are re-imported into Zimbabwe. Since the real prices of the primary commodities exported from Third World countries such as Zimbabwe are constantly falling, relative to the prices of the finished products imported by these countries, they generally face unfavourable terms of trade. The effect on a country such as ours which earns almost all of its foreign exchange through the sale of primary commodities, is that we are constantly having to increase the volume that we export in order to import a constant, or even declining, quantity of manufactured goods. This represents a structural imbalance in our balance of payments as it is virtually impossible to break out of this trap while we continue to export commodities in their raw state and import finished goods.

The falling prices of primary products also limits the growth of the domestic market through the restraint imposed on input costs. Since the falling commodity prices limit the profitability of the mining sector, input costs, including wages, have to be kept to a minimum. This, in turn, limits the growth of the domestic market and forces the developing country to rely on an export market which it sells its products to.

Attempts by Third World countries to maintain profitability in their primary sectors by either offering guaranteed prices (e.g. the maize price, or the 'gold ceiling' price) or by devaluing the local currency, raise different problems. Guaranteed producer prices can either put the cost of food beyond the reach of the majority of the people, or can involve the government in large food subsidy payments which tend to produce large budget deficits, domestic inflation, and balance of payments deficits. Devaluing the currency, on the other hand, can boost the sales of primary commodities but it also increases the cost of vital imports (primary and manufactured goods) without which the country cannot survive.

The Transitional National Development Plan lists as one of its major objectives the promoting of domestic processing of minerals to manufacture finished products. The Secretary of the Ministry of Mines, Cde Chris Ushewokunze, has emphasized the need to move more into 'value-added products' such as the production of stainless-steel. Zimbabwe already produces its own ferro-chrome from chrome-ore; the next step would be the combination of ferro-chrome, steel and nickel to produce stainless-steel.

The major problem in implementing the above has been the lack of expertise, the lack of capital investment, and an adequate (i.e. 20 year) supply of the mineral.

Other projects involving the further processing of domestically produced minerals presently being considered are:
— the production of nickel wire;
— the spinning of asbestos fibre;
— a coal-based chemical industry;
— the upgrading of magnesite;
— the production of tin-plate; and
— the manufacture of refractory products.

The problem of unequal exchange mentioned above (created by the declining terms of trade) could partially be overcome by the development of regional economic integration. The proposals presently being studied by the SADCC mining section (based in Lusaka) envisage a far greater sharing of research and marketing facilities within the Southern African region. The economies of scale generated by the size of the regional market could enable the production and export of numerous products that are not currently viable.

It needs to be remembered, however, that at present the Minerals Marketing Corporation sells mainly to markets outside of SADCC or the Preferential Trade Area (PTA). The reason for this is that these countries are historically not consumers of mineral products. Essentially it is the lack of an industrial structure which would enable the SADCC/PTA countries to utilize Zimbabwean mineral exports that is the obstacle in selling to them.

Another problem in the development of a Southern African market is the need for all the countries in the region to earn hard currency (i.e. fully convertible national currencies, e.g. the US dollar or the British pound) with which to import goods only produced in the First World. It is this need which forces countries to sell their primary products to the developed world rather than to each other.

Eighty per cent of the minerals mined in Zimbabwe are exported in their raw state. These raw minerals are then transformed into finished goods in First World countries and then sold back to Zimbabwe. Because the prices of raw materials are constantly falling while those of finished goods are rising, Zimbabwe actually gets poorer through this pattern of international trade..

Options for Development

Zimbabwe's mining industry can therefore be said to be at a crucial juncture in its development; the recent rapid increases in labour and electricity costs have eroded decades of cheap labour and energy. Furthermore, the declining trend in commodity prices is unlikely to change in the near future. Profitability is therefore being squeezed from above and below, and further undercut by the foreign exchange shortages which delay the purchase of vital spares.

Zimbabwe has two possible options for the future. The first would be to continue to sell the bulk of our commodities on the world market in order to earn sufficient foreign exchange to purchase all our import requirements (mostly producer goods). The problem of declining profitability could be tackled by joint research and marketing with other countries in the region on one hand, and a strategy of guaranteed prices at home to generate high production levels plus a cheaper currency abroad to generate higher sales. This policy mix is unlikely to solve the twin deficit (BOP and budget) problem, and in the long run would probably increase Zimbabwe's dependence on the First World. Such an option would also involve continued government support of an essentially non-viable mining sector.

The second option would be to concentrate on the beneficiation of our minerals and the further use of our raw materials in the production of producer goods. This strategy would involve the development (and protection of) new industries in the producer goods sector, the expansion of the domestic market to absorb the greater volume of production, and the development of barter trade deals with other countries in the region.

Such a move would involve a deepening of import substitution into the producer goods sector and a concentration on export promotion only in so far as the generation of foreign exchange is needed for the purchase of technology which neither Zimbabwe nor the SADCC/PTA countries can provide. Within this option government support would be limited to import controls as a means of protecting infant industries and the promotion of research and development.

References

1. Viewing K.A., *Mining and the Development of Zimbabwe*, Institute of Mining Research, University of Zimbabwe, Harare, September, 1983.
2. Central Statistical Office, *Quarterly Digest of Statistics*, Harare, September, 1986.
3. *ibid.*,
4. RAL Merchant Bank Ltd., *Executive Guide to the Economy*, RAL, Harare, March 1987.
5. *ibid.*, December, 1986.
6. *ibid.*, March, 1987.
7. *ibid.*, June, 1986.
8. *ibid.*, June, 1986.
9. Ministry of Finance, Economic Planning and Development, *Socio-Economic Review of Zimbabwe. 1980-85*, Harare, 1985.
10. *ibid.*, June, 1986.
11. *ibid.*,
12. Standard Chartered Bank, *Standard Chartered Economic Bulletin*, 1987, Harare.
13. MMCZ, *Annual Reports 1983, 1984 & 1985*, Harare.
14. *ibid.*,
15. Viewing K.A., *Mining and the Development of Zimbabwe*, Institute of Mining Research, University of Zimbabwe,
16. Harare, September, 1983.
17. Central Statistical Office, *Quarterly Digest of Statistics*, Harare, September, 1986. (adapted).
18. *ibid.*,
19. Standard Chartered Bank, *Standard Chartered Economic Bulletin*, Harare, 1987.
    Quarterly Digest of Statistics, op. cit.

Chapter 6

THE MONETARY AND FINANCIAL SECTOR

Introduction

The first commercial bank in Zimbabwe opened its doors for business as early as 1892, nearly a century ago. As the country developed, the commercial banks evolved to the extent that, to-day, there exists a full range of financial services available in Zimbabwe, from the deposit facilities of the commercial banks to the specialized banking of the finance houses and merchant banks. The banking sector is capable, allowing for local constraints, of matching traditional bankers anywhere in the world and, in fact, has done so on more than one occasion.

The Role of the Financial Sector

At present the Zimbabwean money and capital market comprises the following institutions: five commercial banks; four merchant banks; two discount houses; five registered financial institutions (finance houses); three building societies; one representative international bank; one export credit insurance corporation; seven major trust companies; one stock exchange; three development finance companies; 59 direct insurers; 8 re-insurers and 17 brokers.

The major role of the financial sector is to channel the surplus funds of households and companies into investments of a financial and productive nature. The deposit receiving institutions act, therefore, as pools or reservoirs of society's savings. The financial sector also has the function of channelling some of the surplus savings into the hands of the government which uses this money for public investments. Through its advisory function the financial sector increases the efficiency of the financial resources that are available. The demands of both buyers and sellers of money are integrated through the operation of the market in financial instruments (treasury bills, AMA bills, negotiable certificates of deposit, etc.) which is facilitated by the institution of the financial market. The latter also provides a measure of security and confidence without which private enterprise could not function.

Definitions of the Money and Capital Markets

The money market is essentially the short-term end of the financial market which is provided by the discount houses, financial houses and the commercial banks.

The capital market, on the other hand, deals with longer-term private and government securities and funds. The capital market is not a geographically distinct market, as the institutions of the money market, mentioned above, also deal in long-term securities. Institutions such as the building societies, development finance companies, insurance companies, the Zimbabwe Stock Exchange and the pension funds deal exclusively in long-term securities and, as such, form the bulk of the capital market.

The Reserve Bank of Zimbabwe regulates both the money and the capital markets.

TABLE 1: Assets of the Principal Institutions in the Money and Capital Market

	Dec. 1985	March 1986
Commercial Banks	$2062,6m	1930,8m
Accepting Houses	407,0m	358,9m
Discount Houses	140,3m	121,4m
Finance Houses	247,0m	263,6m
Building Societies	700,5m	704,8m
Post Office Savings Bank (POSB)	841,0m	874,2m
Reserve Bank	1 053,7m	1 094,0m
*Monetary Banking Sector	3 242,7m	3 125,0m

1

* The Monetary Banking sector comprises of the consolidation of the Balance Sheets of the Reserve Bank, discount houses, commercial banks and accepting houses.

GRAPH 1: Assets of the principle Institutions in the Money and Capital Markets: March 1986

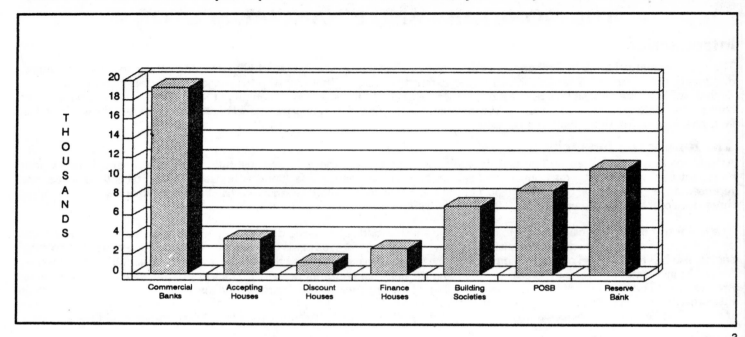

2

From the above Table and Graph it is clear that the commercial banks are the nexus of the banking sector holding approximately 50% of the total assets of the sector as a whole. (Note that the banking sector comprises all deposit receiving institutions including the Agricultural Finance Corporation, but excluding the Reserve Bank).

Contribution to Employment

Employment in this sector of the economy (finance, insurance and real estate) has risen from 1,2% of total employment in 1975 to 1,5% in 1983. In real figures 15 800 people were employed in the sector in 1983, reflecting a growth rate of 3,7% p.a. in employment over the past 20 years.

TABLE 2: State Participation in the Financial Markets

Investments	Equity	
Government Holdings		
BCCZ Ltd	47%	
Zimbank Ltd	62%	
Syfrets Merchant Bank Ltd	62%	(via Zimbank)
Scotfin	62%	(via Zimbank)
Syfrets Real Estate	62%	(via Zimbank)
Syfrets Corporate Trustees	62%	(via Zimbank)
Willis Faber Syfrets	51%	(via Zimbank indirectly)
Reserve Bank Holdings		
Febco	100%	
IPCORN	11%	

Contribution to Gross Domestic Product

The contribution to Gross Domestic Product in 1983 stood at $274m, representing 5,4% of GDP. In real terms the sector has grown at a rate of approximately 10% p.a. over the past ten years.

The rate of growth slowed down as the war intensified between 1977-79 and during the period of drought and recession in the domestic economy (1982-84).

Fiscal Contribution

The insurance, financial and investment companies paid a total of $16,3m in taxation in 1981. This represented 8,6% of total company tax paid.

Institutions in the Money Market

Commercial Banks

There are five commercial banks operating in Zimbabwe at present: five locally registered and one representative international bank. The locally registered banks are the Bank of Credit and Commerce, Zimbabwe Ltd (BCCZ), Barclays Bank of Zimbabwe Ltd, Grindlays Bank (PLC) Ltd, Standard Chartered Bank Zimbabwe Ltd, and the Zimbabwe Banking Corporation Ltd (Zimbank).

The Banque Internationale pour l'Afrique Occidentale (BIAO), a French bank, is the only international bank operating in Zimbabwe. Citibank NA (an American bank), the First National Bank of Boston and the Druzena Beogradska Bank from Yugoslavia all operated for short periods in the country in the early 1980s. The latter was only here during the building of the Sheraton hotel and conference centre, whilst the two American banks left due to the lack of international business.

In terms of the Banking Act (1964) commercial banks are obliged to maintain a paid-up capital and unimpaired reserve fund of not less than $1 million. They must further invest a minimum of 40% of their liabilities to the public in prescribed liquid assets (this increased from 35% on 31st June 1984), and must maintain balances equal to 8% of their demand deposits and 4% of their time deposits with the RBZ.

In addition the banks have entered into an agreement over the joint raising of interest rates paid on deposits, interest charged on advances and the levying of bank charges. The commercial banks, therefore, act as a cartel.

Commercial banking is concentrated in Harare where 77% of all deposits are held. The relative importance of this sector of the money market is underscored by the fact that 37% of the savings of all financial institutions, private and public alike, are held by the commercial banks.

BOX 1: Monetary and Financing Institutions Operating in Zimbabwe

Comercial Banks
Barclays Bank of Zimbabwe Limited
Bank of Credit and Commerce Zimbabwe Limited
Standard Chartered Bank of Zimbabwe Limited
Grindlays Bank p.l.c.
Zimbabwe Banking Corporation Limited

Accepting Houses (Merchant Banks)
Merchant Bank of Central Africa Limited
RAL Merchant Bank Limited
Standard Chartered Merchant Bank Zimbabwe Limited
Syfrets Merchant Bank Limited

Discount Houses
BARD Discount House Limited
The Discount Company of Zimbabwe Limited

Financial Institutions
Fincor Finance Corporation Limited
Grindlays Industrial and Commercial Finance Limited
Scotfin Limited
Standard Chartered Finance Zimbabwe Limited
udc Limited

Representative Offices
Banque Internationale pour l'Afrique Occidentale (BIAO)

The entrance of government into the commercial banking sector (principally through the purchase of Nedbank SA's 61% shareholding in what was then called Rhobank in February, 1981) was intially met with reservations from the rest of the sector. Private banking houses feared that the emergence of a 'Government Bank' might mean a transfer of all government accounts to that one bank, but this appears not to have happened. The entrance of BCCZ (in which government has a 47% share) into the Zimbabwean market, and the advent of the Zimbabwe Development Bank (ZDB) have shown that government is prepared to allow new institutions into the market and to invest in more than one bank in the sector.

The joint government and private sector holdings in institutions such as Zimbank and the ZDB will ensure that the private sector also benefits from the expansion of these government — controlled banks.

As yet the commercial banks have all concentrated on urban banking with little attention being paid to the needs of the rural sector. What little development there has been in the rural areas has been mainly at the growth points or through the provision of mobile units. Many of the institutions currently in the market feel that rural banking warrants special "development banking" attention and that they are not geared towards such an operation. The BCCZ entered Zimbabwe with a specific brief to function in the rural areas; to date this has not happened.

The commercial banking sector is the largest financial sub-sector (see Graph 2) accounting for almost 49% of the total assets of the banking sector in 1985.

GRAPH 2: Commercial Banks in Zimbabwe according to size of Assets as at December 1986

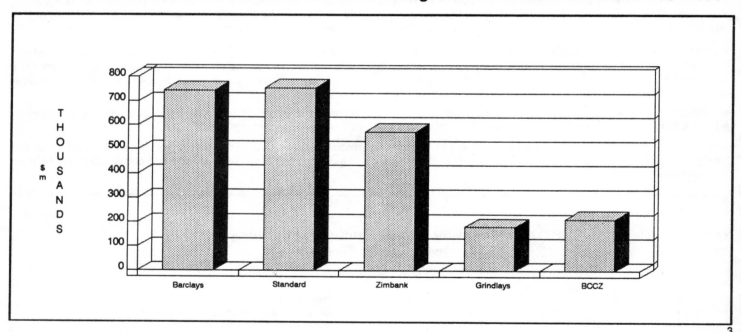

Although the above graph compares the asset structure of the banks on the 31st December 1986, it also accurately reflects their relative market shares.

Table 1 shows the components of a commercial bank's balance sheet. The percentages given are averages based on the Monthly Statement of Assets and Liabilities submitted by all commercial banks to the Reserve Bank.

The Merchant Banking Sector
At present there are four merchant banks operating in Zimbabwe:

— the Merchant Bank of Central Africa Ltd (MBCA) which was originally sponsored by Philip Hill Acceptance

Corporation, a South African wholly-owned subsidiary of a London company;
— RAL Merchant Bank Ltd founded in 1956 by the Anglo American Corporation;
— Standard Merchant Bank of Zimbabwe Ltd, a wholly-owned subsidiary of Standard Chartered Bank;
— Syfrets Merchant Bank Ltd (Sybank) which is wholly-owned by Zimbank.

TABLE 3: Balance Sheet of a large Commercial Bank

Assets		Liabilities	
1. Notes and Coin	3%	1. Demand Deposits	36%
2. Balances with the Reserve Bank of Zimbabwe	7%	2. Savings Deposits	21%
3. Clearing House Balances	2%	3. Time Deposits	24%
4. Balances with banks abroad	0,3%	4. Amounts owing to Reserve Bank of Zimbabwe	-
5. Money at call	0,7%	5. Clearing Balances	6%
6. Government paper (at book value)	13%	6. Amounts owing to banks abroad	1%
7. Other Investments (at book value)	14%	7. Bills Payable	0,2%
8. Bills of exchange	14%	8. Amounts owing to branches	-
9. Loand and advances to the Private Sector	24%	9. Other Liabilities	11,8%
10. Loans and advances to Government and statutory bodies	28%		
11. Balances held with branches	3%		
12. Bank Premises	2,5%		
13. Other Assets	0,5%		
	100%		100%

5

The merchant banks cater mainly for the needs of the business sector. Their principal business is in the field of bills of exchange, hire-purchase financing, medium-term loan financing, foreign market transactions (the financing of imports and exports), stock exchange transactions, portfolio management, company broking and corporate reconstruction.

GRAPH 3: Merchant Banks in Zimbabwe according to size of Assets: 31 December 1986

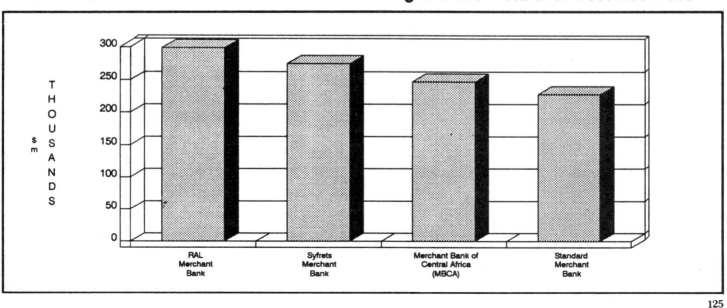

6

Where trade and loan finance is their main area of business, the merchant banks also finance a significant volume of government, AMA, treasury and parastatal requirements.

The assets of the merchant banking sector constituted 9% of the total banking sector in 1985.

Since June 1984 the banks have been required to hold liquid assets equal to 40% of their liabilities to the public.

The fortunes of the merchant banks are closely tied to those of their business clients — thus the decline in corporate profitability experienced from 1982-84 also affected the banks' profitability. In addition, the entrance of government into the field through Sybank, foreign exchange cut — backs, and the collapse of the new issue market have all adversely affected the merchant banking sector.

Discount Houses

The two institutions operating in the discount market in Zimbabwe are the Discount Company of Zimbabwe Ltd (DCZ) and Bards Discount House Ltd.

The discount houses are frequently referred to as the bankers to the banks as their major function is to provide liquidity for the banking system.

The discount house derive their name from their historical function of discounting trade bills. Treasury and AMA bills now form the major part of their business. Other marketable securities dealt with by the discount or money market are bankers acceptances, Government and Local authority stocks, negotiable certificates of deposit (NCDs), treasury bonds and AMA bonds.

By investing their money in treasury bills or in the shortdated bond market, the discount houses provide government with money for its 'ways and means' financing. The discount market also facilitates the expansion of the acceptance business conducted by banks and makes funds available to the hire-purchase or leasing companies. Finally, it provides the whole business community with a sophisticated market in short-term and highly marketable debt instruments.

GRAPH 4: Discount Houses : Share of the Market, as at 28 February 1986

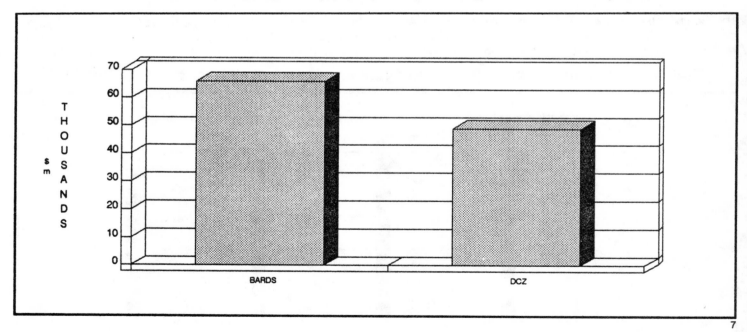

The discount houses do not advance money through loans or overdraft facilities to any of the banking institutions. Instead, their funds are invested in the debt instruments mentioned above (treasury bills, etc.) which in turn provide short-term cash balances to a wide range of institutions in the market.

In order to maintain the efficient operation of this short-term market, the discount houses are compelled to hold 85% of their asset portfolios in liquid form.

This discount houses accounted for 3% of the total assets of the banking institutions at the end of 1985.

Finance Houses

There are five registered financial institutions operating in the market:

— **udc** Ltd, whose holding company EDESA (Economic Development for Equatorial and Southern Africa) is based in the Netherlands;

— Fincor, incorporated in 1961, is based in Bulawayo;

— Scotfin, wholly owned by Zimbank, and is therefore government controlled;

— Grindlays Industrial and Commercial Finance Ltd, wholly owned by the Grindlays group;

— Standard Finance Ltd, wholly owned by the Standard Chartered Bank group.

Most of the funds of the finance houses are deposits from the public. 'Statutory deposits' (liquid assets) must be kept with the Reserve Bank of Zimbabwe and paid-up equity must exceed $0,5m. The finance houses can only accept deposits for periods longer than 30 days.

Although the original business of the finance houses was the provision of hire-purchase (HP) consumer durable financing, most of their business to-day is advancing loans to both the business sector and private individuals. Other financial services offered by this market include revolving credit advances for business, factoring, fixed-term deposits, and import financing arranged with external agencies.

The rise in interest rates and the application of higher sales tax on consumer durables has significantly cut demand for HP and leasing facilities. Export credit finance is a potential growth area for this sector provided external capital funds can be drawn into such an operation. At present foreign exchange and borrowing constraints are limiting the potential development of the sector which could, under favourable circumstances, serve the SADCC market as a whole.

GRAPH 5: Building Societies: Share of the Mortgage Market, 31 January 1987

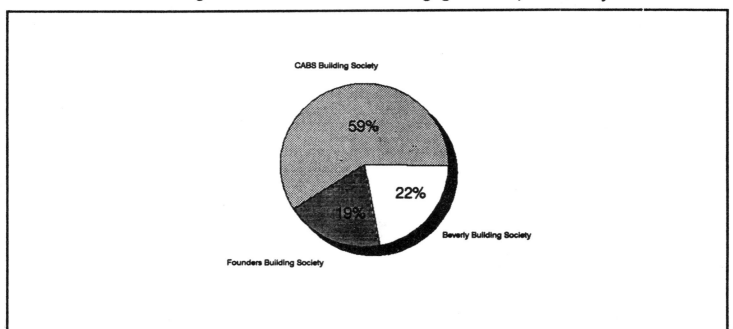

The Institutions of the Capital Market
Building Societies

Three registered building societies are presently operating within Zimbabwe: Beverley Building Society, the Central African Building Society (CABS), and Founders Building Society.

The building societies' funds derive largely from shares and deposits from the public. As with the banks the market is cartelized (i.e. interest rates are set jointly by the various institutions).

Since 1980 the three societies have been trading in treasury bills and to-day about 30% of their funds have been placed with the public sector. Their operations are strongly influenced by the State which, besides determining the liquid asset ratio (15% at present) also governs mortgage allocation, maturities and interest and sectoral allocations (e.g. non-residential property loans must not exceed 20% of total loans). Almost all the liquid assets of the building societies are in the form of short-dated government stock which effectively makes them significant providers of funds to government and local authorities. The building societies also play a major role in the provision of funds for the development of low-cost housing schemes.

The 9% paid-up permanent shares (PUPS) introduced by the government in mid-1986 were designed to channel more money into the building societies in order to finance housing. Of these funds, 25% has to be put into low-cost housing, and the remainder (after the statutory reserves, short- and long-term reserves) can be directed into low-density or commercial building.

By the end of January 1987 approximately $63m had been invested in 9% PUPS. About half of this was new money, and half represented transfers from the 11,25% PUPS (which were not tax deductible).

One difficulty in channelling funds into low-cost housing is the lack of clarity about the meaning of 'low-cost'. Government has not specifically defined it in terms of the value of house, or the borrower's salary or even in terms of house location. Clearly there is a need for more housing in the high density areas, and the money should be directed towards people earning below a stipulated minimum salary. Clearly also, the houses should cost less than a certain sum of money and, of course, the person should not own any other house at the time of negotiating the loan. However, because of the lack of definition, it has been left up to the building societies themselves to make the decisions about who gets loans, where to build, etc. Since July 1st 1986 one building society alone has advanced over $12m as 16 500 low-cost housing loans i.e. approximately $7 500 per house, which is the average cost of low-cost housing in Zimbabwe.

GRAPH 6: Building Societies in Zimbabwe according to Total Liabilities, 31 January 1987

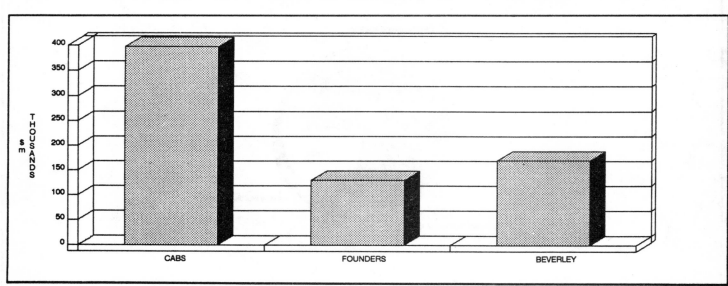

Much of the building of low-cost houses is at present being undertaken by the building brigades. This has the advantage of creating employment, but often means that the cost of the houses is higher than if built by commercial companies.

Another problem with the low-cost housing scheme has been the slow allocation of stands by the municipalities. From the building societies' point of view it would be far easier to loan money in larger amounts to either the municipalities or to commercial companies which would then undertake the building of several hundred houses at once. The houses would then be sold to the public. The advantages of such a scheme would be to reduce building costs and speed up construction.

The Post Office Savings Bank (POSB)
The POSB has recently displaced the building societies as the second most important deposit receiving institution (after the commercial banks) following its rapid growth in the past five years (see Table 4).

GRAPH 7: Savings Institutions: Share of the Market, March 1986

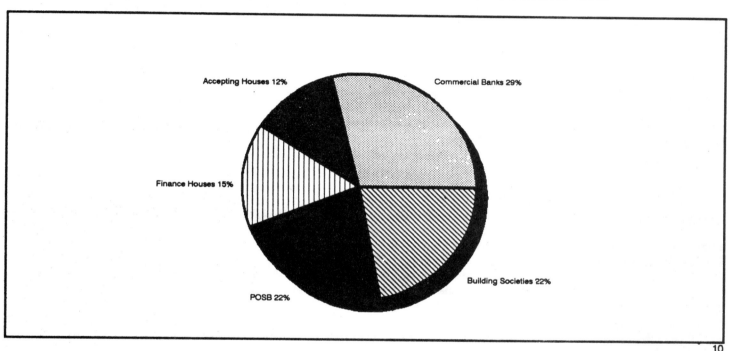

Accepting Houses 12%
Commercial Banks 29%
Finance Houses 15%
Building Societies 22%
POSB 22%

The entire POSB portfolio is invested in government and municipal paper with the exception of minimal working balances which are placed on call with the discount houses. The increased flow of deposits into the POSB since 1980 has assisted in providing a less inflationary source of financing for the budget deficit.

Insurance Companies and Pension Funds
At the end of 1982 there were 59 direct insurers (of which 19 were Zimbabwean companies), 8 professional re-insurers and 17 brokers (15 local companies) spread across all classes of the insurance business.

The insurance sector, with total assets of $772m in 1981, is a major source of funds for private and public investment, which include:

— approved assets: 60% of the assets of the insurance and pension houses must be invested in approved securities which include government stock, treasury bills, municipal stock, securities of public bodies (ESC, AMA, etc) and policy loans;

— mortgage bonds (commercial, industrial and farm) which are loans secured by a mortgage on immovable property;

TABLE 4: Growth in POSB Deposits 1975-85

End of	Deposits			Rate of Growth in Deposits
	Savings	Fixed	Total	
1975	116,7	36,7	153,4	-
1976	129,2	46,1	175,3	14%
1977	140,8	53,9	194,7	11%
1978	146,1	61,9	208,0	7%
1979	159,2	69,4	228,6	10%
1980	174,9	73,6	248,5	9%
1981	203,2	92,4	295,6	19%
1982	254,8	112,3	367,1	24%
1983	287,2	130,3	417,5	14%
1984	363,1	210,6	573,7	37%
1985	455,1	299,9	755,0	32%

11

The increase in deposits shown in Table 4 is largely due to the tax-free interest rates offered by the POSB which enables it to compete on privileged terms.

— debentures, which are loans to companies;

— investment in property;

— company shares;

— short-term money market assets.

Most insurance companies and pension funds would hold a certain proportion of their assets in the short end of the market to enable them to meet their commitments (such as the payment of claims or policies) without having to realize their long-term investments, and for their day-to-day operating expenses.

The pension funds and insurance companies play an important role in the operation of the stock exchange and the capital market in general, by channelling funds to both government and the private sector. In recent years these institutions have become increasingly significant in the provision of non-bank credit to the central government. There are presently about 65 pension funds operating in Zimbabwe with assets (in 1981) of over $450m.

The pension companies are governed by similar government regulations as the insurance companies, requiring them to invest at least 60% of their assets in approved securities. Their assets play a major role in the financing of private and public investments.

The Re-Insurance Market

The function of a re-insurance company is to take the risk of insurance off the shoulders of the insurance companies. The risks of insurance entered into by individual companies might be beyond their capitalization in terms of their share capital. In such a case the re-insurance company takes some of the risk.

In Zimbabwe the insurance market was entirely foreign controlled, and the government, in an attempt to gain greater control over it, launched the Zimbabwe Re-insurance Corporation, as a wholly owned state institution. Government's options were either to nationalize (as Zambia did) or to participate in the insurance market (as Kenya and Nigeria did). Government decided to participate through the formation of the Corporation. This gets 20% of all the business written by the local insurance companies, and in return it pays out 20% of the claims on the individual insurance companies.

Before the Zimbabwe Re-insurance Corporation was established, the insurers would look to their parent companies abroad for cover, thereby incurring foreign exchange costs.

BOX 2: Insurance Companies operating in Zimbabwe as at December 31, 1985

Direct Insurers:
A.A. Mutual Insurance Association Ltd
Alfa Insurance Co. S.A. NV. Ltd
Colonial Mutual Life Assurance Co. Ltd
Commercial Union Assurance Co. Ltd
Crusader Life Assurance Co. (Pvt.) Ltd
C.U. Fire Marine and General Insurance Co. Ltd
Doves-Croker-Morgan (Pvt.) Ltd
Eagle Insurance Co. Ltd
Friends Provident Life Office
Funeral Assurance Society
General Accident Fire and Life Assurance Corporation Ltd
General Accident Life Assurance Limited
Guardian Assurance Company Ltd
Heritage Insurance Company of Zimbabwe (Pvt.) Ltd
Incorporated General Insurance Ltd
IGI Insurance Company Zimbabwe Limited
Insurance Company of North America
Legal and General Assurance of Zimbabwe (Pvt.) Ltd
Lion of Zimbabwe Insurance Ltd
Lloyds Underwriters
The Manufacturers Life Insurance Co. Ltd
Mashfords Funeral Assurance (Pvt.) Ltd
The National Mutual Life Association of Australasia
NEM Insurance Co. (Zimbabwe) (Pvt.) Ltd
Norwich Union Life Insurance Society
Pearl Assurance Public Limited Company
Pearl General Insurance Co. (Pvt.) Ltd
Phoenix Prudential Assurance of Zimbabwe
Protea Assurance Company Ltd
Prudential Assurance Company Ltd
Royal Mutual Insurance Co. Ltd
Santam Insurance Co. Ltd
Shield of Zimbabwe Insurance Co. Ltd
South African Mutual Life Assurance Society
South African National Life Assurance Co. (Sanlam)
South African Trade Union Assurance Society Ltd.
Southampton Assurance Co. of Zimbabwe
Southern Insurance Association
Southern Life Association
Standard General Insurance Co. Ltd
Sun Alliance and London Assurance Co. Ltd
Sun Life Assurance Co. of Canada
Unity Insurance Co. Ltd
Zimbabwe Credit Insurance Co.
Zimnat Insurance Co. Ltd
Zimnat Life Assurance Co. Ltd

Professional Reinsurers:
Central Reinsurance Corporation Ltd
Cologne Reinsurance Co. of South Africa Ltd
Gerling-Global Reinsurance Co. of South Africa Ltd
Hollandla Reinsurance Co. of South Africa
Mercantlle and General Reinsurance Co. of S.A. Ltd
Munich Reinsurance Co. of S.A. Ltd
Reinsurance Union Ltd
Swiss-South Africa Reinsurance Co. Ltd
Zimbabwe Reinsurance Corporation

Brokers:
Associatied Brokers International (Pvt.) Ltd
C.T. Bowring and Associates (Pvt.) Ltd
Greig Fester Ltd
Eldridge Enthoven (Pvt) Ltd
Sedgewick Forbes (Africa) (Pvt.) Ltd
Willis Faber Life and Employees Benefits (Pvt.) Ltd
Willis Faber Syfrets (Pvt.) Ltd
Hudson Adams (Pvt.) Ltd
Minet Insurance Brokers (Zimbabwe) (Pvt.) Ltd
Zimbabwe Insurance Brokers (Pvt.) Ltd

The Zimbabwe Stock Exchange (ZSE)

The Zimbabwe Stock Exchange is a key component of the capital market in that it brings together the long-term financing needs of companies and the short-term investment needs of the market (of investors). Through the stock market, government and the local authorities can raise money for expansion and development by issuing new stocks and shares to the public.

To the members of the public, whether institutions or individuals, the stock market can provide a channel for investment, which should, in normal times, provide protection against inflation which is not provided by fixed interest stocks.

It should be noted, however, that money invested in the stock exchange is risk capital, i.e. the value of shares can go down as well as up.

Shares are bought and sold on the stock exchange by stockbrokers who are members of it. Stockbrokers act as financial advisers to their clients and carry out their orders as agents. Membership declined after Independence to the point where there were only two members left in 1984. However, in 1985, the government introduced new regulations to allow corporations, as well as individuals, to become members of the ZSE, a move which boosted its activity. Membership in March, 1987 had risen to six.

The main centre of trading in the ZSE is in Harare where the bulk of investment takes place. At present 56 companies are quoted on the Exchange, although this number can change . Government, municipal and ESC stocks with a nominal value in excess of $800m are also listed on the Exchange, as are a number of foreign companies.

Since Independence the state of the market has varied. Market values rose to a peak in December 1980, thereafter declining steadily to the lowest point in the past six years in 1984. Market capitalization (the total value of all shares quoted on the stock exchange) stood at $730m in March 1987, midway between the post-Independence high and low marks.

The Reserve Bank of Zimbabwe (RBZ)

The Reserve Bank of Zimbabwe is at the apex of the financial system, and was established in 1956 with a capital stock of $2 million as the Bank of Rhodesia and Nyasaland. Its major functions is to facilitate a high rate of growth while maintaining a minimum rate of inflation. This the Bank achieves through its control of the money supply and the application of monetary policy. Other Bank functions include the issue of note and coin, the control of the country's gold and other foreign assets, maintaining the government's accounts, and acting as lender of the last resort to the banking system.

The Functions of the Reserve Bank

The RBZ is the sole issuer of note and coin in the country. Although, in practice, there is little control over the issue of currency, the proportion of currency to the total money supply is usually in the region of 25%.

The Banks control of gold and other foreign assets incorporates control of the country's scarce foreign exchange resources (as laid down in the Exchange Control Regulations of 1961) in order to ensure adequate foreign exchange reserves to survive in times of difficulty.

The RBZ's function as banker to the government involves maintaining government deposits and raising finance to pay government debts. The weekly tender of treasury bills (approximately $16 million) raises money for government's short-term obligations, while the issue of longer-term securities finances capital projects.

Being lender of the last resort involves the periodic intervention in the money market in times of tight liquidity when the banks might be finding it difficult to meet their financial obligations to their clients. In such an event the Bank would accommodate the market through the re-purchase of its own paper. The RBZ would operate through the discount houses in the performance of its function as the lender of the last resort.

The control of the rate of inflation and the maintenance of a stable economic climate through the medium of its monetary policy is the most important of the Bank's functions. In the pursuance of such a policy the Bank can alter the bank rate, the Statutory Reserve Ratio, and the liquid asset ratio; it can also undertake open market operations; place direct quantitative controls on lending, or use moral persuasion.

The Reserve Bank has, since 1980, acquired more control of the financial system through the operation of monetary and financial policies, and as a result of the country joining international financial organizations such as the International Monetary Fund, the International Bank for Reconstruction and Development (commonly known as the World Bank) and the African Development

Bank (ADB). Borrowing from such organizations is conditional and it is the role of the RBZ to see that the conditions are met. The present PTA clearing facility arrangement, introduced in 1984, provided an additional role for the Bank which, in the interim, has the responsibility of operating this facility for the PTA region.

Recent Developments in Monetary Policy

Although the RBZ enjoys a degree of independence from government in the formulation of its monetary policy, the conditions in the money market are very sensitive to the overall political climate. The Bank will often find itself faced with the need to design its monetary policy in accordance with the political demands of the day.

During the UDI period the government maintained a policy of 'cheap money' designed to stimulate high levels of investment. The bank rate was kept at a constant 4,5% throughout the 1960-80 period. The balance of payments problems and the intensification of the war from 1974-80 mitigated against investment, resulting in a build-up of excess liquidity at the time of Independence.

The new political dispensation of 1980 was met by a policy of accommodation by the Bank. No restrictions were introduced and as a result the money supply increased by 34,2% in 1980. The total increase in domestic credit was over 30%, a dramatic rise over previous years. Net lending to the government accounted for 62% of this increase, while the private sector, still rather cautious in the early days of Independence, increased its lending by only 14%. Most of the financial requirements of the private sector were met from their internal funds which had accumulated over the years of sanctions and war.

In view of the excess liquidity prevailing in the money market, the expected inflationary pressures resulting from the end of the war and the lifting of sanctions, the RBZ had increased the prescribed liquid asset ratios for the commercial banks, accepting houses and building societies to 35%, 30% and 20% respectively in May 1979. Further moves were taken in April 1980 when a more stringent definition of liquid assets was introduced.

Escalating Demand

The immediate post-Independence period, as expected, was one of rapidly escalating demand. This was due to the general spirit of optimism that prevailed and the increased foreign exchange allocations to the business sector.

Consumer spending rose rapidly at the same time. This resulted from the introduction of the minimum wage, free primary education, free medical treatment (for people earning below $150 per month), the reduction of sales tax on all commodities, the removal of tax on basic food items, and the increased peasant sector earnings after the bumper harvest.

In an attempt to control the increased demand and to stimulate greater savings for investment purposes, the RBZ introduced a policy of restraint in 1981. The Bank rate was increased from 4,5% to 6% and the minimum lending rate for commercial banks from 7,5% to 9%. This had the effect of increasing all interest rates and thereby dampening demand. From May 1981 the statutory reserve balances held by commercial banks, acceptance houses, and finance houses with the RBZ were increased in order to limit the supply of credit. The measures were designed to discourage non-essential spending by consumers and to encourage saving in order to make funds available for financing the growing government budget deficit.

The deterioration of the balance of payments position and the continual rise in inflation necessitated another increase in the bank rate in September 1981 to 9%, while the minimum lending rate for commercial banks increased to 13% (see Tables 5 and 6 for Money Market Interest and Lending Rates).

Financing the Private Sector

Real GDP growth had increased from about 11% in 1980 to 13% in 1981, causing an expansion in the credit needs of the economy. Private sector borrowing increased largely as a result of the declining internal reserves which had seen the firms through 1980, necessitating a greater reliance on the banking sector. A large portion of the lending to the private sector was accounted for by a doubling of credit to the AMA for the purpose of funding the bumper harvest of 1980-81 (the AMA borrowed $175 million in the 1980-81 financial year). Financing the export stockpiles, which arose because of the transport difficulties experienced in 1981, accounted for another large portion of the credit expansion.

In addition, in mid-1981 the RBZ began to purchase government paper from the banking system in an attempt to free the funds of these institutions for private sector financing. The tobacco industry urgently required trade financing, and the transport bottlenecks had resulted in the stockpiling of many important export commodities, including maize. The Bank also started taking up a growing volume of commercial paper including AMA bills.

Slower Money Supply Growth

Money supply, having grown at 34% in 1980, rose only 8,7% in 1981. This was well below the rate of inflation (12,6%), and was as a result of:

- the pushing up of interest rates;
- the reduction in public sector borrowing;
- the running down of the country's foreign exchange reserves;
- the shift of private sector funds into long-term deposits;
- decreased net borrowing from the monetary banking sector by government.

The deterioration in the country's balance of payments position in 1981 led to an increase in official short-term foreign borrowing.

TABLE 5: Money Market Interest Rates: 1975-86

End of	Bank rate	Bills		Discount houses					
		Treasury[1]	Agricultural Marketing Authority[2]	Call money[3]	3 month bankers acceptances[4]	Negotiable certificates of deposit[5]			
						3 months	6 months	12 months	24 months
1975	4,50	3,55	4,26	3,00-4,85	4,25	4,15-4,25	4,35-4,50	5,00-5,25	6,80-7,10
1976	4,50	3,60	4,26	3,00-4,00	4,25	4,10-4,35	4,25-4,60	4,65-5,15	5,50-5,75
1977	4,50	3,55	4,06	3,00-3,75	4,25	3,60-3,80	3,75-4,00	4,25-4,50	5,25-5,50
1978	4,50	3,61	3,95	3,00-3,75	4,25	3,60-3,90	4,00-4,25	4,40-4,60	5,00-5,25
1979	4,50	3,57	3,95	3,00-3,75	4,25	3,50-3,80	3,75-4,15	4,60-5,00	5,10-5,55
1980	4,50	3,30	3,75	2,80-3,50	4,00	3,80-4,50	4,05-4,70	4,60-5,20	5,20-6,10
1981	9,00	8,18	8,70	6,50-7,65	9,50	14,00-14,90	14,00-14,60	13,25-14,50	14,00-15,00
1982	9,00	8,29	8,75	7,75	8,90	9,50-11,00	9,75-10,50	10,00-1075	10,50-11,25
1983	9,00	8,66	8,75	8,00-8,75	9,25	15,00	14,25-15,00	14,00-14,25	14,00-14,25
1984	9,00	8,40	8,75	8,10	8,75	9,50-9,75	9,60	-	-
1985	9,00	8,62	9,25	8,00	8,75	9,30-9,75	9,30-10,00	-	-
1986 Jan	9,00	8,79	9,25	8,25	9,25	9,50-10,00	9,75-10,25	10,25	-

12

1. Average rate of allotted tenders for 91 day bills.
2. 180 day bills issued every two weeks.
3. The range of rates paid during the last week of the month.
4. The buying discount rate.
5. The buying yield. The yield on negotiable certificates of deposit issued by different institutions varies and thus the rates represent the spread applicable to the relevant time periods.

Budget Deficits

The government's policy of redistributing income towards the lower income groupings in order to promote greater equality, continued throughout this period despite the country's poor economic performance. It generated large budget deficits in 1981 and 1982 which government hoped would be offset by inflows of foreign aid. When the expected aid failed to materialize large cutbacks in spending had to be introduced. In addition to the shortfall in aid, tax revenue from local companies and domestic spending declined rapidly in 1982 when the real GDP growth rate fell to zero from 13% in the previous year. The high levels of government spending ran down the government's reserves with the RBZ and absorbed the foreign exchange reserves. The RBZ was forced to increase its short-term foreign borrowings to meet the country's foreign debt repayments.

Since 1982 the Bank has had to mobilize funds to help finance the government deficit (in 1982 it provided nearly $200m to government in overdraft facilities). The economic slowdown did not bring down the rate of inflation, which continued to rise to the level of 14% in 1982.

Crisis levels were reached in late 1982 when the government was forced to devalue the dollar, cut subsidies on maize, reduce foreign exchange allocations and cut business and holiday allowances in an attempt to reduce the balance of payments and

TABLE 6: Lending Rates: 1975-86

End of	Commercial banks — Minimum overdraft rate	Accepting houses — Minimum rate on acceptance credits	Finance houses — Hire purchase rates2	Building societies — Mortgage advances1 — Residential property	Commercial property
1975	7,50	6,00	10,00-17,54	7,25	8,00
1976	7,50	6,00	10,00-17,54	7,75	8,50
1977	7,50	6,25	10,00-17,54	7,75	8,50
1978	7,50	6,25	10,00-17,54	7,75	8,50
1979	7,50	6,25	10,00-17,54	7,75	8,50
1980	7,50	6,00	11,00-17,54	7,75	8,50
1981	13,00	11,25	17,00-23,00	13,25	14,75
1982	13,00	10,65	18,00-23,00	13,25	14,25
1983	13,00	11,00	20,00-23,00	13,25	14,25
1984	13,00	10,50	20,00-23,00	13,25	14,25
1985	13,00	10,75	20,00-23,00	13,25	14,25
1986 Jan	13,00	10,75	20,00-23,00	13,25	14,25

1. Rates on loans over Z$12 000.
2. This covers the range of rates charged.

13

budget deficits. Government also tried to save money by cutting back the rapidly expanding civil service and slowing down expenditure on future capital projects.

The fall in interest rates in 1982 reflected an easing of the liquidity situation. Most of the money supply growth in 1982 was a result of the increased lending to the non-government sector. Lending to government declined, as did foreign assets.

Increasing defence commitments in the region in 1983 undercut government's attempts at thrift, which were further undercut by the decision to build the new conference centre.

The declining balance of payments position led to stringent measures being introduced in 1983, such as further cuts in subsidies, increases in sales tax, income tax and import duties and a broadening of the tax base by taxing lower-income workers. There was also growing concern over the government's indebtedness to the monetary banking sector. In order to remedy this, government increased the share of its stocks and bonds which the insurance companies and pension houses had to hold, from 22% to 44%.

Demand for credit remained sluggish throughout 1983, enabling the government to keep within the ceiling for the expansion of domestic credit that was stipulated in the IMF stand-by agreement. Despite reduced demand, the tight liquidity situation that resulted from the decrease in deposits necessitated a reduction in the liquidity ratio for commercial banks from 35% to 30%.

The mobilization of blocked funds, the expected inflow of funds from the external securities pool and the increased size of the budget deficit all led to the increased availability of funds in the monetary banking sector. Government borrowing from the banking sector to finance the budget deficit has been rising steadily from only $106m in 1982/83, to $197m in 1983/84, and $207m in 1984/85. The fiscal deficit is inherently inflationary, especially when financed from bank borrowings. The rate of inflation from 1983-84 averaged 18%.

In order to control the rate of inflation, the Reserve Bank raised the statutory liquid asset ratio of commercial banks and accepting houses from 30% to 35% in May 1984, and to 40% in June. These measures were aimed at restricting the expansion of the money supply in order to control inflation. The Bank also announced that it would issue bills which would be non-rediscountable and non-transferable, in order to prevent any secondary credit creation from taking place. In addition the interest rates and deposit level ceilings for the POSB were increased in order to attract money to the POSB rather than the monetary banking sector.

Total money supply increased by 22,3% in 1984, largely as a result of government borrowing from the monetary banking sector.

Stabilization

The government stabilization programme adopted in 1983 began to pay dividends in 1985 when the rate of growth shot up from only 1% in 1984 to 6% in 1985. The rate of inflation was cut from the 1983 peak of 18% to a level of below 10% in 1985; the current account deficit, which in its worst years was over $530m, turned into a surplus. Three years of stagnation gave way to economic expansion.

Inflation

The increased rate of growth brought with it some of the economic ills associated with periods of expansion. The mid-year wage rises coupled with increased fuel, energy and import prices began to exert pressure on the rate of inflation. The return to prosperity was also accompanied by increased rates of government spending which pushed the budget deficit up to $808m, $550m of which was to financed from the domestic capital and money markets. The combined effect of the faster money supply growth and the wage rises increased domestic demand in a period of severe import constraint, intensifying the upward pressure on prices.

As in the 1980-81 period the maize stockpile tied up a large amount of capital through the AMA, whose borrowings are expected to rise from $700m in 1984-85 to over $1 200m in 1985-86.

The Policy Options of the Reserve Bank

The RBZ, in the face of a liquid situation in the market and rising aggregate demand, had to decide whether to adopt an accommodative stance towards the market in order to allow growth to continue, or whether to tighten liquidity and face the danger of crowding the private sector out of the market. Tightening liquidity would control the rising levels of demand, but it would also force up interest rates which could push private borrowers out of the market. A more accommodative stance on the other hand, would maintain the high levels of liquidity but would, in all probability, drive the rate of inflation up.

The strategy chosen by the Bank was to 'crowd out' consumption spending by restricting bank credit for consumption purposes (hire-purchases etc.) while still making finance available for investment. In order to achieve this the RBZ raised the reserve requirement of the commercial and merchant banks from 8% to 10% and issued increased volumes of non-rediscountable and non-transferable Reserve Bank bills designed to mop up liquidity. These measures pushed the treasury bill rate up from 8,5% to 8,7%.

Slower Growth in 1984

Whilst the 1984-85 budget deficit and parastatal losses had been partly funded by converting the blocked non-resident funds into government bonds, this strategy could not be repeated. The increased levels of government spending in 1985-86, together with increased private sector demand led to tighter liquidity in 1986.

AMA borrowing in order to finance the 1986 bumper harvest will intensify the pressure on a tightening money market. It is expected that the GMB will be holding stocks of 2-2,5m tonnes by the end of 1986 tying up credit of around $400m and incurring annual interest of $50m.

Mounting Deficits

The budget deficit rose by 52% in the 1986-87 budget, with the gap between recurrent expenditure and normal revenues, including grants, having doubled in two years. This widening gap continues to put inflationary pressure on the economy. In addition the current account deficit, after being reduced from $533m in 1982 to $102m in 1984, is once again increasing. These deficits have caused an increase in the inflation rate from 9% in 1985 to 13,6% in the first half of 1986 and it is forecasted to reach 15% by the end of 1987.

The faster money supply growth needed to finance the budget deficit has the effect of worsening the inflation problem and forcing the RBZ to further devalue the currency in order to remain competitive in a period of deflation internationally.

Financing the 1985 and 1986 Budget Deficits

The $1,05bn budget deficit in the 1986-87 financial year was partly a result of the debt service burden which absorbed approximately 25% of total spending. The ever-increasing subsidy bill (11% of the budget) and the growth in education and defence spending are the other major causes. The 1985-86 deficit of $692m was financed without substantial recourse to bank borrowing; $211m was raised by foreign borrowing, $238m from institutional sources (pension funds and insurance companies) and $180m from the POSB. Bank borrowing (the only inflationary component) was estimated at $55m. The net result was a 6,6% growth in the money supply from June 1985 to June 1986.

Financing the 1986-87 budget deficit promises to be very different. Foreign borrowing is only expected to contribute $83m, and the non-bank sector (mainly the POSB and the institutional funders) $550m, leaving $417m to be raised from the money market. The potential for increasing money supply and market liquidity is therefore enormous. With the rate of inflation already estimated to reach 15% in 1986, such pressures can only push it up even further and jeopardize the shaky recovery that the economy is experiencing.

The relationship between the budget deficit and the rate of inflation hinges on two interdependent areas: the competition between the public and private sectors for investment resources, and the additional demand created by government financing its budget deficits from the monetary banking sector which is not met by an increase in supply. The competition for investment resources is only problematic if there is a shortage of liquidity on the market. Over the past six years liquidity has been relatively high, except in 1983 when the RBZ had to lower the liquidity ratios for commercial banks. In general, therefore, the lack of investment is not a result of the public sector taking funds from the private sector, but is rather related to the degree of business confidence and the availability of foreign exchange.

As regards the pattern of deficit financing, what is important is the extent to which public expenditures constitute productive investment which would increase supply and therefore satisfy the increased level of demand. Borrowing for this purpose would minimize the adverse effects of the high levels of government expenditure.

TABLE 7: Rate of Inflation and Real GDP Growth in the 1980-86 period

Year	Growth Rate	Inflation Rate
1980	11%	8,6%
1981	13%	12,6%
1982	0%	13,8%
1983	- 3%	17,9%
1984	1%	16,6%
1985	6%	9,8%
1986	*3%	*15,0%

*Estimates   14

Inflation and the Exchange Rate

The past six years have seen three consecutive rises in the bank rate in an attempt to curb rising demand, after nearly 20 years of interest rate stability. With the export market playing an increasingly important role in generating growth in the domestic economy, the control of the inflation rate becomes more and more essential. High inflation at home pushes up the prices of exports and forces the RBZ to depreciate the currency in order to maintain competitive prices. The continually rising prices of the past six years have resulted in the downward slide in the value of the currency. The high domestic inflation has been brought about by insufficient supply and rising costs (especially import costs). The shortage of foreign currency has limited the growth of domestic output, and in a situation of rising demand due to rising minimum wages, demand has outstripped supply, therefore pulling prices up (known as demand-pull inflation). The resultant inflation has brought about the depreciation of our currency and the consequent rise in the cost of imported raw materials.

The reasoning behind the RBZ's continual depreciation of the Zimbabwe dollar is that a cheaper dollar will stimulate the demand for exports. A cheaper dollar, however, also makes imports more expensive. The demand for imports, in a situation of rising domestic demand, has not abated despite their increasing cost. The result is even greater inflation (cost-push inflation this time) and greater demands made on the scarce foreign exchange resources. Increasing minimum wages have added to the cost-push pressures on domestic prices.

The Long-term Effects of Demand Management

The RBZ's strategy of suppressing local demand and depreciating the price of the currency abroad recognizes the crucial role of exports and tends to emphasize this role as a generator of growth.

It is the long-term benefits of this policy which have to be questioned. Zimbabwe exports mainly raw materials and commodities which are notorious for their price instability. The uncertain nature of the return places the producers of these products in a very precarious position and makes government support essential. The domestic mining sector, for example, would have little chance of survival without government financial and technical assistance while the agricultural sector is competing in a world market which is dominated by the EEC and the North American producers who can afford to subsidize their exports. The world market is therefore flooded with cheap food, making Zimbabwean products uncompetitive.

For the agricultural and mining sectors to generate the export sales that we expect of them, continual government support in the form of technical assistance, financial assistance (low interest loans, concessionary rates of taxation, etc) and government guaranteed prices will be necessary. These very policies, however, have been the cause of our budget deficits and high rates of inflation in the past.

A thriving domestic market could, in the future, absorb many of the products which are produced for export, without the constraint of having to compete against First World producers of food who are able to maintain low operating costs through their mechanization and economies of scale. In the face of high domestic unemployment, trying to match such production policies could worsen the situation.

References

1. Reserve Bank of Zimbabwe, *Quarterly Economic and Statistical Review*, Harare, June, 1986.
2. Graph 1 is based on Table 1.
3. Whitsun Foundation Report, *Money and Finance in Zimbabwe*, Harare, 1982.
4. Information taken from the Monthly Statement of Assets and Liabilities of the four Commercial Banks in Zimbabwe. (December 1986).
5. Information taken from the company reports of the relevant monetary institutions.
6. *ibid.,*
7. *ibid.,*
8. *ibid.,*
9. *ibid.,*
10. Reserve Bank of Zimbabwe, *op. cit.*
11. *ibid.,*
12. *ibid.,*
13. Central Statistical Office, *Quarterly Digest of Statistics*, Harare, September, 1986.
14. *ibid.*

Chapter 7
THE FOREIGN SECTOR

Introduction

The Transitional National Development Plan said the following on the relation of foreign trade to the domestic economy:

"The economy's foreign trade is closely related to the level of GDP. During 1969-1974 the average annual elasticity of foreign trade turnover to GDP is estimated to be 1,3. This means that to achieve an 8% growth rate, trade turnover would have to increase at a significantly higher rate of 10,4%."

An increase in the volume of exports generates the foreign exchange needed to purchase the vital inputs without which domestic industries cannot produce, let alone grow.

The importance of the foreign sector to the domestic economy is illustrated by tracing the historical linkages between Zimbabwe's foreign trade and its domestic growth.

Zimbabwe's Early Trading Relations

The modern history of Zimbabwe is integrally tied up with the question of trade links. Historically it was the demand for raw materials which led imperial Britain in the person of Cecil John Rhodes to acquire control of Zimbabwe's mineral and agricultural resources. The Rudd Concession gave Rhodes and the BSAC access not only to the mineral rights, but also to agricultural land which was to be used to produce agricultural exports using imported capital equipment.

The nature of the early trade links, designed almost purely to suit the needs of the "mother country", is highlighted by the continuous surplus of exports over imports until 1946 (see Table 1). This would support the contention that the early trade links between Britain and Zimbabwe were based on the extraction of raw materials from the colony in order to support the manufacturing industry of the former.

TABLE 1: Total Exports and Imports and Gross Domestic Product:

Year	GDP £ million	Exports £ million	Exports as % of GDP	Imports £ million	Imports as % of GDP
1930		7.43		7.52	
1935		9.00		6.41	
1939		11.80		8.93	
1940		15.16		9.33	
1945		17.95		12.51	
1946		21.27		20.32	
1950		48.25		58.87	
1954	169.6	49.53	29.20	80.36	47.38
1955	189.7	51.64	27.22	81.79	43.12
1956	219.9	54.31	24.70	83.57	38.00
1957	244.9	59.58	24.33	85.00	34.71
1958	254.8	56.12	22.03	86.79	34.06
1959	264.6	64.33	24.31	88.21	33.34
1960	280.5	68.88	24.56	90.00	32.09
1961	299.6	79.35	26.66	91.75	30.03
1962	316.7	79.67	25.16	87.14	27.51
1963	322.0	82.07	25.49	82.14	25.51
1964	332.2	133.47	40.17	108.24	32.57
1965	351.9	157.90	44.87	119.79	34.04
1966	378.8	97.53	25.75	84.71	22.36
1967	366.7	94.40	25.74	93.53	25.51
1968	396.0	87.86	22.19	103.87	26.15

1

The shortage of consumer goods brought about by the Second World War necessitated a greater drive towards self-sufficiency with local capital playing the major role. The services sector was expanded, the economic infrastructure further developed, and the state actively promoted import substitution.

This new policy led to greatly increased volumes of capital equipment which from 1947 generated large trade deficits (see Table 1)

From 1930-39 exports had grown at an annual average rate of 7,5%, and imports at 3,8%. In 1940-50 imports grew six-fold while exports trebled. This brought to an end the period of trade surpluses (exports exceeding imports) and from 1947 the trade section of the balance of payments account reflected a deficit balance (i.e. imports exceeded exports).

From the early days of Zimbabwe's participation in the international economy, gold and tobacco were the major exports. In the 1950s tobacco accounted for over 50% of the foreign exchange earned, and mineral exports 20%.

Trade Links

By 1938 Zimbabwe had already established trade links with 11 other countries outside Africa. Britain, having the advantage of the historical links, remained the major trading partner until 1969 when Japan temporarily took the lead. Other important trading partners in this early period included Italy, West Germany, France, Sweden and Switzerland. Trade links with the developed countries dominated Zimbabwe's trading patterns from 1938-65 (until UDI), as shown in Table 2.

TABLE 2: Trade Links with Developed and Developing Countries: 1938-1965

Year	Developed Countries		Developing Countries	
	Exports %	Imports %	Exports %	Imports %
1938	99	96	1	4
1948	92	93	8	7
1952	94	93	6	7
1953	97	95	3	5
1958	94	94	6	6
1963	94	91	6	9
1965	60	87	40	13

2

Detailed statistics on the direction of trade were not published (for obvious reasons) after the Rhodesian declaration of independence).

Regional Trade

Early trading patterns in the region were largely determined by the colonial powers which controlled the region. British colonies therefore traded with other British colonies rather than with neighbours which belonged to Portugal.

Zimbabwe joined the South African Customs Union (SACU) as early as 1903, together with Basutoland, Bechuanaland and Swaziland. This allowed goods to move freely between member countries although Zimbabwe was allowed to levy duties on a number of goods coming from South africa, including wine, spirits and beer. The SACU resulted in a large increase in the volume of trade between Zimbabwe and South Africa.

During the period of Federation the tariffs acted as a barrier to low cost imports from developed and developing countries alike. Trade with Britain, however, was not affected as Zimbabwe depended on Britain for the import of most of its machinery and technology.

Zambia was the single largest export market in Southern African until UDI. From 1938-65 between 50% and 65% of Zimbabwe's exports to Southern Africa went to Zambia (see Table 3). After 1965 South Africa took Zambia's place as Zimbabwe's major regional export market. In terms of imports from the region, South Africa has been Zimbabwe's dominant supplier since 1938.

The Effects of UDI

The overall effect of UDI on Zimbabwe's external trade was to strengthen trade relations with South Africa. (South Africa, Mozambique and Malawi did not impose any economic sanctions on Rhodesia.) The closing of the Beira and Maputo harbours

TABLE 3: Zimbabwe's Imports and Exports to Southern Africa: 1938-73

Year	South Africa Exports % of Total	Zambia Exports % of Total	Year	South Africa Imports % of Total	Zambia Imports % of Total
1938	37.7	62.3	1938	91.1	8.3
1948	28.4	61.8	1948	91.4	3.5
1952	47.7	47.0	1952	89.8	5.2
1953	45.4	49.8	1953	89.2	7.1
1958	95.2	—	1958	95.8	—
1963	94.5	—	1963	95.91	—
1965	20.78	63.6	1965	78.4	14.31
1966	25.2	27.2	1966	91.67	5.83
1967	73.8	12.6	1968	96.02	2.1
1968	64.4	25.4	1969	97.3	0.8
1969	65.9	24.2	1969	97.2	0.4
1970	65.9	23.2	1970	96.3	0.6
1971	66.5	21.8	1971	96.7	0.3
1972	72.8	11.8	1972	96.6	0.9
1973	76.2	8.1	1973	96.8	0.2

3

after 1975 meant that the distance to the sea doubled for Zimbabwean exports which had to travel through South African ports instead.

Initially the effect of sanctions was to increase the demand for, and production of, local goods. This stimulated the economy from 1968-75, but the shortage of foreign exchange (as a result of sanctions) in an economy heavily dependent on imports of machinery and technology, caused the rate of growth to slow down after 1975.

The Balance of Payments Account
An analysis of the balance of payments account (see Box 1) in the UDI period shows that the visible trade balance (total exports less total imports) was positive in every year, except 1968. The services account, on the other hand, remained in deficit over the entire period, showing the country's dependence on foreign services, particularly transportation.

The UDI period was also marked by a large outflow of financial (investment) capital. The production and services sectors were (as now) largely dominated by foreign capital which, as confidence in the economy declined, was not re-investing its income.

The capital account of the BoP reflects a net inflow of capital throughout the early period of UDI (up to 1976) with the exception only of 1966 and 1972. After 1976, with the intensification of the war, the trend reversed and the capital account recorded net outflows up until 1981. The overall position in the capital account would seem to contradict the negative trend in investment income, and can only be explained by the fact that while some companies with interests in Rhodesia were not re-investing, others recognized that large profits could still be made and were moving in.

The change in this trend after 1976 can largely be attributed to the closure of the Mozambiquan border, and the opening up of the Eastern front. At this point it became clear to most investors that Rhodesia was no longer a viable investment.

The Role of Foreign Capital in the pre-1980 Period
Zimbabwe entered the international arena in the late nineteenth century as a supplier of raw materials and has continued in that role ever since. The only change has been that Zimbabwe now supplies not only Britain but a range of countries. Over 90% of Zimbabwe's trade relations in the period up to 1980 have been with developed western nations. This trading pattern has been influenced by the pattern of foreign investment. Foreign capital inflows have been biased towards production for the profitable export market except in cases where production for the domestic market is more profitable.

An important consequence of sanctions was to increase the degree of overlap between industrial and financial capital, which concentrated the financial, industrial and agricultural resources of Zimbabwe into a small number of powerful monopolistic establishments.

BOX 1: Understanding the Balance of Payments Account
Part 1: The Current and Capital Accounts

The balance of payments account is a summary of a country's trade (imports and exports) with the rest of the world. It deals with merchandise imports and exports; services and income inflows and outflows; unrequited transfers; and capital inflows and outflows (see Table 8, page 148).

The BoP account can be divided into the capital and the current account sections: the capital account deals with long- and short-term capital flows while the current account is made up of goods, services, income and unrequited transfers. Merchandise imports and exports form the major part of the current account and incorporate the purchase and sale of goods, the sale of gold, re-exports (goods which pass through Zimbabwe en route elsewhere), and internal freight. The purchase and sale of merchandise is known as a country's visible trade.

Invisible trade refers to a country's services receipts and payments, income receipts and payments, and unrequited transfers. Zimbabwe's major service payments include the payment of shipping services (port dues and external freight), transport services such as passenger fares and port services, and the payment of holiday allowances. On the credit side Zimbabwe earns services income from tourism and passenger fares from the National Railways and Air Zimbabwe. The payment of dividends to foreign companies which invest in Zimbabwe, and the interest payments on our foreign debt are both part of income payments together with the remittances of former residents. Income receipts are very small in comparison and come largely from interest payments received by the public and private sectors and dividends received by individuals resident in Zimbabwe.

Unrequited transfers refer mainly to one-way transactions; i.e. gifts, donations, migrant workers' remittances, pension payments, etc. Official unrequited transfers are gifts to or from foreign governments.

The balance on Zimbabwe's services account is almost always negative, which is typical for a developing country. The services industry (shipping, air-freight, insurance, banking, etc.) tends to be the domain of the First World. The developing countries' economies are still focused largely on the extraction of raw materials and, in some cases, the processing of these raw materials. Being a landlocked country, Zimbabwe incurs large transport expenses which add to its services deficit.

Capital transactions represent long- and medium-term loans and transfers of securities or capital assets. The loans can be either long-term or short-term and can be negotiated by either the government (official) or the private sector.

TABLE 4: Volume and Value Indices of Exports and Imports and Terms of Trade: 1975-84 (1980 = 100)

Period	Volume		Unit Value		Terms of Trade
	Imports	Exports2	Imports	Exports2	
1975	119,6	107,3	48,0	56,8	118,3
1976	87,4	107,8	54,4	59,3	109,0
1977	80,5	102,4	60,0	61,7	102,8
1978	73,6	106,5	68,2	65,7	96,3
1979	72,6	105,0	93,3	75,5	80,9
1980	100,0	100,0	100,0	100,0	100,0
1981	123,5	95,2	99,5	110,6	111,2
1982	133,0	98,0	99,1	107,3	108,3
1983	111,5	101,5	116,4	121,3	104,2
1984	111,1	100,2	131,2	158,3	120,6

4

In order to assess whether we have improved our current account position in relation to previous years it is not enough to look at the current prices. The volume index (see Table 8) tells us whether we have exported or imported more physical items (i.e. bags of maize). The value index measures fluctuations in price levels. The increase in exports from 1983 to 1984 (from 1 174 to 1 484) does not in itself tell us anything. It does not indicate whether we have exported more maize or gold, or whether it is just that the price of maize and gold have increased thus giving us more money this year than last year.

The drop in the volume index of imports from 1983 to 1984 indicates that we imported marginally fewer goods in 1984. The drop in the volume of exports indicates that we exported fewer goods as well. The rise of export value of $374 million must, therefore, be a result of rising export prices. The value index for exports shows a 30% rise in prices (i.e. 121,3 in 1983 and 158,3 in 1984).

Thus the apparent improvement in export performance in 1984 was largely due to inflation. In real terms less was exported in 1984 than in 1983 (as the volume dropped). The major reason for inflated earnings from exports was that the Zimbabwe dollar fell by over 26% against the US dollar and by lesser amounts against other major trading currencies. This tended to inflate export prices quoted in domestic currency terms.

Import prices rose by about 13%, but the approximately 20% reduction of private sector import allocations, boosted by currency depreciation, resulted in a 15% overall improvement in the terms of trade (see Table 4).

Trends in the Balance of Payments Account in the post-Independence Era

For most of the UDI period Zimbabwe had surpluses in the current account; it was only following Independence that this account moved into deficit. The most important change after Independence was the increased import allocations which brought about a 37% increase in the volume of imports in 1980 and 23% increase in 1981 (see Table 5 which is derived from the complete balance of payments account given in Table 8). The new government expected an increased volume of exports with the lifting of sanctions, and so it increased foreign exchange allocations for foreign travel, remittances of company dividends and profits, and the importation of intermediate and capital goods. Instead of rising, exports actually fell by approximately 5% in both 1980 and 1981 (the 1981 level of exports was the lowest level since 1971).

TABLE 5: Visible Trace Account (Z$ million) 1979-84

Year	1979	1980	1981	1982	1983	1984
Imports	595	861	1059	1114	1087	1237
Exports	734	929	1002	998	1174	1464
Visible Balance	+ 139	+ 68	+ 57	− 116	+ 87	+ 247

5

The fall in exports was due to the 10,5% rise in domestic prices, the fall in commodity prices and world market demand, and increasing competition from other industrializing countries.

Export Composition

Table 6 shows the composition of commodity exports in the years 1978-84. Although the basic structure of exports remained the same in the first year of Independence, significant changes are evident in the proportionate shares of food products and manufactured goods. Food, beverages and tobacco (categories 0 and 1) increased from 28% in 1980 to 40% in 1981, following the bumper harvests of the 1980-81 agricultural season. Manufactured goods, on the other hand, dropped from 37% to 27%.

The major categories of exports were food products (15%); beverages and tobacco — mainly tobacco — (25%); minerals and metals (20%); fuels (1,3%); manufactured products (27%); and other primary products (8,6%).

The percentage share of the major exports (including gold) by SITC sections are shown in Graph 1, while the contribution of the three major sectors of the economy (manufacturing, mining and agriculture) to total exports is shown in Figure 1. The slight

143

TABLE 6: Exports of Principal Commodities by percentage of Total Exports: 1978 - 84 — in current prices

Categories	Years						
	1978	1979	1980	1981	1982	1983	1984
Food Products	19%	17%	13%	15%	16%	15%	13%
Beverages and Tobacco	18%	13%	15,5%	25%	24%	23%	23%
Crude Materials except fuel	23%	22,5%	21,5%	19%	17,5	18%	19%
Fuels and Electricity	1,5%	1,5%	1,5%	1%	1,5%	1,5%	1%
Oils and Fats	1%	1%	*0,5%	*0,5%	*0,5%	*0,5%	0,5%
Chemicals	1%	1%	1%	1%	1,5%	1%	2%
Manufactured Goods	30%	34%	37%	27%	28,5%	33%	33%
Machinery and Transport equip.	2,5%	2%	2%	2%	1,5%	1%	1,5%
Miscellaneous manuf. and commod.	4%	8%	8%	9,5%	9%	7%	7%
Total %	100%	100%	100%	100%	100%	100%	100%
Total $ (current prices)	558 661	645 365	787 526	888 067	807 144	1 025 708	1 271 070
Volume	106,5	105	100	95,2	95	101,5	100,2

6

difference in figures between Table 6 and Graph 1 is due to differences of classification (see explanation given in Figure 1 — the pie charts).

FIGURE 1: The contribution of the three major sectors to Export earnings according to different classifications (1984 figures)

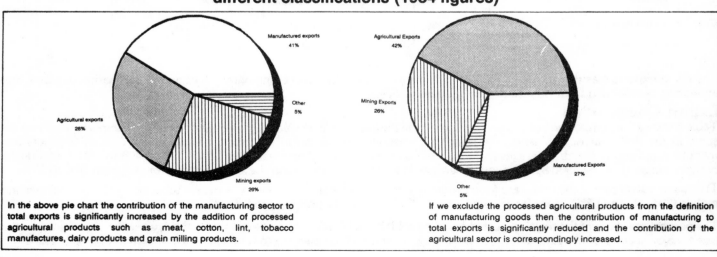

Manufactured exports 41%

Other 5%

Agricultural exports 26%

Mining exports 26%

Agricultural Exports 42%

Mining Exports 26%

Manufactured Exports 27%

Other 5%

In the above pie chart the contribution of the manufacturing sector to total exports is significantly increased by the addition of processed agricultural products such as meat, cotton, lint, tobacco manufactures, dairy products and grain milling products.

If we exclude the processed agricultural products from the definition of manufacturing goods then the contribution of manufacturing to total exports is significantly reduced and the contribution of the agricultural sector is correspondingly increased.

GRAPH 1: % Share of Major Exports by SITC Sector

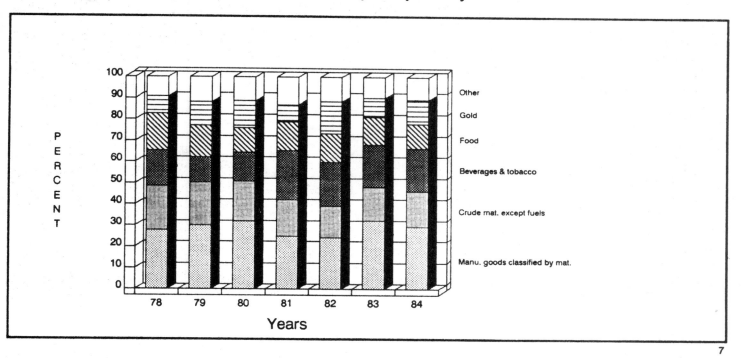

Import Composition

The major increases in imports (see Table 7) in 1980-81 came in chemicals, manufactured products, and machinery and transport equipment. (Note that total imports increased by 26% in 1981, from $809m in 1980 to $1 018m in 1981. So where proportions remained constant, as in the case of manufactured goods, the volume of goods imported would have risen considerably). The only decrease in imports came in food, beverage and tobacco, and in miscellaneous manufactures.

Despite the government's attempts to restrict import demand by introducing measures to curb domestic demand and to promote exports, the negative trend continued into 1983 with the visible balance deteriorating to *minus* $113,4m at the end of 1983. The combined effect of a 26% rise in imports and a 13% rise in exports resulted in a net balance of —$46m, the first adverse visible balance since 1968.

In 1975
107 tonnes of maize, or
16,5 tonnes of cotton   bought one tractor

In 1978
158,3 tonnes of maize, or
27,9 tonnes of cotton   bought one tractor

In 1983
275,7 tonnes of maize, or
27,9 tonnes of cotton   bought one tractor

In 1986
503,93 tonnes of maize, or
117,6 tonnes of cotton   bought one tractor.

Similar to developing countries world-wide Zimbabwe exports ever increasing quantities of raw materials in exchange for ever decreasing quantities of finished goods.

Table 7 shows that imports continued to rise in 1982 in both volume and value terms with the most significant increase being recorded in the machinery and transport equipment sector. Manufactured items comprised 78% of total imports in 1982, up from 74% in 1981 and 69% in 1980.

TABLE 7: Imports of Principal Commodities by Percentage of Total Imports: 1978-84

Category	1978	1979	1980	1981	1982	1983	1984
Food products	1%	2%	3%	1,5%	1%	2%	7%
Beverages and Tobacco	0,5%	0,5%	0,5%	0,5%	0,5%	0,5%	0,5%
Crude Materials except fuel	3%	3%	3%	3%	3%	4%	3%
Fuels and Electricity	23%	30%	24%	21%	16,5%	21%	21%
Oils and fats	0,5%	0,5%	1%	1%	1%	1%	1%
Chemicals	15%	14%	13,5%	14%	11,5%	14%	15%
Manufactured goods	17%	17%	19%	19%	14,5%	14,5%	15%
Machinery and Transport equipment	25%	23%	26%	32%	41%	34%	31%
Miscellaneous Manuf. & commod.	15%	10%	10%	8%	11%	9%	6,5%
Total %	100%	100%	100%	100%	100%	100%'	100%
Total $	403 691	549 265	809 398	1 017 694	1 081 787	1 061 619	1 200 668
Volume Index	73,6	72,6	100	123,5	133,0	111,5	111,1

9

Graph 2 shows Zimbabwe's imports (by SITC section) from 1978-84. From Graph 2 and Table 7 it is clear that the largest category of imports by SITC section throughout the period has been machinery and transport equipment (with the exception of 1979 when fuels and electricity was the largest single section). Petroleum fuels and products constitute the largest single import item, representing 21% of total imports in 1984. Chemical imports (the second major category together with miscellaneous manufactured goods) include items such as resins, medicinal and pharmaceutical products, insecticides, disinfectants and fertilizer material. Most consumer manufactures fall under miscellaneous manufactured goods which represented an import cost of Z$80,4m to Zimbabwe in 1984.

The 1982-84 Recession
1982 proved to be one of the worst years ever with regard to the current account balance, the deficit on visible trade being compounded by a large deficit on both services (a deficit of $192m) and factor payments (a deficit of $162m). The major component of service payments is usually shipment services which includes both port dues and external freight. Dividend payments and profit remittances of foreign companies investing in Zimbabwe form the major item of the category 'Income Payments' (otherwise known as factor payments).

The worsening balance of payments situation led the government to cut import allocations further in the 1982-83 period which resulted in a 16% cut in the volume of imports entering Zimbabwe in the 1983 period. Measures to depress domestic demand were also introduced in an attempt to control the rate of inflation, which together with the cut in import allocations, produced a zero growth rate for 1983.

1984 was the third successive year of drought which, understandably, increased the pressure on the balance of payments. Maize imports, further cuts in foreign exchange allocations, and the curb in foreign factor payments introduced in March 1984 were designed mainly to curb the large outflow of invisibles.

Table 4 lists the major components of invisible trade (see Box 1 for details of the composition of invisible trade) while Table 5 gives a summary of the balance on the invisible trade account over the 1979-84 period. This measures introduced in March 1984 included:

— a temporary suspension in the remittance of dividends, branch and partnership profits;

— a temporary reduction in the settling-in allowance of emigrants;

— the aquisition of the blocked external securities pool;

— the offer to convert blocked funds into long-term government bonds (effectively giving the Government of Zimbabwe the use of that money);

— the temporary suspension of all income remittances other than pensions, alimony payments and expatriate incomes approved by the RBZ.

GRAPH 2: % Share of Major Imports by SITC Sector

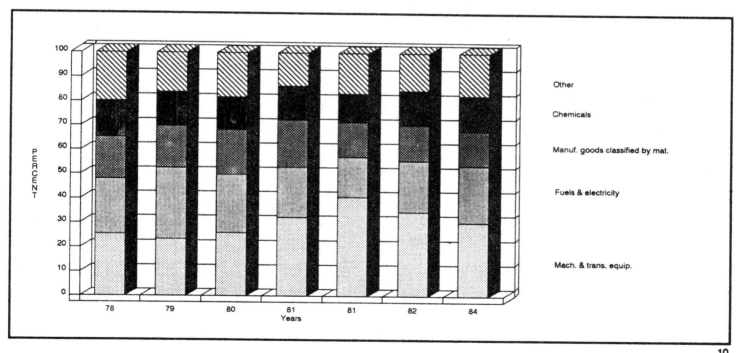

The combined effect of these measures was to move the balance of the current account in a favourable direction, reducing the deficit from —$454,2 in 1983, to —$101,9 in 1984 (see Table 8).

The decline in export performance in the first four years of Independence can be attributed to the following factors:

— a decline in the demand for asbestos, which fell by 50% in 1980-83, largely because of the world campaign against asbestos;

TABLE 8: Balance of Payments: 1979-84

	1979		1980		1981		1982		1983		1984	
	Cr.	Dr.	Cr.	Dr.	Cr.	Dr.	Cr.	Dr.	Cr.	Dr.	Cr.	Dr.
A. Goods, Services and Income												
Merchandise†	734,0	594,9	928,9	860,5	1 001,9	1 059,4	998,2	1 114,3	1 173,9	1 086,6	1 483,7	1 237,1
Export/Imports	645,4	549,3	787,5	809,4	894,6	1 017,5	817,6	1 081,8	1 027,3	1 056,2	1 277,0	1 199,4
Re-exports	3,7	–	6,5	–	7,3	–	20,7	–	20,2	–	22,3	–
Gold	66,6	–	115,2	–	76,3	–	140,5	–	98,9	–	189,6	–
Internal freight	18,3	45,6	19,7	51,1	23,7	41,9	19,4	32,5	27,5	30,4	24,8	37,7
Shipment Services	18,8	46,4	25,9	65,1	16,8	128,6	14,8	122,0	18,0	185,3	22,3	163,9
Port dues	–	21,7	–	21,0	–	30,3	–	33,5	–	35,5	–	40,1
External freight	18,8	24,7	25,9	44,1	16,8	98,3	14,8	88,5	18,0	149,8	22,3	123,8
Other Transport Services	24,9	39,3	38,7	51,4	31,2	52,1	54,5	40,3	60,8	56,5	71,2	62,3
Passenger fares	4,3	21,4	11,0	21,5	16,5	22,2	20,9	16,0	30,2	16,6	36,1	11,3
Port services	20,6	17,9	27,7	29,9	14,7	29,9	33,6	24,3	30,6	39,9	35,1	51,0
Travel	5,6	71,8	15,9	102,4	16,8	103,4	20,4	78,9	25,8	73,4	31,2	83,0
Business and holiday allowance	–	63,7	–	92,3	–	89,5	12,5	64,4	8,2	56,2	9,4	58,5
Tourism	5,5	–	15,7	–	16,6	–	2,0	–	3,0	–	6,1	–
Other	0,1	8,1	0,2	10,1	0,2	13,9	5,9	14,5	14,6	17,0	15,7	24,5
Direct Investment Income	23,4	42,0	26,7	50,0	33,6	79,2	35,5	95,3	39,1	92,2	39,7	14,9
National Railways	22,9	–	26,0	–	32,2	–	34,6	–	37,9	–	38,4	–
Dividends and profits of companies and persons	0,5	42,0	0,7	50,0	1,4	79,2	0,9	95,3	1,2	92,2	1,3	14,9
Other Investment Income	18,4	24,3	37,8	32,9	31,0	64,5	25,1	122,9	30,4	184,6	8,8	205,6
Interest: public sector	10,3	4,1	22,7	5,9	16,7	27,5	14,4	75,2	12,1	127,7	12,3	166,9
private sector	1,0	5,5	1,5	8,9	1,5	15,9	1,5	24,4	3,9	33,6	2,8	25,6
Dividends - persons	6,5	–	9,0	–	12,3	–	8,9	–	14,2	–	13,7	–
Former residents' remittances	0,6	14,7	0,6	18,1	0,5	21,1	0,3	23,3	0,2	23,3	–	13,1
Other	–	–	4,0	–	–	–	–	–	–	–	–	–
Other Goods' Services and Income												
Official	0,7	2,1	15,8	3,6	8,3	14,3	20,9	11,4	21,6	22,5	30,8	24,8
Private	10,8	51,7	15,2	55,3	19,9	74,3	27,4	82,2	28,4	92,4	33,5	103,3
Labour Income	0,8	23,4	2,5	23,5	0,2	3,5	0,4	2,8	0,7	2,2	0,6	3,0
Property Income	0,7	7,0	1,8	8,8	1,4	9,5	1,1	12,9	1,0	12,7	0,8	9,0
Other	9,3	21,3	10,9	23,0	18,3	61,3	25,9	66,5	26,7	77,5	32,1	91,3
B. Unrequired Transfers												
Private	29,7	**67,7**	33,0	110,5	47,7	133,2	50,7	147,4	73,0	187,33	125,3	183,2
Migrants' funds	0,7	**13,7**	0,3	23,9	0,4	26,6	0,7	30,1	0,1	30,8	0,6	23,0
Non-commercial remittances	7,2	**0,4**	6,0	0,8	0,5	–	1,7	–	–	–	–	–
Pensions	5,1	13,5	3,5	29,7	2,6	37,3	2,5	54,4	2,7	64,9	3,2	71,3
Other	12,2	13,1	21,1	17,2	25,8	15,4	23,5	12,0	52,7	41,5	100,2	38,7
Other Goods' Services and Income												
Official	0,7	2,1	15,8	3,6	8,3	14,3	20,9	11,4	21,6	22,5	30,8	24,8
Private	10,8	51,7	15,2	55,3	19,9	74,3	27,4	82,2	28,4	92,4	33,5	103,3
Labour Income	0,8	23,4	2,5	23,5	0,2	3,5	0,4	2,8	0,7	2,2	0,6	3,0
Property Income	0,7	7,0	1,8	8,8	1,4	9,5	1,1	12,9	1,0	12,7	0,8	9,0
Other	9,3	21,3	10,9	23,0	18,3	61,3	25,9	66,5	26,7	77,5	32,1	91,3
Official	–	–	37,1	–	68,9	6,4	38,6	4,2	71,7	16,1	117,8	8,0
Government	–	–	33,5	–	59,2	–	32,3	4,0	64,0	–	117,8	–
Non-commercial transactions	–	–	3,6	–	9,2	–	6,3	–	7,7	7,2	–	–
Other	–	–	–	–	0,5	6,4	–	0,27	–	8,9	–	8,0
Net balance on current account	–	73,9	–	156,7	–	439,3	–	532,8	–	454,2	–	101,9
C. Capital Account												
Government	128,6	10,6	33,0	54,6	150,7	46,3	257,6	99,1	267,5	77,9	302,5	150,9
Other public authorities	0,5	6,9	0,7	3,7	57,9	2,2	192,2	2,8	317,1	225,3	171,3	80,0
Private transactions including statistical discrepency	81,5	19,4	126,5	26,1	220,4	70,3	339,5	169,0	98,2	80,9	99,0	75,7
Net balance on capital account	173,7	–	75,8	–	310,2	–	518,4	–	298,7	–	266,2	–
Net balance on current and capital account	98,8	–	–	80,9	–	129,1	–	14,4	–	155,5	164,3	–

— the decline in demand for nickel, chrome and steel;

— the drop in meat exports as a result of the spread of foot and mouth disease in some parts of the country;

— the rise in domestic demand due to rising money wages which directed potential exports to the domestic market;

— Zimbabwe's manufactured exports to SA have been constrained by the size of the preferential quotas established in the trade agreement with SA. More recently (since 1984) the decline in the value of the SA rand had made Zimbabwe's exports less competitive there (i.e. local goods are now cheaper than Zimbabwean goods).

— traditional exports such as coffee, sugar and beef have been restricted by quotas in international agreements;

— transport difficulties in Mozambique.

1984 saw a recovery in the performance of both metals and manufactured products. Other than maize, the demand for agricultural products also increased. These increases were largely due to the world economic recovery, the easing of the drought, the depreciation of the Zimbabwe dollar and the introduction of the Export Revolving Fund. (For more details on the Export Revolving Fund see Box 3 on page 93 in Chapter 4 — the Manufacturing Sector).

GRAPH 3: Foreign Trade: 1978-86

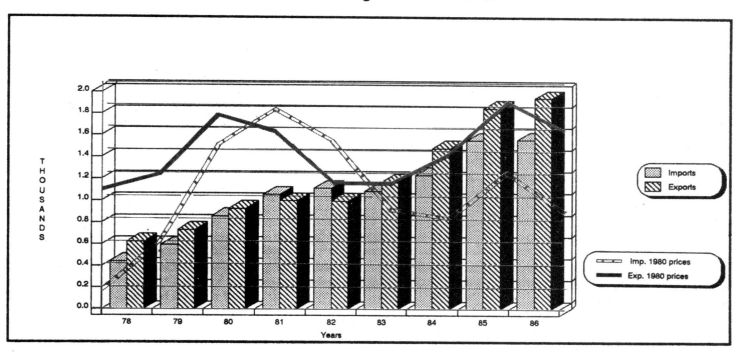

The post-1984 Recovery

Graph 3 shows a marked improvement in the current account balance since 1983. The solid line on the graph indicates the value of exports at 1980 (constant) prices while the dotted line indicates the value of imports at 1980 (constant) prices. Zimbabwe's exports in 1985, including gold sales, are estimated to be in the region of $1 767m (23,5% higher in money terms, than 1984) while imports are estimated at $1 447m. Unmanufactured tobacco was the largest single contributor to export earning in 1985 (30,5% of total). Maize exports were constrained by rising competition from other countries in the region such as Malawi and Kenya. During the 1985-86 marketing year, 285 000 tonnes of maize were exported, of which 200 000 were sold to South Africa. Although the visible trade account has registered a healthy surplus (see Graph 3) provisional figures indicate that the overall current account will register a deficit of approximately $145m due to rising service payments. (See Table 9 for the rising deficit balance on invisible trade; Table 9 has been drawn from figures given in Table 8).

Expressed in SDRs (Special Drawing Rights — the IMF currency) both exports and imports have declined from their 1981-82 peaks. Graph 4 indicates that the buying power of exports in 1986 was little different from the 1980 level (despite the dramatic rise of the Zimbabwe dollar value of exports) while the economy's import capacity fell by a third from its 1982 peak (see Graph 5).

TABLE 9: Invisible Trade Account: 1979-84 (Z$m)

Year	1979	1980	1981	1982	1983	1984
Receipts	132,3	246,1	274,2	287,9	368,8	500,6
Payments	345,3	471,2	656	704,6	910,3	849,1
Balance on Invisible Account	- 213	- 225	- 382	- 417	- 542	- 349

13

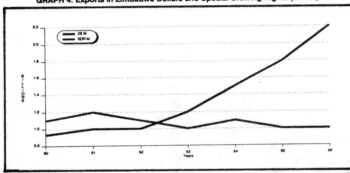

GRAPH 4: Exports in Zimbabwe Dollars and Special Drawing Rights (SDR's)

14

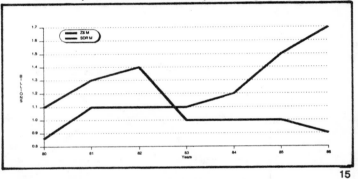

GRAPH 5: Imports in Zimbabwe Dollars and Special Drawing Rights (SDR's)

15

The current account will, however, remain in deficit due to the rising deficit on invisibles. Graph 3 shows that despite the substantial rise in merchandise trade in Zimbabwe dollar terms (at current prices), the volume of trade actually declined in 1986 in real terms (i.e. at constant 1980 prices).

Manufactured goods earned the country 28% of total export earnings in 1985 and 24% of total export earnings in the first nine months of 1986. On the import side machinery and transport equipment accounted for 30% of total imports for the years 1982-85 and closer to 40% in 1986.

Paying for the Deficits

The deterioration of the current account of the balance of payments which plunged the entire balance of payments account into deficit in 1980-83, necessitated a dramatic increase in foreign borrowing from a level of $353,3 million in 1979 to a new high of $1 437,7 million in 1984 (see Table 10). The rapid rise in foreign borrowing began during the last few years of the war (1978-80) and continued after 1980 as the new government borrowed externally in order to finance both the reconstruction programmes and its programme of social reforms. The new debt was increasingly financed from private and commercial sources with short repayment periods. In addition Zimbabwe made use of the International Monetary Fund facilities drawing SDR 175m under a stand-by arrangement, SDR 56m under the Compensating Financing Facility, which is specifically for countries which experience a temporary decline in export earnings due to crop failures, etc., and a further SDR 2m from tbe Buffer Stock Facility which provides loans to countries wanting to finance commodity stocks.

The Zimcord conference held in March 1981 pledged aid of nearly US$2,2 billion to Zimbabwe. By the end of 1984 less than a fifth of this had been disbursed. The reasons for the slow rate of disbursement include:

— lack of adequate co-ordination between government ministries leading to confusion about the functions of different branches of government and a lack of information on what money was available;

150

— a poor costing of projects and lack of proper project management;
— the need within aid agencies to refer minor problems to their head offices;
— the reluctance of aid agencies to use local expertise;
— the insistence by these agencies on international competitive bidding.

TABLE 10: Domestic and Foreign Borrowing 1975-84

Year	Domestic Borrowing	Foreign Borrowing	Total
1975	601,8	93,8	695,6
1976	710,4	78,1	788,5
1977	779,4	88,5	867,9
1978	926,0	223,8	1149,8
1979	1129,0	353,3	1482,3
1980	1428,5	414,8	1843,3
1981	1584,4	514,3	2098,6
1982	1639,9	841,4	2481,3
1983	1866,4	986,6	2853,0
1984	2309,0	1437,7	3746,7
1985	2812,4	1828,9	4641,3
1986	3087,7	2172,1	5259,8

16

Zimbabwe's debt-servicing obligations from 1987-90 have been estimated at Z$850m — Z$900m annually. Based on an estimate for export earnings at $2,8bn in 1987 the debt-service ratio (debt-service payments as a proportion of export earnings) will be around 32%. With debt-servicing consuming such a large proportion of Zimbabwe's export earnings the likelihood of increasing import allocations to anywhere near the required level over the next four years is very slim.

The Direction of Trade (Zimbabwe's major trading partners)

The period before UDI was one in which the United Kingdom dominated Zimbabwe's import and export trade. Up to 50% of our exports were sold to the UK and more than 50% of our imports came from there. The pattern ever since has been one of increasing diversification in both import and export markets, with Zimbabwe no longer being dependent upon a single market.

Export Trade

Table 11 divides export trade into three categories: trade with Africa, trade with the western industrialised countries, and trade with other countries (which includes developing countries and a small but growing volume of trade with socialist countries).

Trade with South Africa has dominated African trade ever since UDI. The pattern changed in 1985 when South Africa slipped into second place in the export market, buying only 11,4% of total exports.

SADCC trade, after remaining virtually constant from 1981-84, increased slightly in 1985 and even further in 1986. Imports from Zambia in 1985 increased by 28%, purchases from Botswana by 6,5%, while imports from Mozambique and Malawi declined. Commodity aid programmes under which Zimbabwe could successfully tender for supply contracts helped to increase the overall level of exports to SADCC countries. (See Box 3 on SADCC for details on the aims and major project areas of SADCC).

The declining export trade with South Africa appears to have been compensated for by an increasing volume of trade with industrialized countries (from 49% to 52%) and socialist countries. Trade within the PTA (see Box 4) also appears to have declined, from 15% in 1982 to 12% in 1984.

Trade with the industrialized countries has been increasing steadily over the past five years, with the UK in 1985 having taken over as Zimbabwe's major trading partner. Trade with Italy has also been increasing steadily while trade with the USA and West

Germany has remained constant. The importance of our trade with the industrialized world is illustrated by the fact that over half our present export trade is with this block of nations and that four of our five largest trading partners are from the industrialized countries. Zimbabwe's trade with EEC countries is governed by the terms of the Lome Convention (see Box 2 for details).

Table 12 indicates that South Africa has moved back into being Zimbabwe's biggest export market in 1986, buying 15,7% of exports and supplying 20% of imports.

TABLE 11: Direction of Zimbabwe's Export Trade 1981-85 (%)

Country/Region Exported to:	1981	1982	1983	1984	1985
1. Africa	34,09	32,14	32,94	30,54	n.a.
of which - South Africa	21,64	17,07	18,72	18,27	11,4
SADCC	10,22	10,99	10,39	10,47	N.A.
PTA (incl. SADCC)	12,45	15,07	14,22	12,27	N.A.
2. Industrialised Western Nations	46,92	49,76	52,85	52,33	n.a.
of which: West Germany	8,22	8,0	7,73	8,59	9,8
U.S.A.	7,86	7,88	6,7	6,21	7,9
Britain	6,90	9,53	11,64	12,79	12,9
Italy	4,96	4,43	5,17	5,06	6,2
3. Other Nations (including developing and socialist countries)	18,49	18,1	14,24	17,13	n.a.
Total	100%	100%	100%	100%	100%

17

NOTES:
1. All figures in percentages of total exports for that year.
2. Data for years 1980 - 84 have been extracted from the Statistical Yearbook published by the CSO. 1985 data is from the RAL Executive Guide to the Economy.

TABLE 12: Major Trading Partners

$ million	EXPORTS		IMPORTS	
	1985	Jan-Sep 1986	1985	Jan-Aug 1986
South Africa	166,5	184,0	273,2	217,4
U.S.A.	125,8	79,7	146,7	65,1
U.K.	200,3	175,7	151,1	127,5
West Germany	153,4	101,6	100,5	109,5
Japan	71,4	63,6	56,4	49,9
Italy	91,5	80,8	43,8	31,7

18

Import Trade

The western industrialized countries form the single largest block from which Zimbabwe imports goods, with the USA predominating. The volume of import trade with the UK has remained relatively constant since Independence (with the exception of 1982), while imports from the USA have been increasing steadily from the 1981 level of $74,4m (7,3% of import trade) to the 1985 level of $184,9m (12,3% of import trade).

BOX 2: Zimbabwe and the Lomé Convention

Zimbabwe first joined the ACP (Asia, Caribbean, Pacific) group of countries in 1981 and has benefited from the EEC's aid to this group through the Lomé Convention. Since Independence the type of aid received through Lomé has included:
— reconstruction of rural infrastructure;
— the promotion of agricultural extension services;
— the construction of rural health clinics;
— the importation of food items;
— commodity imports;
— the construction of the Veterinary Science faculty at the University.

In the agricultural field Zimbabwe has been allocated a sugar quota of 25 000 tonnes and a beef quota of 8 100 tonnes. The outbreak of foot and mouth disease in some parts of Zimbabwe prevented the country from immediately taking up the beef quota, but by September 1985, beef exports to the EEC were underway.

The EEC also provide an export stabilization facility (Stabex) which guarantees member countries a basic minimum price for their exports of raw materials to the EEC (i.e. it operates in much the same way as the producer prices for agricultural commodities within Zimbabwe). Most of Zimbabwe's exports are, however, not affected by the scheme with the exception of iron and steel which was introduced in the Lomé III Convention, signed in December 1984.

BOX 3: The Southern African Development Co-ordination Conference (SADCC)

SADCC was formed in Lusaka in April 1980 primarily in order to reduce the dependence of Southern African countries on South Africa. The member countries are Angola, Botswana, Lesotho, Malawi, Mozambique, Swaziland, Tanzania, Zambia and Zimbabwe. SADCC has isolated three major areas for co-operation between member states and has allocated primary responsibility for each of these areas to a different member state: Mozambique has been charged with the task of co-ordinating the use and rehabilitation of the existing transport and communication network; Zimbabwe is in the process of working out a food security plan; while Tanzania has been given responsibility for harmonising industrial development.

Because of the landlocked nature of most of the member countries of SADCC and the dependence on South Africa for almost all import and export traffic, a special commission was established to look into this area, the Southern African Transport and Communications Commission (SATCC) which is being co-ordinated by Mozambique. The major task of SATCC is the establishment and financing of additional regional transport facilities with a view towards breaking the dependence on South Africa. The Botswana-Zambia road, the Swaziland earth station for satellite telecommunications, and the rehabilitation of the Beira harbour are examples of projects undertaken by SATCC. In all, 120 projects have been identified.

Zimbabwe's special responsibility is in the area of food security, with the major priorities being to deal with drought in the region, and to adopt long-term measures designed to improve productivity, storage capacity and distribution. Projects which have been proposed include the development of:
— an early warning system for drought;
— regional resource information systems through regular workshops, seminars and courses;
— an inventory of agricultural resource bases;
— food processing technology;
— food reserves for the region;
— post-harvest loss reductions;
— a marketing infrastructure.

Tanzania's task in harmonising industrial development is essentially aimed at reaping the benefits of economies of scale by developing industries which serve the whole region instead of duplicating industries in member countries.

Zimbabwe's exports to the SADCC region have increased from Z$96m in 1982 to Z$146m in 1984, while imports have remained relatively constant at around Z$80m. Zimbabwe's most important trading partner in SADCC is Botswana accounting for 42% and 46% of imports and exports respectively, followed by Zambia, accounting for 29% of exports and 37% of imports in 1984.

TABLE 13: Direction of Zimbabwe's Import Trade 1981-85
(in percentages)

Country/Region Imported from:	1981	1982	1983	1984	1985
1. Africa	35,23	29,69	32,64	25,88	n.a.
of which - South Africa	24,78	22,13	24,48	19,3	18,3
SADCC	7,75	7,56	8,16	6,58	n.a.
2. Industrialised Western Countries	45,85	54,57	48,62	48,9	n.a.
of which: Britain	10,02	14,97	11,46	11,95	10,1
U.S.A.	7,31	9,57	9,46	9,29	12,3
West Germany	7,25	8,19	7,35	6,86	6,8
Japan	6,05	5,21	4,75	5,27	3,8
3. Other Nations (including developing and socialist countries)	18,92	15,75	18,89	25,22	
Total	100%	100%	100%	100%	100%

19

NOTE: 1. All figures in percentages calculated as proportion of total imports.
　　　　2. Data extracted from the same sources as table 2.

BOX 4: The Preferential Trade Area (PTA)

The PTA was formed in 1982 by a group of 18 Eastern and Southern African countries in an attempt to reduce dependence on the industrialized countries and to promote greater economic co-operation among African states. The PTA is not only concerned with trade but hopes to promote co-operation in the areas of transport and communication, agriculture, natural resources and monetary affairs. Since its formation 15 countries have ratified the PTA treaty: Burundi, Rwanda, Comoros, Djibouti, Malawi, Mauritius, Lesotho, Ethiopia, Kenya, Somalia, Uganda, Tanzania, Swaziland, Zambia and Zimbabwe. Countries which have not yet ratified the treaty but are expected to join are: Botswana, Angola, Mozambique, the Seychelles and Madagascar.

The PTA aims at a gradual reduction and eventual elimination of customs duties and non-tariff barriers within member states. Preferential treatment applies only to goods originating from within member states which are produced by companies under local management and with majority local ownership (i.e. 51% of the shares must be locally owned). The restrictions on participation by foreign-owned corporations is in line with the PTA's emphasis on promoting self-reliance, but in order to allow for a period of transition the restrictions will be imposed gradually. In the case of Zimbabwe, within the first two years of the treaty a local ownership minimum of 30% applies, rising to 40% for the following two years and 51% at the end of the fifth year.

Zimbabwe's trade with PTA member states has remained relatively stable with exports being in the region of Z$65m and imports Z$40m in the years 1982-84. The historical links which most PTA member states have with industrialized countries and their consequent need for foreign exchange has acted as a constraint on the development of intra-PTA trade. Commodity import aid schemes which make available foreign exchange to import from specified sources only (usually from the country giving the aid) have not helped matters at all.

In order to overcome the foreign exchange constraint the PTA established a PTA Clearing House (based at the RBZ) in order to facilitate the use of national currencies in intra-PTA trade. Only the net balance at the end of a transactions period will be settled in foreign exchange. The clearing facility came into operation on 1st February, 1984 (the transactions period is two calendar months). At the end of each two month transactions period the net debtor/creditor balance is converted to UTAPA, the official unit of account for the PTA. The UTAPA is equivalent to an SDR, and final settlement is made through the Federal Reserve Bank, New York. Member states are thus able to exchange their UTAPA for hard currencies where they are in surplus, or sell hard currency in exchange for UTAPA where they are in deficit in order to settle their account with the Clearing House.

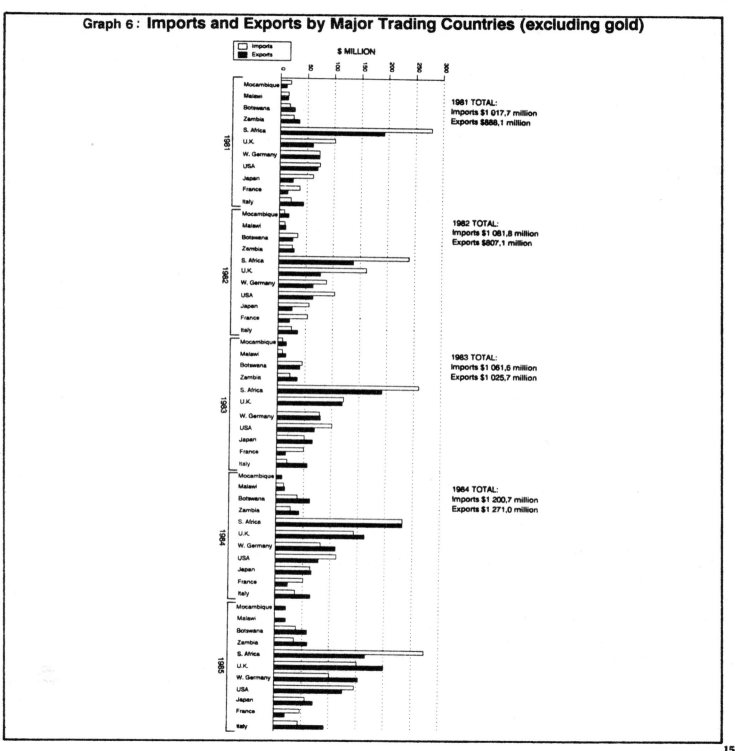

Graph 6 : **Imports and Exports by Major Trading Countries (excluding gold)**

Imports
Exports

$ MILLION

1981 TOTAL:
Imports $1 017,7 million
Exports $888,1 million

1982 TOTAL:
Imports $1 081,8 million
Exports $807,1 million

1983 TOTAL:
Imports $1 061,6 million
Exports $1 025,7 million

1984 TOTAL:
Imports $1 200,7 million
Exports $1 271,0 million

Although imports from South Africa have been decreasing, it remains the major partner in import trade. Trade with the rest of Africa equals only one third of imports from SA. Trade with African countries other than those in the SADCC or South Africa are not given in published official statistics which implies that the volume of this trade is even smaller than the 0,03% of import trade with Swaziland. Trade with socialist countries (Bulgaria, China, Romania and Yugoslavia) represented 1,5% of total imports in 1984. (See Box 4)

Table 13 gives details of Zimbabwe's import trade with African, western industrialized and other countries. The major trend in import trade is away from African countries (although SADCC trade is increasing slowly) and towards either the industrialized or the industrializing countries.

Graph 6 indicates Zimbabwe's trade balance with its major trading partners and with selected countries in the SADCC and PTA regions. (See Box on page 154 for details on the PTA).

Trade Routes

Table 14 indicates the changing nature of Zimbabwe's trade routes over the past half century. Most of the changes have resulted from political rather than economic factors. The figures for 1939 in Table 14 show that in this early period Zimbabwe routed most of her foreign trade through the closest ports, i.e. Maputo and Beira in Mozambique. The South African ports, being much further away, received only 16% of Zimbabwe's export traffic and 39% of its import traffic.

TABLE 14: Zimbabwe Railway Traffic by Route in Selected Years 1939-83 (in percentage)

Route			1939	1967	1970	1975	1980	1981	1982	1983
1.	via South Africa	In	39,2	27	38	51	99,5	92	79,5	93
		Out	16,1	13	22	25	83	73	50	64
2.	via Mozambique	In	59,4	71	62	49	0,4	7,5	19,5	6,5
		Out	65,2	53	51	69	2	17	38	25
3.	via Zambia	In	1,4	2	—	—	0,1	0,5	1	0,5
		Out	18,7	34	27	6	15	10	12	11
	Totals (%)	In	100%	100%	100%	100%	100%	100%	100%	100%
		Out	100%	100%	100%	100%	100%	100%	100%	100%

21

NOTES;
1. The totals are all in percentages.
2. The import and Export totals of all three countries concerned include goods in transit.

The figures for 1967 reflect the changes that came about as a result of the formation of the Federation of Rhodesia and Nyasaland. Trade routes had not yet been affected by UDI in 1965. Both imports and exports through South Africa had declined while exports were increasingly routed through Mozambique and Zambia. The large increase in exports through Zambia also represents the increased sales to Zambia and Malawi, which were a result of the formation of the Federation.

The 1970 and 1975 figures reflect the impact of sanctions, as more goods were being re-routed through South Africa and proportionately less through Mozambique and Zambia. By 1980 the border with Mozambique had been closed for a number of years, explaining why virtually no imports or exports were going via this route. The Independence of Zimbabwe and the end of the war normalized relations between countries in the region and slowly the trade routes used by both importers and exporters began to change — shown by the increased use of Mozambiquan ports in 1980 and 1981 largely at the expense of the southern routes.

The dramatic reversal of this trend in 1983 followed increased MNR activity which reduced the flow of imports through

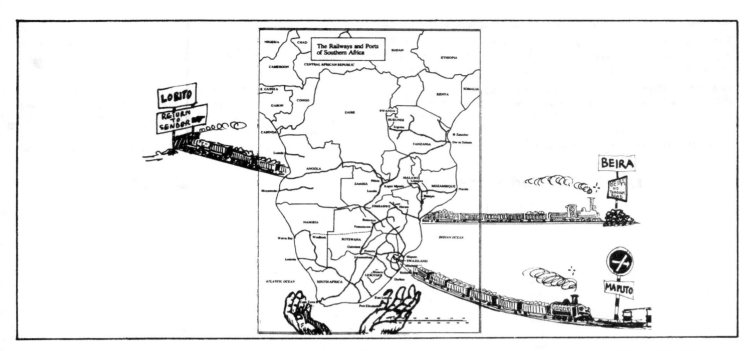

Mozambique from 19,5% to 6,5% of total import volume. Likewise, the export volume decreased from 38% to 25%. The large increases in export and import trade through Mozambique in the 1980-82 period indicate the potential of this route were it not for the destabilizing effect of the Renamo bandits.

Foreign Exchange Rationing

The present system of foreign exchange allocations was intially designed by the previous government in order to prevent large outflows of currency after the dissolution of the Federation and the imposition of UDI. The allocations are determined by an inter-ministerial committee chaired by the Ministry of Finance, Economic Planning and Development, which sets quantitative limits on the total allocation of foreign exchange and then divides this amongst the eligible users. The extent of the rationing indicates the degree to which demand exceeds the supply of available foreign currency.

TABLE 15: Import Allocation ($ millions) 1979-85

	1979	1980	1981	1982	1983	1984	1985
Total allocations	555,3	746,0	854,0	730,6	729,3	707,9	770,0
of which —							
Building projects	0,9	2,9	2,9	3,4	4,7	2,6	3,5
Industrial projects	13,3	18,9	20,2	16,2	17,9	14,1	14,9
Mining projects	*	10,0	8,8	3,9	3,4	3,0	4,0
Commercial imports	105,5	155,6	183,2	135,8	111,8	74,9	66,5
Industrial imports	137,4	216,1	251,8	195,2	169,3	138,4	159,7
Public sector project	*	9,9	12,1	47,5	12,9	13,0	11,3

22

The current system is biased towards the historical users of foreign exchange and, as such, restricts the growth of new and potentially more efficient users. The critical shortage of foreign exchange also leads to excessive profits being made by some of the recipients. This has, in some cases, been countered by price controls, but this method compounds the need for administrative control which often leads to delays and inefficiency.

Table 15 shows the increase in import allocations from 1979-85. The figures, in current prices, show an initial increase until the beginning of the recession in 1982. The 1985 alloaction of $770m was still significantly below the 1981 peak. In view of the sharp devaluation of the Zimbabwe dollar and rising import prices, the 1985 level represents a 58% drop since 1982.

The cuts in import allocations were most severe in the commercial and industrial sectors; the level of commercial allocations in 1985 was 60% below its level in 1981, whilst that for industrial allocations was 45% below the 1981 level in nominal terms. Given that inflation had eroded virtually 60% of the buying power of the allocation in real terms (see Table 16), the commercial sector was receiving 20% and the industrial sector 27% of the allocation they received in 1981. Due to the fact that a large proportion of commercial imports are for industrial use, the effect on industry in terms of reduced imported inputs was much more severe than in apparent from the figures.

TABLE 16: Import Allocations at Current and Constant Prices: 1979-85

Year	Import Allocations	
	Current Prices (Z$m)	Constant (1980) prices (Z$m)
1979	555,3	609,9
1980	746,0	746,0
1981	854,0	768,7
1982	730,6	578,0
1983	729,3	505,4
1984	707,9	437,5
1985	770,0	442,0

23

Table 16 shows the value of the import allocations at constant (1980) prices. The current prices have been deflated using the GDP deflator, thereby giving an indication of the real value of the import allocations.

Future Strategies in Balance of Payments Management

The degree of openness of an economy can be seen as both a strength and a weakness. A high degree of integration into the world economic order can ensure that the level of productivity and the development of technology in the domestic economy match those of the developed economies and, therefore, enable the domestic economy to participate on world markets. This would, however, also mean that fluctuations affecting the international markets would also affect the domestic market. In an open economy such as we have in Zimbabwe (where imports and exports are generally in the region of 25-30% of GDP) the aggregate size of domestic production and income is determined to a very large extent by the conditions prevailing in the international market, and especially by trends in the international commodities market.

The TNDP estimated that in order to achieve a growth rate of 8%, a 10,4% growth in trade was necessary (giving Zimbabwe an average annual elasticity of foreign trade turnover to GDP of 1,3). A decline in exports would mean a decline in foreign currency available for imports which, in turn, would slow down our rate of growth. The demand for imported inputs is exacerbated by the import restrictions that existed in the past as these led to a huge backlog of suppressed import demand.

The major priority in any medium-term strategy for growth in Zimbabwe must be the attempt to maintain balanced balance of payments and budgetary positions. The large budget deficits of the past few years have increased the inflationary pressures in the domestic economy thereby necessitating the continual depreciation of our currency in an effort to remain competitive on the world market. A cheaper currency increases the costs of imported inputs causing local prices to rise even further and necessitating further adjustments in the currency's value. Devaluation also serves to worsen the external debt problem by increasing the size of the debt-servicing. Since the foreign debt is denominated in US dollars, a 10% drop in the value of Zimbabwe's currency effectively increases the size of the foreign debt by 10%.

Table 17 show the rate of depreciation of the Zimbabwe dollar against the currencies of its major trading partners. Depreciation against the US dollar in the first five years of Independence was at a rate of 11,2% per year; for the pound sterling it was under 10% p.a. but for the German mark it was over 12% p.a. The Zimbabwe dollar strengthened against most regional currencies with the exception of Mozambique and Tanzania. Appreciation against the South African rand (at a rate of 35% between 1982-85) was largely a result of the rapid depreciation of the rand in 1985.

TABLE 17: Foreign Exchange Depreciation/Appreciation rates for Zimbabwe Dollar (per cent) 1979-86

	1979-78	1980-79	1982-80	1982-81	1983-82	1984-83	1985-84	1985-82	1987-86
Japanese Yen	–	–	–	–	–	–	- 26,6	–	- 17
US Dollar	0,1	6,9	- 12,1	- 15,8	- 16,8	- 26,4	- 8,5	- 44,0	+ 5,5
Pound Sterling	- 8,7	- 0,2	9,9	- 8,1	- 7,2	- 8,3	- 25,9	- 37,0	- 7,5
SA Rand	0,0	- 4,6	13,1	- 12,8	- 5,6	19,5	19,8	35,2	- 3,3
Deutschemark	- 7,3	24,4	0,8	- 17,5	- 5,1	15,0	- 28,2	- 42,1	- 2,1
Swiss Franc	- 1,3	6,2	- 11,0	- 13,1	- 9,6	- 12,6	- 26,6	- 42,1	- 2,2
French Franc	- 4,1	20,8	11,2	- 8,3	2,6	- 14,9	- 28,0	- 37,2	- 14,7
Italian Lira	- 3,0	23,1	13,7	- 11,0	0,2	- 14,4	- 20,0	- 31,3	- 1,8
Mozambique Metical	–	–	- 4,0	- 16,7	- 10,1	- 22,4	- 13,4	- 39,6	n.a.
Botswana Pula	–	–	–	- 6,3	- 9,1	- 0,9	26,4	14,0	- 3,7
Zambian Kwacha	–	–	–	18,3	34,7	8,4	134,7	342,7	2,7
Tanzanian Shilling	–	–	–	- 10,5	8,9	6,2	- 16,3	- 3,3	n.a.

24

The budget deficit for 1985 was significantly lower than predicted ($691m instead of just over $800m) due to higher than expected tax revenues and successful cuts in capital expenditure. The projected deficit for the 1986-87 fiscal year of over $1 200m indicates, however, that the budgetary problems are far from over.

The overall balance of payments position improved from a surplus of $164,3m in 1984 to a surplus of $203,5m in 1985 (i.e. a 24% improvement). This was largely brought about by increased capital inflows.

The dependence on imported inputs and the lack of foreign exchange to purchase sufficient quantities of these inputs can only be overcome by a simultaneous diversification and expansion of exports. At present, most exports are of agricultural, mineral and processed metal products, all of which face either stagnant or only slowly growing world markets (see Box 5).

Increase in the volume of trade (essentially exports) are limited by the following factors:

Transport: Zimbabwe is dependent on foreign countries for access to world markets. Domestic resources in the field of transport cannot handle the large volumes of imports and exports, especially in years of bumper harvests.

Dependence on imported raw materials: the sectors which generate growth in the economy (manufacturing, mining and agriculture) are all dependent for their continued expansion on an adequate supply of imported inputs.

Foreign exchange constraints have prevented the expansion of trade with other African countries and have meant that most of it has been with the developed world. The direction of trade has in turn influenced its nature; the developed world needs raw materials which it transforms into finished good and sells to the developing world. Zimbabwe's manufactured goods have difficulty in competing with those of the First World, leaving it in the position of being an exporter (primarily) of primary commodities.

Import controls within Zimbabwe necessitated by the shortage of foreign exchange, have in certain cases limited the importation of essential inputs for goods aimed at the export market.

The import controls have in this way led to a decline in the proportion of manufactured goods in total exports.

Box 5: The Future Prospects for Major Export Items

1. **Tobacco** remains our single largest export earning 20% of the export revenue in 1984. The tobacco market has, however, been a buyers market which has not grown for the past three years. Despite the high quality of Zimbabwe's tobacco, world tastes have moved away from the crop (largely for health reasons). The potential for expanding tobacco exports are not therefore very good.

2. **Gold** moved into second place above ferrochrome in 1984 generating 11% of total export revenues. As long as the gold price remains in the region of Z$400 per ounce or more and the government continues its 'price support' fund the future prospects for the gold industry remain good. The technical and financial assistance provided by the Ministry of Mines has helped to ensure the existence of many small mines throughout the country.

3. **Ferro-Alloys** earned Zimbabwe $155m on the export market in 1984 (10% of export revenues). The demand for stainless steel is growing internationally and Zimbabwe's share of the world market could expand if regional tensions do not disrupt the import of vital inputs from South Arica. Competition from South Africa (in the event of international sanctions not being effective) could pose a major problem due to the cheap Rand.

4. **Cotton Lint** generated 8% of Zimbabwe's total export earnings in 1984. Zimbabwe's cotton, being hand-picked to ensure high quality, commands high prices on the world markets. The rising world prices; the labour intensive production methods, and the suitability for small scale production all make this a good prospect for future expansion. One major problem at the moment is that South Africa buys 32% of Zimbabwe's cotton export. Regional tensions and the imposition of sanctions could necessitate the search for new markets.

5. **Asbestos** earnings at $74m generated 5% of export earnings in 1984. Were it not for the effect of asbestos products and asbestos mining on health this product would represent a major potential growth area. Reserves of good quality asbestos in Zimbabwe are high which together with efficient new willing facilities place Zimbabwe in a highly competitive position. The reality however is that the international market for this product is declining with a total ban on all asbestos products being a future possibility.

BOX 6: The Valuation of the Zimbabwean Dollar

The direct relationship between the availability of foreign exchange and the level of growth highlights the need for flexibility in the area of exchange rate determination and foreign exchange allocations.

Since 7th March, 1980, the Zimbabwe dollar exchange rate has been determined on the basis of a transaction-weighted basket, with weights corresponding to Zimbabwe's patterns of trade. The six currencies determining the value of the Zimbabwe dollar are the South African rand, the Swiss franc, the British pound, the US dollar, the German mark and the French franc. The weight of the different transactions (determined in January 1982) is as follows:

US dollar	..	55%
SA rand	..	25%
UK pound	..	12%
German mark	..	5%
Swiss franc	..	2%
French franc	..	1%

The government has used exchange rate management to maintain stable export prices on the international market. The high rates of domestic inflation in 1982 and 1983 were compensated for by successive devaluations which countered the effects of the inflation.

At the end of May 1986 the exchange rate of the Zimbabwe dollar against the US dollar was 56,4% down from November 1982 and 10,1% down from May 1985. Compared with the OECD currencies as a group the Zimbabwe dollar depreciated by 15% in the year to May 1986.

The sharp depreciation of the South African rand has meant that Zimbabwean goods have found it difficult to compete on the South African market and that Zimbabwe has lost competitiveness vis-á-vis South Africa. South Africa's position as a major trading partner has meant that a depreciation of the rand has contributed to the recent depreciations of the Zimbabwe dollar.

Whereas this continual depreciation should have improved the country's export performance and helped to protect domestic jobs which were in jeopardy due to loss of export markets, the poor world prices for most of Zimbabwe's export commodities have negated any benefit brought about by depreciation. The problems of lack of growth in the material sector and increasing input costs (especially rising wage costs) have had to be countered by further depreciation of the Zimbabwe dollar against the currencies of its major trading partners.

A third method, popular with the IMF, is that of wage constraint. Rising minimum wages increase production costs and can price exports out of the market. Advocating wage restraint in the export sector in Zimbabwe would be directly contrary to the government's policy of growth with equity. The bulk of exports are either agricultural or mineral products, and wages in these sectors (especially agriculture) already tend to be lower than in other sectors of the economy.

How Foreign Trade can restrict Progress

Increasing the volume of exports in a situation of declining terms of trade and high domestic inflation could well mitigate against government's efforts to raise standards of living and redistribute incomes. The declining terms of trade refer to the rate of exchange between exports and imports. Terms of trade are said to be declining when more and more exports are needed in order to purchase the same volume of imports. The rapid rise in oil prices in the middle and late seventies, for example, meant that Third World countries such as Zimbabwe had to sell ever larger volumes of primary commodities in order to purchase a constant quantity of oil.

The high domestic inflation rate influences the volume of exports demanded; if prices in Zimbabwe are rising faster than those of competing countries, then although this has a positive effect on the terms of trade, export demands will drop (as prices are too high), and the net result is a deterioration of the trade balance as exports decline.

Producing for a highly competitive export market can mean keeping wages low in Zimbabwe in order to keep the prices of the finished products low. The demands of the export market, therefore, generate greater inequalities in the domestic market.

Alternatively, if wages are allowed to rise within the context of the open economy, the entrenchment of workers is the only alternative for producers who are desperately trying to remain competitive in the face of stiff international competition. Producers tend to hire fewer of the more highly paid workers and mechanize in order to maintain production levels. The result is an increased demand for imported luxuries from the labour aristocracy (those highly paid few who still have jobs), and an increased demand for capital equipment from the producers; both of which increase the demand for foreign exchange and the negative pressure on the balance of payments . If this pressure continues over the long term the value of the currency will fall, thereby increasing import prices even more. So although wages rose, increasing the standard of living of a few, the lot of the majority worsened significantly.

A further complication of the open economy strategy is that export promotion goes hand-in-hand with an increased volume of imports. Competition from imports can, and often does, inhibit domestic employment as local firms are put out of business by foreign rivals (the effect of Dandy chewing gum on the local market for chewing gum is a case in point).

Competing on the world market demands that the domestic methods of production are in line with the methods used in the developed countries. Capital intensive techniques which employ small quantities of skilled workers and demand large quantities of foreign exchange replace labour-intensive methods which use few imported inputs and hire large quantities of workers. The result is often large-scale unemployment which, in turn, reduces the size of the domestic market and forces producers to sell an ever-increasing proportion of their products on the world market, necessitating further mechanization and more advanced technology. The results of this pattern of trade are in direct contrast to the aims of the policy of growth with equity.

The years of sanctions under UDI followed by the continued shortage of foreign exchange in the post-independence era, has forced the business community to operate with outdated and over-worked equipment. This has made it very difficult to break into the highly competitive export market.

Reducing the Openness of the Economy

If an increased volume of trade leads to a greater degree of inequality then measures need to be taken to reduce, rather than increase, the degree of openness of the economy. The most important element of such a strategy would be to concentrate growth on areas which use less imported inputs. The service sectors of the economy are not significant consumers of imported inputs. This includes the distributive industry, the banking, financial and insurance sectors, real estate, education, health, and public administration. Of the directly productive sectors, agriculture, non-metallic minerals, mining and quarrying, foodstuffs, beverage and tobacco, textiles and the coal industry, all have an import dependence of less than 15%.

At the other end of the scale, the rubber, chemicals, electrical machinery, transport and equipment sub-sectors all have an import dependency of more than 30%. (Transport and equipment having the highest import dependency ratio of 41,6%).

In general the allocation of foreign exchange should be in support of projects which in the long run save rather than consume foreign exchange, i.e. industries which have the capacity to expand with minimum import content.

By making the allocation of foreign exchange contigent on proof that the goods cannot be produced locally, production techniques that are based on the maximum use of local material would be encouraged. Since most capital intensive techniques would generally be import-intensive, labour-intensive methods of production need to be encouraged. Reducing the tax benefits on capital intensive techniques would go a long way towards shifting the emphasis more towards labour-intensive methods.

Where the use of capital equipment is unavoidable its potential can be more fully exploited by making it available on a hire basis through leasing agreements, or by sharing equipment between a number of manufacturers.

Exports need to be diversified into areas of rising demand. This could include the export of clothing to the developed countries, of manufactured consumer goods to the African market (primarily the PTA countries), and of capital goods to the SADCC region. Such expansion would require significant government support in the form of policy support and financial incentives.

Another major problem facing Zimbabwe in the export market stems from the nature of the goods exported. Primary commodity exports are continually being exchanged for smaller and smaller quantities of finished goods (see page 145), resulting in declining receipts from trade (worsening terms of trade) and lower domestic rates of growth. The traditional response to the above problem, that of export promotion, has been, therefore, problematic.

An alternative approach might well be to attempt to process raw materials domestically. This would save on the foreign exchange needed to purchase the finished goods (largely capital goods) but assumes the technology and expertise to produce these (capital) goods in the first place. Most of the companies that would be in a position to develop such technology are branches of the same multinationals that are currently producing such capital goods in other parts of the world and making profits by selling this equipment to Zimbabwe. The major problem with the local production of capital equipment is the size of the market. Production for the Zimbabwean market alone would not be at all feasible as the production runs would be too small, making the equipment far too expensive. Production for export is a possibility, but foreign companies have hesitated because of the shortage of foreign exchange for imported inputs, the relatively high labour costs, the distance from world markets, and the lack of export financing from the government. If raw materials are to be used domestically for the production of capital goods then the government will clearly have to play a far greater role than it is doing at present — either through the provision of tangible incentives to foreign companies or through direct government involvement in research and development and possibly even finance.

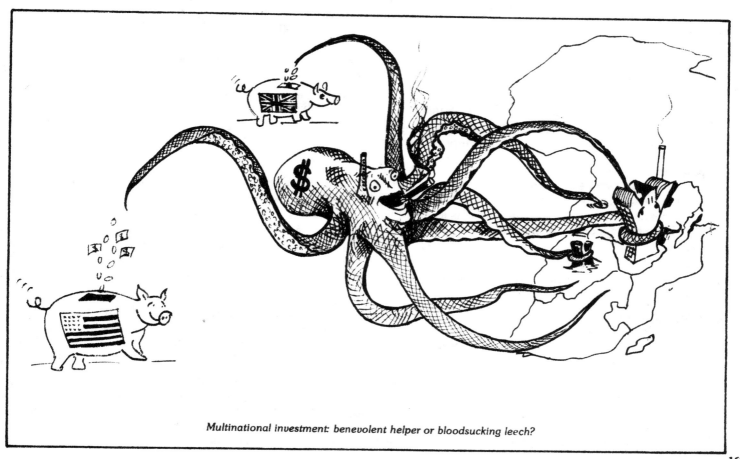

Multinational investment: benevolent helper or bloodsucking leech?

163

The most effective solution to the problem of worsening terms of trade is to diversify the range of exports so that a decline in the price of some commodities is offset by a rise in others, or a decline in one market does not affect the overall demand. The present product type and destination of exports is related far more to the international interests of the multinationals which dominate the export sector than to the BoP needs of the Zimbabwean economy; changing the export-mix might therefore be easier said than done. This once again points to the need for greater government participation in the field of direct production in order to ensure that the interests of Zimbabwe predominate.

Countering the Anti-Export Bias

The system of protection that followed the imposition of sanctions has led to an anti-export bias within the local economy that is reinforced by the lack of foreign exchange for inputs. If Zimbabwe is to capture new export markets for her manufactured goods then a system of incentives will be needed to overcome the strong orientation of the manufacturing sector to the domestic market. The duty drawback scheme and the export revolving fund are steps in the right direction. Further measures could include a system of credit guarantees for export financing and the creation of a facility which would enable exporters to provide longer credit terms to purchasers of their products. This could be especially important in the promotion of a regional market, such as SADCC, for our capital goods.

Altering the Import Mix

The major categories of imports are petroleum products (±20%), intermediate goods (±40%), and machinery and transport equipment (±35%). Where the overall level of imports cannot be reduced without reducing the growth rate, a medium-term strategy could aim at increasing the import of machinery and transport equipment which would allow Zimbabwe to produce more of the previously imported intermediate goods. Although the overall usage of foreign exchange might remain constant, or even increase slightly, the growth of employment and domestic demand resulting from the increased import substitution would generate higher levels of growth.

With regard to petroleum inputs, an increased usage of coal and a more efficient use of energy should enable petroleum product inputs to grow at a slower rate than GDP, thereby reducing the proportion of petroleum imports to total imports.

The urgent need for investment growth will need to be satisfied if long-term growth is to be achieved (see Appendix 1). This will increase the demand for all above categories of imports, especially machinery.

The change in the composition of both imports and exports in order to enhance the process of import substitution and to move into export markets that have greater growth potential, are therefore key elements of a medium-term growth strategy.

Export Promotion

In the face of BoP deficits one can either decrease imports, or one can promote exports. One method of doing the latter is to make them cheaper, by devaluing. By decreasing the value of the dollar in relation to foreign currenices (more Zimbabwe dollars can therefore be bought with the same volume of foreign currency) Zimbabwean goods effectively become cheaper on the world market. This should increase export sales and decrease import purchases, thereby correcting the imbalance in the BoP.

It is possible, however, that other countries will also decrease the value of their currency (or simply drop the prices of their goods) necessitating further devaluations to maintain the viability of the export sector. Each successive devaluation increases import prices and fuels domestic inflation. High inflation acts against the devaluation and renders our exports less competitive. (Box 6 indicates how the value of the dollar is determined).

If the demand for imports declines as a result of devaluation this will result in a saving of foreign exchange. Zimbabwe's principal imports in 1984 were fuels and electricity (21%) and machinery and transport equipment (31%). Increasing the import prices of these necessary commodities would result in more than less foreign exchange being spent on imports. On the other hand, cut-backs in foreign exchange allocations for these items would act as a brake on the growth of the domestic economy.

A second method of promoting exports is through export subsidies. These have the advantage of making the exports cheaper while not increasing import prices. The problem, however, as with all subsidies, is the dependence they generate. Maintaining subsidies over a long period of time reduces the incentive to increase efficiency and cut costs. Limited subsidies which decline by a given percentage each year could overcome this problem. An additional problem with export subsidies is that they induce competing nations to impose retaliatory subsidies in order to maintain their market share.

References

1. Whitsum Foundation, *Trade and Development in Zimbabwe*, Harare, 1980.
2. *ibid.,*
3. *ibid.,*
4. Reserve Bank of Zimbabwe, *Quarterly Economic and Statistical Review*, Harare, June, 1986.
5. *ibid.,*
6. Ministry of Finance, Economic Planning and Development, *Socio-Economic Review of Zimbabwe. 1980-85*, Harare, 1985.
7. Central Statistical Office, *Quarterly Digest of Statistics*, Harare, September, 1986.
8. *ibid.,*
9. *ibid.,*
10. *Socio-Economic Review of Zimbabwe, op. cit.,*
11. *Quarterly Digest of Statistics, op. cit.,*
12. RAL Merchant Bank Ltd., *Executive Guide to the Economy*, Harare, March, 1986.
13. *Quarterly Digest of Statistics, op. cit.,*
14. Standard Chartered Bank, *Standard Chartered Economic Bulletin*, Harare, May, 1987.
15. *ibid.,*
16. *Quarterly Digest of Statistics, op. cit.,*
17. Central Statistical Office, *Statistical Yearbook of Zimbabwe 1985*, CSO, Harare, 1985.
18. *Executive Guide to the Economy, op. cit.*
19. *Trade and Development in Zimbabwe, op. cit.,*
20. *Socio-Economic Review of Zimbabwe, op. cit.,*
21. *Trade and Development in Zimbabwe, op. cit.,*
22. *Socio-Economic Review of Zimbabwe, op. cit.,*
23. *Socio-Economic Review of Zimbabwe, op. cit.,*
24. *Socio-Economic Review of Zimbabwe, op. cit.*

CONCLUSION

The Transition Revisited

Having set out to write a book on the economics of transformation it is necessary to comment on the process of that transformation. As stated in the introduction, the transition is not simply a transfer of power from one elite to another, but rather the transfer of economic and political power to the mass of the people. For this to take place, changes are necessary at both the objective and subjective levels. The objective level incorporates changes at the level of ownership: the people themselves, through their representatives, need to take control of the nation's assets. Whether this control takes the form of nationalization of existing assets, the expansion of the state sector side by side with the private sector, or the gradual emergence of a cooperatively-owned sector of the economy, remains a question for debate. The crucial issue in this debate revolves around the transfer of the effective power of ownership of the nation's assets.

Change at the subjective level concerns the development of political and class consciousness. The struggle for national liberation in Zimbabwe was spearheaded by the peasantry mobilized around the land question. The consciousness of the rural perople was raised through focusing on the contradictions which emerged in the pattern of land ownership in pre-independent Zimbabwe. The post-liberation struggle for economic independence will require the mobilization of all Zimbabweans in an effort to take control of the nation's economy and to chart an independent path of development. Such a struggle will demand the alliance of all progressive classes (including the national bourgeoisie) under the leadership of the working class.

A discussion of the economics of transformation is therefore not complete without a thorough examination of these subjective factors. The absence of such a discussion from this book was largely determined by practical reasons of space and the need to publish the material before it became out-dated. The author hopes, however, to continue the discussion on the economics of transformation in a later volume dealing specifically with the questions of the development of political and class consciousness in post-independent Zimbabwe.

Important Dates in the History of Zimbabwe

1870s: *Prospectors from South Africa begin to cross the Limpopo in search of gold in what they believed might be a 'second-Rand'.*

1887: *Piet Grobbler, an agent of the Transvaal Boers, claims that he has signed a treaty of friendship with Lobengula which would give the Boers complete freedom of movement in Matabeleland.*

1888: *John Moffat, a missionary and agent of the British government, claimed that he had concluded a treaty with Lobengula in which the king agreed to ask British permission before signing any future agreements with any other party. This treaty was a fraud as Lobengula was misled about the terms of the treaty.*

1888: *Rhodes sent his agents Rudd, Maguire and Thompson to Matabeleland to persuade Lobengula to sell all the mineral rights in his territory to Rhodes. Lobengula signed the treaty in the belief that only ten men would mine gold for a limited period. This was the notorious Rudd Concession.*

1889: *The British South Africa Company (BSAC) is formed and is granted the right to make treaties and promulgate laws in the name of the British Empire through the Royal Charter of 1899.*

1890: *On 12th September, the settler invasion force, organized by Rhodes, raised the Union Jack on Harare Hill in Salisbury.*

1893: *The settlers invade Matabeleland.*

1893: *The imposition of a hut tax in all company territory (Imperial sanction for the tax is received in 1894).*

1894: *Lobengula dies; this marks the end of Ndebele resistance.*

1894: *The Colonial Office gives authority to a Land Commission to establish the first reserves in Matabeleland.*

1895: *The name Rhodesia is first used for the territories of Matabeleland and Mashonaland.*

1895: *The first provincial labour bureaux are organized in order to recruit labour for the mines.*

1896: *The Ndebele and Mashona uprisings begin in opposition to Company rule.*

1898: *Rhodesia is renamed Southern Rhodesia.*

1898: *The death by hanging of the spirit mediums Kagubi and Nehanda marks the end of the war.*

1898: *Native reserves are extended to the whole country (these reserves were subsequently entrenched in the 1923 Southern Rhodesian constitution).*

1899: *The Labour Board of Southern Rhodesia is formed.*

1899: *African workers on the Red and White Rose Mine stage a go-slow demanding an improvement in the conditions of service.*

1901: *Striking workers are Camperdown Mine succesfully block an attempt to reduce their wages.*

1903: *Mine owners form the Rhodesian Native Labour Bureau (RNLB) which is responsible for recruiting labour for the mines and making sure that they stay on the job.*

1904: *The hut tax is doubled bringing the African contribution to State revenue up to 41%.*

1905: *A strike at Bonsor Mine fails and wage cuts are enforced.*

1908: *An Estates Department is established in order to promote European settlement in the colony.*

1909: *Africans living on 'unalienated land' had to pay rent to the Chartered Company (those living on white farmland paid even higher rent).*

1909: *The strike at Ayrshire Mine fails to revise a wage reduction.*

1912: *The Dog Tax is introduced.*

1912: *The Land Bank is set up with a share capital of £25 000 to make credit facilities available to European farmers only (it was only in 1945 that the Land Bank began to extend loans to farmers in the African Purchase Areas).*

1914: *A Company ordinance makes cattle dipping compulsory in any area where this is the wish of the majority of white farmers. Fees for dipping range from one to two shillings per head.*

1918: *Strikes begin at Wankie Colliery which continue sporadically until 1921.*

1918:	Strikes take place at the Globe and Phoenix Mines.
1919:	White mine workers successfully strike for a 25% wage increase and a 48 hour working week.
1920:	The Rhodesian Bantu Voters Association is formed to work for the advancement of the Bantu Peoples.
1921:	A white mine-workers' strike at Shamva is defeated and management locks workers out the mine.
1923:	Responsible government is introduced into Southern Rhodesia which marks the end of Company rule. The Settler State that emerges represents an alliance between settler and international capital.
1924:	Sir Charles Coghlan becomes the first Prime Minister of Southern Rhodesia.
1927:	A branch of the South African based Industrial and Commercial Workers Union (ICU) is started in Bulawayo and called the Rhodesian Industrial and Commercial Workers Union (RICU).
1930:	The Land Apportionment Act is passed. This represents the first legal sanction by Parliament of the division of the country into reserved areas for blacks and whites. The act designated 51% of the land as European land; 22% as Native Reserves; and 8% as Native Purchase Areas.
1931:	The Maize Control Act (1931) and its subsequent amendments protect and subsidize the European producer at the expense of the African producer.
1933:	The Reform Party wins the general election.
1934:	The Industrial Conciliation Act is passed. The act excludes Africans from its definition of employee so that they cannot be members of recognized trade unions.
1934:	The first African National Council of Southern Rhodesia is formed by Aaron Jacha.
1936:	The Native Registration Act is passed which is designed to tighten up the already existing pass laws.
1936:	The Sedition Act is passed which is intended to halt the spread of subversive and seditious propaganda and literature.
1938:	The State in Southern Rhodesia takes over the refrigeration plant and works of the Imperial Cold Storage Company through the newly established Cold Storage Commission (CSC).
1942:	The Cotton Research and Industry Board is set up in order to buy the local crop and alleviate the problem of securing cotton imports.
1942:	The government nationalizes the scrap-iron and steel works which were controlled by ISCOR of South Africa.
1944:	Government takes over the Triangle Sugar Estate and a Sugar Industry Board is formed.
1945:	The Railway Workers Association organizes a strike of Railway workers throughout the country. The leaders of the strike are first dismissed and then arrested when police crush the strike.
1947:	Rhodesia Railways is nationalized and the line to Maputo (then Lorenco Marques) is built (the line is only completed in 1955).
1948:	The country's first general strike breaks out led by Benjamin Burombo. The strike collapses in the face of harsh government repression before it achieves anything.
1951:	The Land Husbandry Act is passed which forces African farmers to destock their land and to modify their land tenure practices. As a result of this act many men are forced to seek wage employment as migrant workers.
1953:	The Federation of Rhodesia and Nyasaland comes into being.
1955:	The City Youth League is formed.
1956:	The Youth League organizes a successful African bus boycott after which over 200 people are detained.
1957:	The Youth League and the ANC merge under the name of the ANC. Nkomo is elected President and Chikerema Vice-President.
1959:	The government passed new laws (e.g. the Industrial Conciliation Act) which allows black workers to form unions but prohibits them from striking. As a result the unions do not gain much support
1959:	The ANC is banned.
1960:	IPCORN Industrial Promotion Council for Rhodesia and Nyasaland – re-named in 1964 Industrial Promotion Corporation of Central Africa – is formed to provide medium-term capital and managerial advice.

1960: *The National Democratic Party (NDP) is formed.*

1961: *The NDP is banned and ZAPU (Zimbabwe African People's Union) is formed on 17th December.*

1962: *The Rhodesian Front party is formed.*

1962: *ZAPU is banned.*

1962: *The Rhodesian Front wins the national elections and Winston Field becomes Prime Minister.*

1963: *The IDC (Industrial Development Corporation) is formed to assist new and selected existing enterprises with long-term capital and managerial supervision.*

1963: *ZANU (Zimbabwe African National Union) is formed.*

1963: *The Federation is dissolved as Nyasaland and Northern Rhodesia both vote to withdraw.*

1964: *Field is forced to resign and is replaced by Smith.*

1964: *ZANU's armed wing, the ZANLA Crocodile Commando, kill the first white in an act of war which launches the second Chimurenga (second war of liberation).*

1964: *ZANU is banned.*

1965: *11th November, UDI (Unilateral Declaration of Independence) is declared.*

1966: *The United Nations imposes selective mandatory sanctions on Rhodesia.*

1967: *The 'Tiger Talks' take place between Wilson and Smith on the HMS Tiger. No agreement is reached.*

1968: *The United Nations imposes comprehensive mandatory sanctions against Rhodesia.*

1968: *Wilson and Smith meet again for talks in an attempt to resolve the situation on the HMS Fearless (known as the 'Fearless Talks'.)*

1969: *The Land Tenure Act is passed which once again changes the racial allocation of land. Approximately 46% of the land is allocated as African land; 46% as European land; and the rest as national land.*

1970: *The Agricultural Finance Corporation (AFC) is formed by merging the Agricultural Land Bank and the Agricultural Loan Fund.*

1971: *The Home-Smith agreement is concluded setting out proposals for a settlement. The African National Council is formed in order to oppose the agreement; Muzorewa is elected leader.*

1972: *The Pearce Commission, which set out to test the acceptability of the Home-Smith agreement, finds that the majority of the people reject it.*

1973: *The border between Zambia and Zimbabwe is closed as the liberation war intensifies.*

1975: *Mozambique becomes Independent under the Frelimo government.*

1975: *The Victoria Falls conference takes place in yet another attempt at reaching a settlement.*

1976: *Mozambique closes the border with Rhodesia as ZANLA guerillas begin to operate from Tete, Manica and Gaza provinces. The only trade route left for Rhodesia is through South Africa.*

1976: *The Patriotic Front is formed and the Geneva conference opens (it is adjourned in December of 1976).*

1977: *Smith rejects the Anglo-American proposals.*

1978: *The Internal Settlement agreement is reached between Smith, Chirau, Muzorewa and Sithole.*

1979: *Muzorewa wins the internal elections.*

1979: *Lancaster House: an all party conference held in London under the Chairmanship of the British Foreign Secretary, Lord Carrington, to agree a new constitution, a cease fire and transitional arrangements for a new election. Agreement was reached on 21st December.*

1980: *Robert Mugabe wins the British supervised elections and Zimbabwe becomes Independent.*

APPENDIX 1: Foreign Investment in Zimbabwe

Introduction

The post-Independence era has been beset by many different economic problems among them the foreign exchange shortages, growing unemployment, falling commodity prices, drought, recession, etc. Few of the problems, however, are as serious in their implications and long-term effects as the drop in the level of real investment. Fifteen years of sanctions took their toll on the economy's capital stock which by the time of Independence was urgently in need of replacement or repair. Zimbabwe's reintegration into the world economy means that our exports are competing against those of countries producing with far more up-to-date technology, forcing us to continue to devalue in order to maintain competitiveness. The following attempts to examine the attitudes of both government and the private sector to this crucial problem and poses tentative solutions.

TABLE 1: Falling Levels Of Real Investment

Gross Fixed Capital Formation in real terms. 1974 - 1983 (1980 = 100)											
1974	1975	1976	1977	1978	1979	1980	1981	1982	1983	1984	1985
938	899	728	552	442	443	528	723	780	649	n.a.	n.a.

1

The falling trend in the pre-Independence years shown in Table 1 reflected the reluctance of the business community to invest in the midst of the war period; the post-Independence recovery was cut short by the drought and recessionary conditions which set in in 1983.

It has been estimated that it costs in the region of Z$10 000 to create one job in the formal sector. The official statistics for unemployment estimate that approximately 300 000 people are unemployed at present (1984 figures). In the four years (between 1980 and 1984) only 7 000 new jobs were created each year, while in the region of 30 000 people were looking for work in each of those years. Since much of the economy is working below full capacity it is probably reasonable to assume that the money spent on investment (see Table 1) was used primarily for the replacement or repair of existing capacity. In order to employ 30 000 school-leavers additional investment of $300 million would be needed each year, over and above the present level of approximately $700 million. As the number of job seekers increases (due to the population growth rate) so too must the level of investment.

In the 1974-83 period the population increased by almost one third (from 6 180 000 to 8 181 000) yet the number of people in formal employment decreased by 6 500 and the level of investment in real terms decreased by 31%. Unless something is done to reverse the falling trend in investment levels there is little hope of resolving the problem of unemployment.

The Trend in Investment Spending

Two important trends have emerged in investment spending during the period in question:
(i)   the share of investment in material production (agriculture, mining, manufacturing, electricity and water, construction, distribution and transport and communication) has been declining in favour of investment in non-material production (the services sector)
(ii)   the private sector's share of total investment has declined from 71,4% in 1974 to 45% in 1983; government's share has correspondingly increased.

The overall trend in Zimbabwe at present is, therefore, one in which consumption spending is increasing at the expense of investment spending; the investment which is taking place is increasingly coming from government which is spending the money on the services sectors rather than on increasing the nation's productive assets. Although government has been increasing its share of material production in recent years, (particularly in the past six months) this has been through the purchase of existing companies in the productive sector (Astra, Mardon, etc.) rather than by new investment which would create new employment.

Government's Attitudes towards Private Sector Investment

From the above it is clear that what is needed in Zimbabwe at present is an increase in investment which has the capacity to generate profits and create employment. Such investment could either come from the locally controlled private sector, the multinational corporations which are presently in Zimbabwe, new multinational investment, or from the government itself.

170

The government's attitude to private sector investment, (spelt out in its investment guidelines — September 1982), is one of acceptance of its contribution in all economic spheres, and a recognition that this sector is motivated by the economic return to investment. In an effort to encourage investment which is 'conscious of and dedicated to the economic and social advancement of Zimbabwe ...' government has laid down the following investment priorities for foreign capital (note that government defines as 'foreign' any corporation which has more than a 15% shareholding by a non-resident/non-citizen of Zimbabwe, i.e. this includes almost all the manufacturing sector, 90% of the mining sector, approximately 70% of the financial sector, etc.):
— investment in rural areas;
— investment in new enterprises which involves the transfer of foreign technology into Zimbabwe;
— investment in new enterprises on a joint venture basis with domestic capital or a state equity participation;
— investment in existing enterprises which does not dilute local ownership or pass control from one foreign investor to another;
— investment in undertakings which make extensive use of local raw materials;
— investment in labour intensive technology;
— investment in areas in which exports can be generated.

The present exchange control regulations allow foreign companies to remit 50% of after-tax profits in the form of dividend payments. These remittances are further subject to a 20% non-resident shareholder's tax.

All investment (as defined above) by foreign companies needs the approval of the Foreign Investment Committee which is a committee of ministers headed by the Minister of Finance, Economic Planning and Development. It is not only new foreign investment that has to be approved by this committee but also any acquisition of shares which would increase the foreign holding of an existing company; the acquisition of the whole or any portion of a Zimbabwean business by the purchase of the assets of the business; the transfer of shareholdings in a Zimbabwean company between different foreign owners; and even joint ventures with government.

Private Sector Attitudes towards Investment
The sanctions years left Zimbabwe almost entirely self-sufficient in the production of consumer goods. Further investment would, therefore, have to look more to production for the export market, or alternatively, the production of capital goods. Major problems in both these areas would, however, first have to be overcome. Zimbabwe does not provide conditions which are favourable enough to attract foreign corporations which are planning to produce goods for export to the southern African region. For example:
— wages in Zimbabwe are significantly higher than they are in neighbouring countries (see the accompanying graph for the minimum daily wage rate for tea workers employed in major tea producing countries of the world).
— restrictions on the hiring of skilled expatriate labour, and on the firing of labour also often act as disincentives to potential foreign investors;
— the repatriation of profits is limited (compared with other developing countries); taxation is high; and bureaucratic control — not to mention delays — also discourage investors.

The production of capital goods for the Zimbabwean market alone is not feasible as the market is too small to warrant an economically viable scale of production. If Zimbabwe were to be used as a base from which capital goods could be exported then conditions for investors would have to be significantly improved. Besides the problems of wages, taxes and bureaucratic control mentioned above, export financing is a vital component of securing any export order. Any export of capital equipment from the OECD countries is supported by loan finance for the buying country granted by the exporting country i.e. the seller raises the finance. Generally these are government guaranteed loans over periods ranging from five to ten years at preferential rates of interest ($\pm$ 6,5%). For Zimbabwe to compete on the capital goods export market the Zimbabwean government would have to be prepared to provide such loan facilities to the importing countries. A recent export order for the Tazara railway line fell through because of government reluctance to make such a guarantee.

A further problem in developing Zimbabwe as an export base is the question of which export market to aim at. The regional market is far too unstable for serious consideration: the bandit problems in Mozambique and Angola rule out the two largest territories in the sub-continent, while the ever-present threat of sanctions make the landlocked countries a poor investment for anyone interested in the export market. Moreover, the need that all SADCC countries have for hard currency also complicates inter-regional trade.

Finally, the question of the profitability of investments in Zimbabwe needs to be considered. A foreign company with money to

GRAPH 1: Comparative Minimum daily Wage Rate for Tea Workers

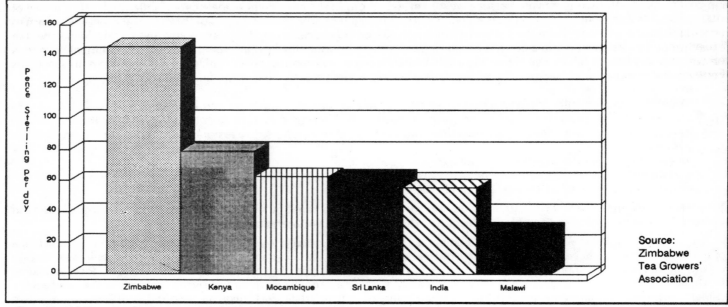

Source:
Zimbabwe
Tea Growers'
Association

The wage value are the Sterling pence equivalent of the minimum daily wage rates ruling in the countries concerned at November 1986. Minimum 2
wage rates do not necessarily reflect daily earnings.
It is notable that the Zimbabwe tea plantation worker receives the highest daily wage of all tea workers employed in the plantation industries of the
major tea producing countries in the world.

invest would be looking for at least a 15/20% interest rate as this is what they would get by investing in their domestic money markets. Taking the risks of investing in this part of the world into account (the political and economic instability; the shortages of foreign exchange with which to service their investments; the unfavourable labour legislation) an investor would want a return of

---

BOX 1: Attempts to Increase the Level of Investments

The Minister of Finance, Economic Planning and Development, Bernard Chidzero, recently announced new measures designed to stimulate investment in Zimbabwe. Since these measures were announced after the writing of this article on investment they are summarized below for the reader's information. Although many of the measures are temporary stop-gap measures designed to alleviate the present critical shortage of foreign exchange, some of the measures which government is in the process of considering are on the lines of the necessary reforms mentioned in Appendix . . . . . .

Cutting the proportion of after-tax profits that foreign investors are allowed to remit from 50% to 25% and dropping the interest rates that foreign investors can earn on the surplus funds they cannot remit from 8 to 5% will not be viewed very positively by potential investors and can hardly be described as measures designed to attract new investment. These measures have been necessitated by the lack of incentives offered in the past, and although necessary, will not make it any easier to attract investment in the future.

On the more positive side government has removed some of the restrictions it had previously placed on the use of these surplus funds, hoping to divert them into export generating or import substitution projects. Companies with foreign funds are being encouraged to buy essential imports through the use of these funds (i.e. no currency involved importation); although, whether companies which have unutilised surplus funds inside Zimbabwe will be prepared to effectively bring more foreign capital into the country is uncertain to say the least.

Other important measures announced include:
— that steps were being taken to speed up the granting of price increases;
— that government was investigating ways to improve its system of import allocations;
— that guidelines pinpointing appropriate areas for new investment would be published soon;
— that negotiations were continuing with the World Bank on the extension of the export revolving fund;
— that the 25% cut-back on remittances would not affect any new investment in this country since 1st September, 1979.

3

approximately 25/30% as the minimum acceptable pre-tax profit rate. Assuming a 30% rate of return on an initial investment of $100 million, the company would earn a pre-tax profit of $30m; after paying the 52% company tax this would leave $15,6m; a 50% dividend payment and the non-resident shareholder tax of 20% would mean that only $6,24m of the original $100m deposit could leave the country as a return to the investor. A foreign corporation therefore has to weigh up an investment in Zimbabwe with all the complicating factors mentioned above and a 6,4% return on initial investment a relatively simple investment in the First World money markets which would earn in the region of 15 to 20% return.

Is it possible for Zimbabwe to exist without Foreign Investment?

The high rate of growth generated through the import substitution policies of UDI was only possible because of the accumulated capital stock (both in the form of machinery for production and spares) built up in the days of Federation. Once the narrow phase of import substitution was over, i.e. that of producing consumer goods which had formerly been imported, the rate of growth began to slow down. By 1980 much of the capital stock was badly in need of replacement and stocks were very depleted. Because we lack the expertise to produce the capital goods domestically we either have to earn enough foreign exchange, through exports, to import all our capital good requirements, or we need to attract foreign investors who would bring the technology we need with them. In the present climate of falling export prices, continual devaluation and foreign exchange cutbacks the possibility of Zimbabwe being able to replenish its capital stock through its own resources is somewhat slim. Yet without capital stock and a continual improvement in our production methods that would enable us to keep pace with our competitors, our chances of expanding, or even maintaining our export markets, are small. The possibility of Zimbabwe developing beyond its present stage of exporting raw materials is also very limited, without an injection of foreign technology through foreign investment.

The Costs of Foreign Investment

The cost of foreign investment can be calculated in both economic and political terms. In economic terms one needs to consider the benefits to the host country in both monetary and technical terms (the acquisition of expertise) compared to the costs in terms of the money the host country could have earned, had it undertaken the venture itself, rather than invited in a multinational company. The loss of foreign exchange to the multinational in the form of dividend payments, management fees, license fees, etc., is part of the cost of foreign investment.

Since Zimbabwe clearly cannot afford, in foreign exchange terms, to import the technology we need in order to expand, it is only necessary to consider the economic cost of foreign investment in terms of the money remitted. The following example is drawn from Delta Corporation's financial statements;

TABLE 2: Analysis of Delta Corporation's Financial Statement

DELTA CORPORATION	1976 - 1980	%	1981 - 1985	%
Products and services supplied	$337m	100,0	$1385m	100,0
Products and services bought	$161m	47,8	$639m	46,2
Value Added	$176m	52,2	$745m	53,8
PAYMENTS FROM VALUE ADDED:				
Payments to Government in income tax and excise .	$80m	23,7	$454m	32,8
Payments to employees	$50m	14,8	$195m	14,1
Payments to shareholders	$18m	5,3	$31m	2,2
Interest payments	$5m	1,5	$10m	0,7
Balance reinvested	$23m	6,8	$56m	4,0
Value Added	$176m	52,2	$746m	53,8

In the case of Delta, a company in which approximately 75% of the shares are foreign owned, 95% of the value-added benefited Zimbabwe directly during the 1981-85 period compared to 90% for the 1976-80 period. These benefits were in the form of payments made to government as taxes; payments made to employees; interest payments to local banks; and money re-invested in the Corporation. The input into the economy which arises from the purchase of products and services by Delta and the value of the products and services supplied are considerable. These benefits need to be weighed against the costs of the remittances; 5,3% of the value added in the first period, and 2,2% in the second period.

Ways in which Government could encourage Foreign Investment
The most serious problem confronting local industry at the moment, affecting both local and foreign investment, is undoubtedly the low levels of foreign exchange available for inputs. Increased levels of foreign exchange allocations are therefore an absolute precondition for the revival of investment levels.

The present labour legislation which prevents firms from firing redundant workers also discourages them from expanding their output as they are afraid that they will not be able to lay off additional workers, if market conditions change. Allowing business people to hire workers for a fixed period (i.e. on contract) that could be extended if warranted by business conditions, would generate more employment and a greater volume of exports.

Easing the restrictions on investment by foreign companies could generate much greater levels of investment through the utilization of the surplus funds which these companies are holding within Zimbabwe. Government restrictions imposed through the Foreign Investment Committee are largely designed to promote local ownership and to only allow further foreign investment with money brought in from outside Zimbabwe (thereby generating more foreign exchange). The lack of any investment whatsoever, with the exception of government investment, brought about by these restrictive measures should be sufficient argument for a liberalization.

A major complaint from the private sector is that project approval by the relevant government committees is far too slow. "It is very rare for any application to be processed in less than three months; the norm is more like a year," said one experienced merchant banker in town. Streamlining the procedures would be a step in the right direction.

Most important, however, is the need for government to lay down specific conditions and incentives for foreign investment. Government would need to stipulate more precisely in what sectors investment is desirable and in what sectors it is not. A climate of certainty needs to be created that will enable the foreign investor to plan ahead knowing that for the next ten years his investment will be secure and the return guaranteed. The provision of forward cover by the Reserve Bank in order to offset the repeated devaluation of the dollar would, for example, help to create a more secure environment.

The Chinese Experience
In 1979 the Chinese introduced Special Economic Zones (SEZ) i.e. areas within China in which foreign investment would be welcomed and would be given preferential treatment. The major objective was to modernize Chinese industry by giving it access to foreign technology and to earn foreign exchange through the export of the products from the SEZs. Within four years, 1980-84 there were 3 018 agreements entered into with foreign investors amounting to a total investment of HK$15 billion? The amount of capital that had been invested by 1984 was HK$3,6 billion. Of the 100 investment projects already in operation by 1984, 84% had begun to make profits at an average rate of 15%.

Investors in the SEZs may enter into joint ventures with the Chinese government, run co-operative enterprises and even undertake sole ventures. They have the freedom to employ locals or expatriates. (The present wage rate in China is advertised as being about 50% of the wage paid in Hong Kong.)

The income tax levied on enterprises in the SEZs is calculated at a rate of 15%; enterprises with an investment amount of over US$500m and those operating with advanced technology and a long capital turnover period can apply for a tax reduction of between 20% and 50%. All enterprises are exempted from local surtax and investors reinvesting their profits in the SEZ for more than five consecutive years can apply for reduction or even exemption from income tax for the part of their profits that are reinvested.

All imported machinery, spares, raw materials, and other items used in the process of production are exempted from any import duty. In addition, all imported daily necessities (with the exception of tobacco and spirits) for personal use are exempted from tariffs. Finished and semi-finished products which are manufactured in the special zone for sale abroad are exempted from export duties. All foreign investors are expected to enter into a fixed time contract which may be renewed at the time of its expiry. The contract period for an industrial venture is usually 25 years, while that for commerce and service ventures is shorter.

While all firms investing in the SEZ are encouraged to produce for export, under certain circumstances investors can apply to sell their products in the domestic market.

An important pre-condition Whether the firm has a joint venture with the Chinese Governmentise. The proportion of home-marketed products allowed increases if advanced technology and equipment is provided by outside investors; if the products are badly needed in the home market and if they will replace large scale imports; and if the products are made from raw materials and components from inland China and if the quality of the items are superior to similar products produced in China.

The Chinese further publish details of areas in which investment is welcome. These include:
— the manufacture of high-tech electronic products such as computers, peripherals and integrated circuits;
— the manufacture of petro-chemical products;
— the manufacture of building materials such as float glass and cable;
— the manufacture of high-quality cigarettes, beer, plastic products and corrugated paper;
— the processing of high-grade cotton, woollen and chemical fabrics and high-quality garments;

The degree of certainty created by the very specific conditions of investment and the very tangible benefits offered by the Chinese appears to be generating the required level of investment. Could Zimbabwe not learn from this pragmatic handling of the "foreign devils" by People's Republic of China.

References

1. *Commercial and Legal Quarterly*, Vol 1 No 4, Harare, July 1987.
2. Zimbabwe Tea Growers' Association, reprinted from the 1986 Tanganda Annual Tea Report.
3. Measures announced on 28 May, 1987.
4. RAL Merchant Bank, Harare, Zimbabwe.

APPENDIX 2: Are Zimbabwe's Social Reforms Inflationary

Inflation has become a pressing issue for the man in the street, prices seem to be continually rising; salaries never seem able to keep pace with the price rises and the family budget gets more and more difficult to balance. Is there a foreseeable end to this trend of unequal distribution or are we destined to get ever-poorer.

TABLE 1: Zimbabwe's Inflation Rate: 1980-86

1980	–	8,6%
1981	–	12,6%
1982	–	13,7%
1983	–	18,0%
1984	–	16,6%
1985	–	9,2%
1986	–	*15,0%

1

*1986 rate based on Reserve Bank estimate.

The above table gives an indication of the rate at which prices have been rising in Zimbabwe. The percentage figure explains the price rise in relation to the previous year.

For example: a pair of shoes which cost $20,00 in 1980 would only have cost $18,42 in 1979. The price, since 1979 rose by 8,6% (ie; $1,58). We can further trace the price of that same pair of shoes over the years;

In 1979 it would have cost $18,42	In 1983 it would have cost $30,22
In 1980 it would have cost $20,00	In 1984 it would have cost $35,24
In 1981 it would have cost $22,52	In 1985 it would have cost $38,41, and
In 1982 it would have cost $25,61	In 1986 it will cost $44,17

In practical terms therefore a pair of shoes that cost you $20,00 just 6 years ago will now cost you $44,17. This represents a 121% increase in price. $44,17 in 1986 is therefore worth the same as $20,00 in 1980 once we have compensated for the effects of inflation. This is known as deflating or expressing the value in real terms. $44,17 expressed in 1980 terms (1980 prices) is therefore equal to $20,00.

The same amount of money in 1986 ($20,00 for example) will buy less than half the goods it would have bought in 1980. If you earned $500,00 p.m. in 1980 you could have bought 25 pairs of shoes at $20,00 each. In 1986, $500,00 will only buy you 11,33 pairs of shoes, i.e. less than half of what you buy in 1980. The value of your money has therefore fallen by 121%. Your salary would now have to stand at $1 105 p.m. (a rise of $605) in order for your standard of living to have remained constant. At a salary of $ 105 p.m. you can still purchase 25 pairs of shoes; this indicates a constant standard of living. For you to have improved your lifestyle your salary would have to be above $1 105.

The Standard of Living of the Average Citizen

In order to calculate the wealth of the nation as a whole (in order to see the effects of inflation on the whole country) we use the Gross Domestic Product (GDP) which is the sum total of all the goods and services produced within Zimbabwe in the space of one year. This GDP figure first of all needs to be deflated (ie; expressed in 1980 terms) and then divided by the total population in Zimbabwe. This will indicate the income per capita (per person), in real terms, in Zimbabwe.

Table 2 indicates that real income per head in 1975 was higher than in any year after 1980. 1981 was the best post-independence year yet even in that year real income per capita was $15 lower than in 1975 (ie, 3% lower). Since 1981 real income has declined

TABLE 2: GDP per Capita: 1975-86

Year	1975	1980	1981	1982	1983	1984	1985	1986
GDP at current prices ($m)	1 973	3 226	4 049	4 409	5 081	5 686	6 700	7 700
GDP at constant (1980) prices ($m)	3 112	3 226	3 645	3 646	3 522	3 515	3 939	4 160
Population* (000's)	6 390	7 480	7 730	7 985	8 248	8 520	8 801	9 091
GDP per capita ($)	487	431	472	457	427	413	447	458

* Population figures post 1981 are based on an annual population growth rate of 3,3%.

steadily until 1984 when it began to climb. The 1986 (expected level) is still below the 1981 peak, and far below the 1975 figure.

Table 2 highlights a very serious problem for Zimbabwe: the population growth rate at 3,3% p.a. has outstripped the growth in real GDP resulting in a declining real GDP per capita. The GDP growth since 1982 has averaged at 1,3% p.a. The population growth rate on the other hand has averaged at 3,3% p.a. This means that Zimbabwe has been getting poorer to the tune of 2% per annum since 1982.

The Causes of Inflation

Economists tell us that inflation falls into two basic categories; cost-push and demand-pull inflation.

Cost-push inflation occurs when the factors of production increase in price necessitating a rise in the price of the final product in order to maintain the same level of profits for the entrepreneur. This rise in factor prices can come about for the following reasons;
— a shortage of the commodity locally,
— increased costs of production of the input,
— a rise in the price internationally (eg; a rise in oil prices), or
— a devaluation of the Zimbabwe dollar (which would raise import prices).

Traditionally Economists believed that wage increases were the single-largest cause of cost-push inflation. The workers demand an increase in wage which would cause the employers to increase prices (in order to maintain profit ratios) which would undermine the wage increase in wages necessitating a further demand for increased wages, which would once again be met by a price increase, and so on. This brings about what is known as the wage-price spiral which causes inflation.

This view however is not held by all Economists. Socialist Economists believe that it is the demand by entrepreneurs for excessive profits that cause cost-push inflation. These Economists point to the gap between what a worker earns and what the entrepreneur takes home in the form of profit and question who can best afford a cut-back.

In a country where 35% of all workers in formal employment earn wages below the poverty datum line this is a convincing argument. The poverty datum line (PDL) in Zimbabwe (last calculated in December 1984) for a family of two adults and five children living in Harare, was set at $240 00 p.m. The average wage in Agriculture (1984 figures) stood at $88 00 p.m. while the average wage for domestic servants stood at $74 00 p.m. These two sectors alone constitute 35% of the labour force. An aggravating factor in Zimbabwe is the low level of formal sector employment. Of a population estimated to be in the region of nine million people in 1986 (see table 2) only 1,03 million people are in formal employment. The rest are either unemployed or self-employed either as peasant farmers or in the informal sector.

There are estimated to be in the region of 800 000 families totalling some four million people living in the communal areas. Together with the people in formal employment that accounts for five million people. Of the four million left, 2,5 million would be below the age of 15 (assuming that 50% of Zimbabwe's population is below the age of 15) leaving 1,5 million people either unemployed or working in the informal sector.

The second category of inflation is *demand-pull inflation* which occurs when the demand for goods and services exceeds supply. The excess demand then pulls up prices. The level of demand is determined by peoples disposable income (ie, income after compulsory deductions such as tax, pension and medical aid payments) and varies with the number of people employed and the size of the average wage.

One might well ask at this stage why a country such as Zimbabwe that has such high unemployment would suffer from **excess demand** (note that the size of the labour force — people employed — in mid-1984 was smaller than it was in 1974 despite a 38% increase in the size of the population.) Why is it not possible for the producers to increase the supply of goods and services thereby catering for the excess demand and employing some of the unemployed?

The answer is relatively simple. The value of goods produced in Zimbabwe (especially manufactured goods) depends to a large extent on the import of various inputs. Cars, radios, fridges, stoves, T.V. sets and even tea-bags have imported components. The foreign exchange regime presently in operation and the exchange controls imposed by the reserve Bank severely restrict the free exit of foreign capital and as a result very little foreign capital enters Zimbabwe of its own accord. This creates shortages of foreign currency with which to import the inputs required to produce manufactured goods.

Demand-pull inflation in Zimbabwe therefore results from insufficient supply rather than from excessive demand.

Controlling Inflation

Measures to control inflation are based on the causes of inflation and the economic and ideological perspectives of the government in power. Measures designed to control cost-push inflation would aim at restricting the increases in prices of the factors of production. Governments concerned with maintaining the principles of free-enterprise tend to concentrate on measures designed to control the rise in wages whereas governments which are involved in the building of socialism would restrict the rise of prices while attempting to increase wages towards a more equitable level.

A rise in the price of imported inputs (oil, machinery, technology, etc.) is more difficult to control. Measures can however be taken to minimise the effects of imported inflation including the search for substitutes for imported items (import substitution) and maintaining a stable value of the currency. Devaualtion of the national currency in order to promote export sales leads directly to a rise in the price of imported inputs.

The two major measures used to control demand-pull inflation are demand management and control of the money supply.

Demand management aims at reducing peoples' buying power by reducing their disposable income.

An increase in income tax would for example reduce aggregate demand. Demand management can also be aimed at encouraging producers to produce greater quantities of goods in times of recession. Tax benefits, investment grants and employment grants are used to this end.

Up until the early sixties inflation would only occur during periods of expansion in business activity when the level of employment was high. During contractionary periods the opposite conditions prevailed; inflation was low and unemployment was high. Contractionary measures (ie; measures which contract demand) could therefore be introduced during periods of high inflation without fear of causing excessive unemployment as employment levels were high. Stimulatory measures could similarly be used in periods of recession without fear of fueling inflation as inflation levels were very low in such periods.

All this changed in the late sixties. We now have inflation in periods of high unemployment (as is presently the case in Zimbabwe). Measures designed to curb inflation simply add to the already high unemployment, while measures designed to stimulate employment simply fuel inflation. This makes it very difficult for governments who are primarily concerned with the unemployment issue to tackle the problem of inflation. The Thatcher government, apparently unconcerned about the level of unemployment, has managed to reduce inflation to practically zero levels at the cost of record unemployment. Such measures would be totally unacceptable to a Socialist government which has as a basic principle the generation of 'growth with equity'.

The second major measure used to control demand-pull inflation is control of the money supply. Excessive growth in the money supply can be caused either by;
— excessive public sector borrowing,
— excessive private sector borrowing, or
— large balance of payments surpluses.

All of the above lead to more money in peoples pockets (as borrowed money is eventually used to pay salaries while a large balance of payments surplus means that export production has increased, or spending on imports has decreased, both of which would increase the domestic money supply) which in turn leads to a greater level of demand. If the increase in demand is met by an increase in supply then economic growth (without excessive inflation) would result. If however the increased spending comes largely from government in the form of budget deficits (as is the case in Zimbabwe) then the net result would be an increase in demand without a corresponding increase in supply as the value of government services is often far below the cost of production. Where the budget deficit is financed by borrowing from the banking sector (as appears will be the case with the over $1 Bn deficit in the 1986/87 fiscal year) the net result must be high levels of inflation.

A Solution for Zimbabwe

In the long term the supply of goods and services have to be increased if Zimbabwe is to avoid both excessive inflation and rationing of goods (which is inevitable if the government opts for controlled prices rather than inflation). The likelihood, and indeed the desirability, of dropping the exchange control measures in order to increase supply is very slim. The alternative would seem to lie in greater import substitution and an increased drive towards the development of local technology, both of which would enable us to increase supply without relying on greater inflows of foreign capital.

Some form of both wage and price control seems inevitable. An increased level of efficiency in the setting of these prices and wages is however essential if private sector producers are to be encouraged to maintain production and investment levels.

The solution to the budget deficit problem is more far-reaching. Government spending arises out of its programme of social reforms which is both overdue and necessary if long term stability and growth are to be achieved in Zimbabwe. The issue is who should fund the governments spending programme?

Should Government be competing with the private sector for money and in so doing divert resources away from productive investment, which has the capacity of reducing unemployment, into social spending which is catering for the victims of unemployment?

Should Government be increasing the supply of money to finance non-productive spending and thereby fueling inflation, which in the long run decreases our export sales thereby reducing domestic growth and generating more unemployment? Or should Government rather be attempting to build schools which are self-financing (ie; schools on farms which can feed themselves and produce a surplus which can be sold); technical training institutions which serve the community directly rather than drain the countries resources; parastatals which are run efficiently and at a profit; running factories which make profits and therefore contribute to Governments finances rather than deplete them?

This is not to imply that all services can be produced at a profit. Some, such as sanitation, defence, law and order, etc could never cover costs let alone produce a surplus. Others however, such as education, transport, technical training, and even the Post Office and Air Zimbabwe have the potential to produce a surplus. It is also important for the state sector under socialism to extend beyond the provision of services into material production. The Zimbabwe Mining Development Corporation is a step in this direction.

The point here is that the state sector *can be productive*. Socialism speaks about production as well as distribution, and if that production (including the production of services) cannot be done efficiently and at a profit, then we are building a society that is destined for bankruptcy. As long as Zimbabwean socialism deals only with the distribution of the surplus produced by the capitalist sector, both nationally and internationally, it cannot hope to survive.

References

1. CSO Digest of Statistics based on CPI data
2. *Commercial and Legal Quarterly*, Vol. 1 No. 2, January, 1987.

APPENDIX 3: The Unemployment Crisis in Zimbabwe

The past six years have seen a dramatic increase in the school population and a consequent increase in the number of secondary school leavers entering the job market. Raising the educational stndards of our school leavers has had the effect of raising their expectations which the economy has been hard pressed to meet. Each year the number of school leavers increases, and each year the prospects of finding employment become bleaker. The following article examines the growing crisis in unemployment in Zimbabwe and attempts to locate a solution.

High Population Growth rate

At the heart of the employment crisis lies Zimbabwe's rapid population growth rate of 3,3% per annum. The strains of a rapidly growing population lies in the ratio of dependants to working population (the dependancy ratio). In a developed economy such as the USA approproximately 25% of the population would be below the age of 15 (i.e. dependants); 65% of the population would fall between the ages of 16-60) (i.e. working population) and 10% would be over the age of 60. In Zimbabwe, by contrast, almost 50% of the population are below the age of 15; the remaining 50% therefore bear the burden of supporting the whole country. The higher the growth rate, the higher the proportion of the population below the age of 15.

Diagram 1 indicates the age distribution of the Zimbabwean population. Particularly important is the wide base of the pyramid indicating the high birth rate and the concentration of the population in the 0 — 14 year categories.

The effects of the high growth rate on the standard of living in Zimbabwe is indicated by Table 1 (below). In real terms, as Table 1 shows, the high population growth rate has meant that we are no better off (per capita) in 1986, than we were in 1980. The real per capita figures take the population growth rate into account, so despite the 3% growth in real GDP experienced in 1986, GDP per head growth was nil. (Note that GDP = Gross Domestic Product which is the value of all the goods and services produced within Zimbabwe in the period of one year.)

DIAGRAM 1: Population Pyramid for Zimbabwe (August 1984)

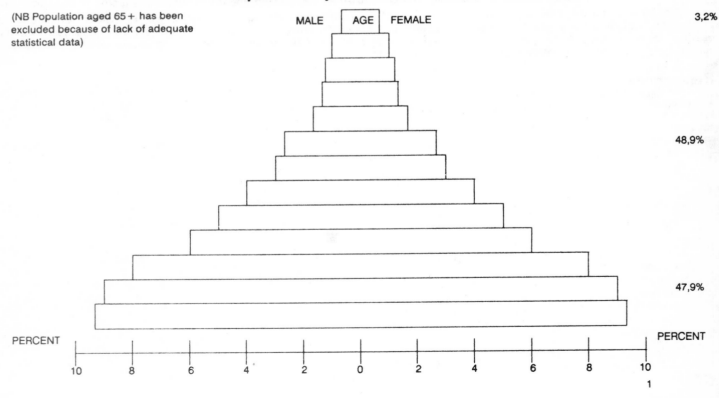

(NB Population aged 65 + has been excluded because of lack of adequate statistical data)

MALE   AGE   FEMALE

3,2%

48,9%

47,9%

PERCENT

PERCENT

10 8 6 4 2 0 2 4 6 8 10
1

Employment trends

Graph 1 compares the increase in population with the size of the labour force in Zimbabwe. If all the people are to be employed, the two curves on the graph should have the same slope. Using 1984 as the base year, the graph shows that except for the years 1965 and 1956, the early UDI years saw employment generation grow at a faster rate than population growth. From 1975 the trend changed and employment began a rapid decline until 1979. Between 1979 and 1981 employment grew at a faster rate than population — but from 1981 the size of the work-force has remained constant at 1,035m while the population has continued to grow. The explanation of these trends lies in the performance of the economy in the above period. The import substitution policies of UDI boosted local production and hence local employment. By 1975, however, the war began to take its toll and the economy entered into a downturn.

TABLE 1: Real Growth in the Zimbabwe Economy

Year	1980	1981	1982	1983	1984 +	1985*	1986*
Real GDP (1980) Z$m	3 226	3 646	3 522	3 560	3 775	3 890	
Real GDP growth (%)	11,0	1,0	nil	- 3,5	1,0	6,0	3,0
Real GDP per head (1980) Z$	448	492	478	448	440	454	454
GDP per head growth (%)	8,0	9,8	- 3,0	- 6,0	- 2,0	3,2	nil

+ = provisional   * = projected

2

The 1984 level of employment (at 1,035m) is still below the 1974 level of 1,039m and the 1975 peak of 1,05m. Since 1975 the population of Zimbabwe has grown by 2,25m people, ie, by 36% yet the size of the work-force has remained more or less constant.

Rapidly expanding education — a common trend in post-colonial societies

The demand for more education is a common feature throughout the ex-colonies which all went through periods when education was restricted to only the elite. Educational policy in the period after political independence has followed the same basic pattern all over Africa. Independence allows a growing segment of the population to use education as a vehicle for social and economic mobility. As the demand for education exceeds the supply, pressure is put on the new government to expand the education system. In a situation of limited financial resources, increasing investment in education is only possible by witholding investment from other sectors of the economy.

As the output of aspirants to jobs in the modern economic sector increases, the deficit between job seekers and available jobs becomes more acute. Demands and threats are made by the unemployed; the demand for work and the threat of riots. The response is usually to expand the administration (government sector) to absorb the unemployed and/or to expand the 'further education institutions'.

Both of the above solutions merely postpone the problem. Inevitably the output of the educational system significantly exceeds the available jobs; more jobs are demanded, frustration builds up, and instability results.

TABLE 2: Total Enrolments from 1979 to 1985

Institutions				Year			
	1979	1980	1981	1982	1983	1984	1985
Primary schools	819 128	1 235 994	1 680 143	1 934 614	2 044 487	2 147 898	2 229 396
Secondary schools	73 540	74 966	145 363	224 609	316 438	422 584	497 766
Teacher Training Colleges	3 002	2 824	3 484	4 373	6 481	12 923	4 504
Agricultural College	171	173	169	530	528	745	838
Technical Colleges	3 663	3 469	6 048	6 962	7 791	9 452	18 213
Apprenticeships	805	965	665	942	854	1 463	—
University of Zimbabwe	1 481	2 240	2 525	3 091	3 620	4 131	4 742

3

The case of Zimbabwe

The tremendous increase in the size of the school population, from less than a million in 1979 (892 668) to approximately 2,7 million in 1985 is shown in table 2 below. The ratio of working population to school population in Britain is 2:1 (the working population being twice the size of the school population) and still Britain cannot absorb the number of school-leavers emerging. In Zimbabwe the ratio of 1:2,76 (i.e. the school population is 2,76 times larger than the working population) is five times worse than in Britain. How can we possibly hope to provide this level of jobs.

TABLE 3: Secondary School Leavers Projected to 1994

Year	Form IV	Form V	Form VI	Total
1983	24 509	2 189	2 890	29 583
1984	71 014	3 112	2 911	77 037
1985	91 763	3 246	3 200	98 209
1986	93 092		4 000	97 092
1987	141 593		4 200	145 793
1988	152 122		4 500	156 622
1989	180 047		4 800	184 847
1990	267 677		5 100	272 777
1991	325 448		5 400	330 848
1992	306 714		5 800	312 514
1993	301 165		6 200	307 365
1994	303 626		6 200	309 826
Total	2 258 770	8 547	55 201	2 322 518

4

Table 3 gives an indication of the number of jobs which have to be created yearly in order to meet the demands of the school-leavers now and in the immediate future. In 1986 e.g., Table 3 shows that there were 97 092 school-leavers. Of this number approximately 45 000 will find places in further education institutions, while approximately 20 000 students from the further education institutions will complete their training and enter the job market. This leaves 72 092 people looking for work. Even with an annual attrition rate of 3% (i.e., 2,5% of the work-force resign annually, while 0,5% die, therefore 31 000 jobs become vacant each year) this still leaves over 40 000 people looking for work early in 1987.

In the past few years the economy has, on average, created 7 000 new jobs per annum. At that rate, in 1986 alone, an additional 34 000 people joined the mass of unemployed. The *Annual Review of Manpower* (1984) estimated the level of unemployment as follows:

1. Total Population 7 998 470
2. Potential Labour force 3 911 251
   (i.e., people between the ages of 15-64)
3. Persons engaged in formal employment 1 035 000
4. Persons engaged in communal farming 1 400 000
5. Persons engaged in the informal sector 63 032
6. Total persons employed (3 + 4 + 5) 2 498 032
7. Total persons unemployed in 1984 (2 — 6) 357 000
8. Unemployment rate (1984) 12,5%

This rather conservative estimate is largely based on the large number of persons engaged in communal farming (4). It was assumed that each of the 700 000 families in the communal areas included at least two people who were fully engaged in farming activities. Given the overpopulation in the communal areas, it can safely be assumed that the majority of this figure of 1 400 000 worker/peasants are seasonally under-employed.

By 1990 the number of school-leavers will reach 272 777. Assuming that as many as 70 000 new places are created in further education, and approximately 40 000 students complete their further education; the economy will have to create in the region of 200 000 new jobs. Even if half of these 200 000 were absorbed into the communal and informal sectors — which is highly unlikely — the formal economy would still have to provide an additional 100 000 jobs.

Even when real GDP equalled 13% (in 1981) the growth in employment was only 2,8% or 29 000 new jobs created. Based on these figures the economy would have to grow at a rate of 40% in order to create 100 000 new jobs. Alternatively, the rate of investment would have to increase radically.

Declining Investment

In monetary terms the level of investment has increased from $421m in 1974 to $1 051m in 1983. In real terms however (ie, at constant 1980 prices) investment has declined from $938m in 1974 to $649m in 1983. This represents a 30% drop in real investment over the ten year period. During the same period, private consumption expenditure (spending on consumer goods) rose from $1 960m to $2 813m in real terms. So, although spending was on the rise, investment was on the decline. During the same period (74 — 85) that investment dropped by 30%, the population of Zimbabwe increased by more than 30%.

In order for new jobs to be created there has to be additional investment. It has been estimated that it costs approximately $12 000 to create one job in the formal sector. To employ the 40 000 school leavers who will be looking for work in 1987, $480m of new investment will be needed. This is over and above the investment capital spent on replacing old and worn out machinery which serves to maintain previous levels of employment — not to create any new employment. If 100 000 new jobs have to be created in 1990, then $1 200m of new investment will be needed.

In order to create full-employment in Zimbabwe (using the Ministries 1984 estimate of unemployment) $4,3 bn of investment will be needed.

Over the past four years investment in the productive sectors of the economy (agriculture, mining and manufacturing) have been on the decline. In real terms investment in Agriculture in 1983 was at the same level as it was in 1976, and in the same ten year period had laid off almost 100 000 workers. Investment in the Mining sector in 1985 at $54m (real terms) was way below the 1974 level of $75m. Employment during this period had dropped from 62 000 workers to just over 60 000. Manufacturing has managed to increase employment levels despite investment in 1983 being less than half of what it was in 1974.

The private sector is clearly not investing. The key reasons for this drop in investment include:
* the desperate shortage of foreign exchange for investment purposes;
* the shortage of skilled staff, partly due to the inability to raise wages;
* cut-backs in labour due to the increases in minimum wages which in some cases have led to a replacement of workers with machinery;
* the decline in profitability due to increased wages and controlled prices
* lack of confidence in Zimbabwe's socialist future;
* lack of foreign investment due to all of the above factors, and due to the limitation on the remittance of profits.

Towards a Viable Alternative

The problem, in brief, incorporates the following factors; the rapid population growth rate; growth of the educational sector outstripping growth in the economy; the education system not preparing people for employment; declining levels of investment, and the general apathy of the private sector.

The rapid population growth rate is more of a symptom than a cause of the problem. Large families serve as a form of security when the economy provides little hope for future prosperity. An improvement in employment prospects and a raising of the general standard of living and education should, in time, help to slow-down the population growth rate.

The structure of the educational system in Zimbabwe at present is such that the O-level school-leaver, after approximately 11 years of schooling, is not trained for anything specific and is thus dependent on the economy to create employment for him/her. Primary schooling merely serves to prepare one for high school; high school in turn prepares the student for work. Those who have dropped out along the way — those who either failed and left school early, or those who were pushed through to O-level and then failed the final exams, or even those who passed their O-level exams but could not find places in further education, are therefore completely unprepared for work at the time they leave school. In Zimbabwe at present, over 60% of the students who start school in grade one drop out before receiving a skill which adequately prepares them for work.

Julius Nyerere, past President of Tanzania, suggested that developing countries could not afford the luxury of an education system which did not prepare people for work. Nyerere suggested that primary education become a course in itself which prepared students for playing a productive role in their communities once they left (primary) school. Furthermore, while at their schools, whether primary or secondary, the student must be productive. The students must grow their own food, make their own furniture and sell whatever surplus they have to buy whatever else they might need. All the chores in the school, the washing, cleaning and even the cooking, must be done by the students themselves, especially at the secondary and tertiary levels. If new buildings are needed, the children, together with the people (the local community) would build them.

GRAPH 1: Comparison of Population of Growth Rate and Employment in Zimbabwe 1964-1986

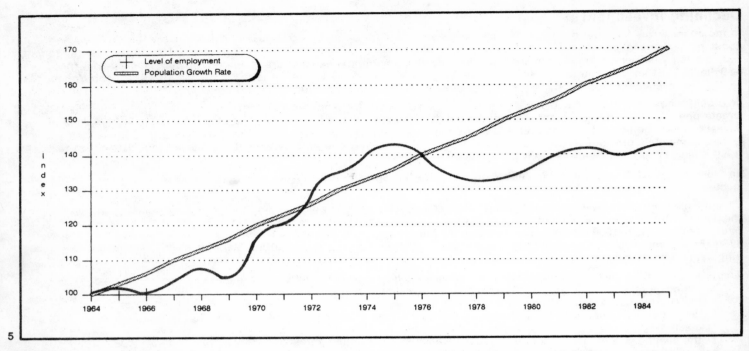

The student, once completing primary and secondary education, is now capable of looking after him/herself; of doing a job of work; of being self-sufficient; and most important, of creating work. The important benefit of a system such as Nyerere describes is the burden of financing education off the shoulders of the state alone makes it possible to further expand education without the fear of creating an unemployable mass.

It is clear that in Zimbabwe at present that private investment is not forthcoming to solve the unemployment crisis; it is also clear that government could not possibly create employment for all in the formal sector. The answer therefore lies in preparing people for self-sufficiency; for creating their own work in the informal sector. A schooling system which is designed to equip people not only with academic skills but with a range of practical skills like building, farming or carpentry brigades in which the school-leavers are provided with the management expertise, the initial contracts and sufficient working capital to enable them to establish themselves; or the state could encourage the school leavers to establish producer co-operatives. Backed by a co-operative bank (provided for in the Five Year Plan) which makes capital available, then armed with their technical skills they learned at school, the school-leaver can immediately become an active participant and contributor to the nations wealth rather than a drain on the economy and a potential threat to the future.

References

1.   Annual Review Manpower, Ministry of Labour, Manpower Planning and Social Welfare, Harare, 1984.
2.   *Economic Bulletin*, Standard Chartered Bank, October 1985.
3.   Central Statistical Office, Harare, 1985.
4.   Statistics Unit, Ministry of Education, Harare.
5.   *Commercial and Legal Quarterly*, Vol. 1 No. 3, April 1987.